THE CHALLENGE OF L'ARCHE

THE CHALLENGE
OF L'ARCHE

*Introduction and Conclusion
by Jean Vanier*

Darton, Longman and Todd
London

362.3

Published in 1982 by
Darton, Longman and Todd Ltd
89 Lillie Road, London SW6 1UD

© 1982 L'Arche International

ISBN 0 232 51560 3

British Library Cataloguing in Publication Data

The Challenge of l'Arche.
1. Arche (*Association*)
2. Mentally handicapped—Institutional care
I. Vanier, Jean
362.3'85   HV3004

ISBN 0–232–51560–3

Phototypeset by Input Typesetting Ltd, London SW19 8DR
Printed in Great Britain by The Anchor Press Ltd
and bound by Wm Brendon & Son Ltd
both of Tiptree, Essex

CONTENTS

ILLUSTRATIONS

Jean Vanier, a Canadian, founded l'Arche in 1964. He had previously served in the Royal Canadian Navy, and then studied at the Institut Catholique in Paris before taking up a teaching post at St Michael's College, University of Toronto. Jean now makes his home in Trosly, France, where he was the community leader until 1980. He has spent much time with the communities throughout the world.

He also founded and continues to work with Faith and Light, a movement which brings together mentally handicapped people, their families and friends, for times of sharing, celebration and prayer. This movement began in 1971 with an international pilgrimage to Lourdes which brought together some 12,000 people, one third of whom were mentally handicapped. Faith and Light communities meet in many countries. In 1968 he was asked to animate a retreat for priests, religious, and lay people at Marylake, Ontario which came to be called Faith and Sharing. Since then he has given many other Faith and Sharing retreats. This has become an important movement, especially in North America. Most Faith and Sharing retreats are now given by other people.

For younger people, Katimavik[1] was started in France in 1972, when Jean and other members of a prayer group in Paris wished to meet for an extended time of prayer and sharing. These gatherings, which are similar to the Faith and Sharing Retreats, have now spread to other countries where they are frequently led by a group of young people.

During a sabbatical year Jean lived and worked at Le Forestière, Trosly. This house welcomes profoundly handicapped people.

[1] An Eskimo word meaning "meeting-place".

INTRODUCTION

Jean Vanier

L'Arche began in August 1964 after I visited Père Thomas Philippe who was then chaplain of the Val Fleuri, a home for mentally handicapped men. We had known each other for several years as it was he who welcomed me into a Christian community after my departure from the Royal Canadian Navy in 1950. In 1964 Père Thomas introduced me to a world I had totally ignored, the world of the poor.

Before long I was able to buy a little house in the village of Trosly-Breuil, where the Val Fleuri was situated. After having visited a number of institutions, asylums and psychiatric hospitals, I welcomed two mentally handicapped men, Raphael and Philippe into this new house.

And so, the adventure of l'Arche began.

I had no previous knowledge of handicapped people. In so many ways I was ignorant. I had a great deal to learn both about handicapped people and life in community.

In that first Arche home, we lived poorly as we didn't have much money. I did the cooking with Louis, a Canadian architect, and Henri, who is French. The food was not particularly good! But we were learning to live together, to care for each other, to listen, and to have fun. Some people in the village cared for us because we were poor. Old Mme Bertrand would bring us soup every Friday; Mlle Gzell gave us apples and once we even received lamb chops in the post! The house was old and ramshackle and needed much repairing. In the attic, we had to make bedrooms and a bathroom. All this took time.

But it was from Raphael and Philippe that I really began to learn. I suppose in receiving them from an asylum I felt good, a sort of "saviour". I had, so I thought, the right to tell them what to do. They were in some way under my power and they should fit into my project. Without any doubt, in starting l'Arche, I wanted to create a Christian community. I had to discover little by little, however, that this was not Raphael's and Philippe's major concern. They needed friendship and security, someone who really cared for them and who listened to their needs and desires and to what they had to say. I had to learn that l'Arche was not just my project but also Raphael's and Philippe's and that of many others who were to come to l'Arche and put their roots down there. I had to discover something about welcome and respect for people, something about liberation of hearts and patience. I had much to learn about myself and my faults and defects, my need to dominate and command after spending eight years in the navy. I had to learn about human growth and suffering, about sharing, and about the ways of God.

In March 1965, the director of the Val Fleuri and most of his staff resigned. I was asked to replace him. I was thus plunged into a chaotic world of thirty handicapped men. There was much depression and violence there and I felt terribly inadequate. Little by little, people came to help: never many, just enough. Meals gradually became times of celebration. We started to pray together in the house and we went on a pilgrimage to Lourdes. Peace began to enter into the hearts of people. Work in the workshops became more serious and important. Seeds of hope started to spring up. L'Arche was becoming a family for those who did not have one, and a place of growth for all.

The Val Fleuri had been founded in 1961 by M. Prat for his son, Jean-Pierre. Dr Préaut, an eminent psychiatrist, was at his side helping him. The Val had grown quite quickly and ended up welcoming thirty handicapped men. Such a big house in such a small village caused worry for the villagers. They looked on it a bit like a house of "mad" people. And the fact that the doors were locked only enhanced this opinion. The first thing I did when I became director was to open wide the doors, allowing the men to move about freely in the village which of course brought fear to some village people. I must say that if I was conscious of the needs

of the handicapped people, I was not sufficiently aware of the
needs of the village. As I look back now, it is not surprising that
the villagers were, if not terrified, at least highly suspicious of our
people and of l'Arche in general.

We still have not completely repaired the damage. It isn't any
use creating a beautiful home unless there is some sort of free
relationship with the neighbours. This implies that the handicapped
person must adjust but also that the neighbours must sense his
gifts and uniqueness. It implies a co-operation between our home
and the village people, in which we are mutually respectful of each
others' gifts, able to work together.

Over the years I have learned that the same thing should happen
with the parents of the handicapped people we welcome. To begin
with, I tended to judge them. Hadn't they rejected their son?
Wasn't it because of their cultural values and lack of competence
that their son felt unappreciated, unworthy and useless? As it took
me time to understand the village people, so also it took me time
to really know the sufferings of parents. How important it is for
a community like ours to co-operate with the families of the men
and women we have welcomed, to sense their sufferings and needs.
A handicapped person who senses a division between his family
and so-called educators will be confused and lost. Frequently educators are more open to the growth of handicapped people than
parents are, because they have chosen this life and because they
have more means at their disposal. A handicapped person can be
attracted to an educator because he feels his worth in that person's
presence. He is lost in the face of the irritability of his parents who
are confronted day-in and day-out by trying situations with which
they can hardly cope. Yet the handicapped person needs the love
and confirmation of his parents. It is indispensable that educators
and parents discover each others' gifts and work together.

In 1967, Steve and Ann Newroth came to Trosly. We had met
in Montreal, at an ecumenical meeting of future priests and ministers. Steve and Ann are Anglicans. They started the third home
in Trosly, "Les Rameaux", where they welcomed three handicapped men. Steve was also in charge of all the building repairs.
After a year, he and Ann went to the ecumenical centre of Bossy

in Switzerland and then back to Canada, hoping to begin an Arche there. In 1968, Sister Rosemary Donovan, then superior general of Our Lady's Missionaries, attended my first retreat at Marylake, near Toronto. It was a time of great grace. At the end of the retreat, Sister Rosemary was inspired by God to offer l'Arche a rather large home near Toronto which the sisters had used as a novitiate. So it was that Daybreak, the first Arche community in North America, was created under the warm and competent guidance of Steve and Ann.

Steve and Ann taught me a lot. They led me into the vast and beautiful field of ecumenism. I had never really lived with people of other Christian churches. Of course, in the navy we lived together with people from different backgrounds but we did not share specifically as Christians. In many ways, I had regarded Protestants as people to be converted rather than as sisters and brothers with whom I was called to live and grow in Christ. Little by little, I discovered the marvels of grace in people and how the spirit of Jesus is guiding all Christians. That did not diminish my love for Roman Catholicism. On the contrary, as my heart grows to new dimensions, my love for the Church of Rome, for the Pope as shepherd of shepherds, has grown.

As Arche communities increasingly welcomed handicapped men and women from different Christian traditions, we learned much about the sufferings of disunity; living together but not able to drink from the same chalice. We have learned to yearn and strive for unity and to discover the beauty of the Spirit residing in each one. And each one is learning to grow in love and in Jesus.

Since Daybreak began, many other Arche communities have sprung up in North America and there are twenty-four different communities there.

Perhaps the most surprising place of growth was in India, through Mira. Mira is an Indian woman I had met in Montreal and who came to l'Arche in 1965. Her father was Moslem and her mother Hindu. She had become Roman Catholic at the end of her school years and deeply desired to find a style of life close to the Beatitudes. When her father fell sick, she felt called to return to Madras but was torn because she felt so attached to l'Arche. There

Jean Vanier

seemed to be only one solution: start a little Arche community in Madras where she could also be present to her father. That foolish idea which sprang up during a conversation with Mira, touched the heart of Gabrielle also. Gabrielle is a German woman who was then in charge of "Carrefour", a centre for foreign students in Montreal but who had deep yearnings to go to India. Mira and Gabrielle had known each other in Montreal.

We had no funds and few contacts for such an adventure, but in February 1969 Roby Kidd, whom I knew in Toronto, put me in touch with General Spears of CIDA who was responsible for distributing government funds to voluntary agencies. He informed me that money was available if I could present a project and a budget. Within a few weeks we received a cheque for over $30,000. We were no longer faced with just a hypothesis; we had started a project and there was no turning back. I must say I was a little frightened as we moved from dream to reality.

Mira and Gabrielle went to Bangalore in October 1969. I joined them a month later. I had already been in correspondence with Major Ramachandra from a Gandhi Institute who was keen that something be done for handicapped people in India. When I arrived in Bangalore, there was a letter from him telling me he would be in Bangalore the following day. When I met him, he told me of a property that he could let us have. I could hardly believe my ears. We visited it. There was a good house, with two wells, just outside the city. I gave a few talks in Bangalore and I asked those who seemed interested in l'Arche if they would form a board of directors for a future home. In a few months the hypothesis had become a very concrete reality. L'Arche in India, known as Asha Niketan, had been founded.

So l'Arche began to enter into a deeper understanding of the needs of handicapped people in India and in other developing countries. With Gus and Debby, Dawn started l'Arche in the Ivory Coast, Robert in Haiti, Nadine in Honduras.

At the same time Arche homes were springing up in Europe. Agnes and Adriano had begun a community near Cognac and Marcelle had begun another near Boulogne. My sister Thérèse began one near Canterbury, and Father Hviid another in Copen-

hagen. Father Roberti asked that his community in Brussels become part of l'Arche. And so there are now over fifty communities
bound together by ties of friendship in what we call the International Federation of l'Arche. Some are large like my own community. Others are small like the one in Ouagadougou. Most of
our communities welcome mentally handicapped men and women,
offering them a real home and place of growth; others – like those
in Haiti, Honduras, Ivory Coast, Upper Volta, and Madras, India
– have welcomed children; still others have welcomed physically
handicapped people. Most of our communities in more industrial-
ized countries are funded by the government. New communities
growing in these countries are struggling to be self-supporting,
everyone sharing his or her salary or pension. It is difficult to be
self-supporting in India or Africa but we are trying with our
chicken farm in the Ivory Coast. We are struggling to get government subsidies and to raise funds locally. But we also need to find
gifts in order to continue to respond to needs.

I suppose nobody is more surprised than myself by the growth
of l'Arche. I never meant it or planned it. In some ways I just
stumbled upon the world of mentally handicapped people. It was
clear I wanted to create a Christian community. But if circumstances had been different, I might have begun with former pris-
oners or delinquents or underprivileged people. Looking back I see
that the hand of God was there.

Since the beginnings in 1964, I know I have made many mistakes
and errors of judgment and in the process have hurt people. I have
also learned very much. In spite of my mistakes, ignorance and
pride, God seems to have blessed our work and guided us. And,
of course, each community of l'Arche is so different; each has its
own history; each one is composed of mortal and fallible people.
God seems to have guided us in and through all our mistakes.
Collectively we are learning and growing.

God guided us in the early days when we were poor materially
and in reputation, fragile and easily crushed. We were small; nobody paid much attention to us. Now we are not so poor financially; we have a large budget from the state, and we are rich in
the strength that is born from solidarity and friendship. We have

many friends and a certain reputation. But we are poor in many other ways.

In the Conclusion I mention the ambiguities, poverties and insecurities which face us. If we needed the presence of God at the conception and birth of l'Arche; if we needed his continual guiding hand during our younger days, I would say that we need him even more now because who knows where we are heading. We have a sense of direction and a certain orientation, but so much is still unclear. The last chapters of l'Arche have not yet been written. Can I ask you to be indulgent and to pray that we keep our hands in the hands of Jesus; that we look not so much on what has been accomplished and take pride and pleasure in it, but rather that we look at all that has yet to be done and thus feel humbled and inadequate. I ask you to pray that we will never stifle the Spirit and become defensive; hiding behind our achievements, protecting ourselves, our values and our ways. Pray that we continue to walk in insecurity, hand in hand with those who are in distress, who are weak, insecure and yearning desperately for friendship.

L'Arche will die if we no longer live and walk with wounded people. L'Arche will die if we do not see them as prophetic, calling us to change; l'Arche will die if we do not discover, in their weakness, the presence of the eternal. I ask you to pray that we may continue to walk in fidelity and humility.

This book is about l'Arche and some of its many facets. It has been written by nineteen of us who have chosen to live with our wounded brothers and sisters. It could have been many others who have been with l'Arche for a number of years, but we had to make a choice and that always leaves out some who could have done as good a job. It is not a history of l'Arche but it tells what we are and what we want to live. It tells of those we have chosen to live with and all they have taught us about life.

But I ask you to be indulgent if you visit an Arche community. Do not be surprised if you find tension, pride and a lack of sharing and welcoming. Do not be surprised to discover that the ideal Arche community does not exist. Each one is made up of people who are struggling, hoping and growing. Obviously, some communities need help to remain dynamic and hopeful. How quickly we can be frightened and close up on ourselves. As Ann Shearer says in Chapter 17, good ideas can lead to bad institutions. Not one of our communities is exempt from this danger and we need help to remain faithful to God and to the initial vision – and particularly to our brothers and sisters. To live as we do at l'Arche is a daily struggle and we need help to do it. We need constructive criticism as we need the wisdom and compassion of the Father to hear, to sift, to evaluate, and to use what we learn for growth.

When l'Arche began in 1964, I just wanted to live with a few handicapped people in a Christian spirit. Since then, I have discovered many new dimensions of l'Arche. I have discovered that to live with the poor and the weak is very demanding, precisely because they are asking me to change, to grow and to be more compassionate and wise. I have learned how much I must die to my own ideas and to myself in order to listen to them and live with them. I have learned about the need for precision and firmness so that we can all grow. I have discovered how difficult it is for assistants to put down roots. I have learned about l'Arche in developing countries and how much we must respect and love other cultures and how easily we judge and impose our ways. I have discovered the importance of integration into neighbourhoods and the importance of co-operation with families. Above all, I have discovered how handicapped people can be a source of peace and unity in our terribly divided world, provided we are willing to listen to them, to follow them and to share our lives with them.

As you read this book you will begin to discover what l'Arche is all about. But do not be surprised if you get confused. Even the name "Arche" has many meanings. L'Arche is a French word for "the ark", and of course I was thinking of Noah's ark and the covenant that God made with his people. People with a mental handicap are so often drowned in the deluge of civilization. They need a place of refuge where they can grow. The name, "l'Arche", refers to the first home in Trosly. The name also refers to the large community around Trosly – twenty different homes and workshops. And an Arche community is one that has in some way been born from or modelled on this first home and community.

This book is dedicated to the Raphaels and Philippes in all our communities. They are the ones who have made l'Arche possible. They are guiding us, if we will but listen.

But it is dedicated even more to the Raphaels and Philippes who are still in large institutions or roaming the streets; who are oppressed and wounded. They are waiting for an Arche or for someone else to welcome them. Obviously l'Arche is not the only organization working in this field; many other people and organizations are creating excellent homes and workshops. This book is dedicated also to all those who are sharing their abilities and their lives with handicapped people and who are yearning and struggling for justice with them.

But handicapped people are not the only oppressed group. I have just read Sheila Cassidy's book[1] in which she speaks of the oppressed in the slums of Chile. Then there are those who have been oppressed because of physical disabilities; the abandoned children the world over, those who have entered into the world of drugs, delinquency and mental sickness; all those who are outcasts and marginal. There are those oppressed by poverty, dominated by brutal totalitarian forces which suppress freedom. This book is dedicated also to them and to all those who walk with them.

It is dedicated, too, to all those who have a dream – a dream of peace, a dream that man is not made for war, hate and oppression, a dream that love is possible, that people can live and share as brothers and sisters in spite of many differences, racial, physical, intellectual or psychological. This book is dedicated to all who have this dream and this hope and who are prepared to work towards a better world and to walk behind, or close by that extraordinary prophet of the Beatitudes, Jesus. I believe he is God, the Word made flesh, born of Mary; others see him as an extraordinary prophet; others see him as a god; and still others as a revolutionary. Whatever we may call him, he is our Master and he has told us that if we walk with the poor, we walk with him; and if we walk with him we walk with the poor.

[1]Sheila Cassidy, *Audacity to Believe*, Collins 1977.

"LIVING WITH"

Sue Mosteller

Sue Mosteller is a Sister of St Joseph who made the first Faith and Sharing retreat in Marylake in 1968. Shortly after, she joined Steve and Ann Newroth in their community of Daybreak. In 1975, at a meeting of the International Federation of l'Arche, she was called to become International Coordinator. As such, she co-ordinates the International Council composed of all regional coordinators, and visits different Arche communities throughout the world. She continues to live and make her home with the community at Daybreak.

Jean Michel, a young mentally retarded man at l'Arche in France, asked Jean Vanier after a conference on "Community": "But how do we live together?' Jean's response has been my experience. "Perhaps," he answered, "it is you, Jean Michel, who should tell us how we live together."

My experience in l'Arche has been one of learning from the Jean Michels of this world to live close to the moment, trying to extract from it its essential gift, and then to accept it, to integrate it, and to love it. It's terribly idealistic and the reality is always far from the ideal but the challenge, for me, is true, and the experience, profound.

"Living with" is doing all the things that everyone else is doing, so I ask myself what I can write about. But there is a way of entering into the rhythm of the day, an attitude which gives the dynamism and energy to continue in the humdrum and to find sources of water that slake the inner thirsts of my being.

My complaint against Paul was always the same. Why doesn't the man take a shower when he comes in off the farm for supper? I hate sitting beside the barnyard, while trying to enjoy my meal!

His theory was different. If this is my home, and I am to be myself here, then stop telling me what to do when I come in from a full day of work. At the table one night when I was particularly hot and bothered, and Paul particularly smelling of the barn, we had a battle royal, with shouting and fighting that stopped all other conversation in the dining room and was very unpleasant for all. Paul finally left the table in a huff and we all tried to reconstruct the familial sense of sharing and enjoying the meal together. After dinner and after the dishes, Frank called me aside and took me to his bedroom where it was quiet and where I might better understand his difficult speech. He said, "I see you are having trouble with Paul," and I defensively replied, "Never mind that, Frank, Paul and I will have to work it out." But he held me with his eyes and said, "You know, if you want to help Paul, you have to start loving him."

Work is important and there is a time for work in our days. Some of us work together in the garden or the workshops or the houses, and we have much to share on the job. One may share the ability to do the task, while the other may express a certain enthusiasm not just for the task but for life itself. Sometimes the job is physically hard, but good, and we experience a mutual fulfilment in the accomplishment of the task together. This becomes a bond between us. Often the job is boring, but we simply undertake the task at hand together.

It was hot and boring, picking strawberries that day in June when Peter had just come and Don, a new assistant, was trying to teach him the importance of the job. At coffee break Don, frustrated but eager, asked what he should do and was told to be strict, but loving. When they returned to the strawberries, Peter expressed how he felt about the job by sitting on a strawberry plant and crushing the ripe berries into red blotches on his trousers. Don took his hand, pulled him to his feet and, eyeball to eyeball — especially since Peter doesn't see very well, — he said, "Peter, if I'm going to pick strawberries, you're going to pick strawberries, so let's get going!" Peter, who had hardly spoken a word in the two months he had lived at Daybreak, gently shook his head in the affirmative and mumbled in a quiet but audible voice, "What's good for the goose is good for the gander!"

Others of us work in factories and in competitive jobs with all the other people who have to work for a living and here there is a greater sense of the importance of one's work.

In all the world of work, however, we have so much to learn about the sense of identity and the sense of purpose which is given through meaningful work. We must grow in our expectations of the other. We must think creatively about the types of work that our people can successfully accomplish. And we must not cease to grow in our ability to teach the necessary skills to perform a given task.

When John Durand set up his first workshop for handicapped people in the USA, he spent the first two days trying to teach a young man to count to five, so as to be able to package five objects in a box. No success. John was beside himself with frustration. He had to get out for a break. As he left, he said to one of the retarded women in passing, "See if you can teach George to count

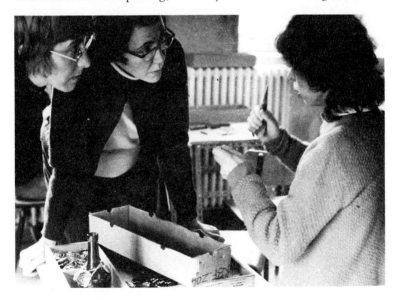

Sue Mosteller, visiting a workshop at La Merci, near Cognac, France

to five." Before he had left the room, he overheard her say to
George, "How many fingers do you have?" George began to count
laboriously, beginning with his thumb, "One, three, sixteen,
thirty-four, twelve." "That's right," she said matter-of-factly,
"put that many in the box."

But "living with" is not only at work. At home there are meals
and all that they entail. Often, we prepare the meal together, two
or three of us for the rest of the family. There is an attitude which
we try to have as we prepare, because we've learned that it influences the quality of the nourishment actually contained in the food.
We try to become conscious of the act of preparing for those we
love, conscious that we can give life through this act of preparing
the meal.

Ted described the situation in Bangalore, India, when they engaged a lady to do the cooking for them so as to have true Indian
meals for the Indians in the home. He explained that she was a
very angry lady and seemed not to like people in general or herself
in particular. He remarked that they could actually "taste" the
anger in her food, that the food was angry food and disagreed
with some of the community members, who were often sick as a
result. Gradually they became aware of what was happening and
after this particular woman was asked not to cook any longer,
their health and their spirits improved.

In these days of fast foods, it is sometimes difficult to grasp the
significance of this gesture of preparation, but it is an ideal that
has deep repercussions. This ideal, for us, is often only an ideal
and we have the "fast food" mentality, hurriedly preparing so as
to get the meal on the table before the next thing we had planned
in our day.

The meals themselves are a time of utmost importance, for the
bodily nourishment and for all it signifies. We discover that it is
also a time for our deeper hungers to find satisfaction. Perhaps
here, at the table, our strongest experience is the taste of our
solidarity. The stories, the bantering, the remarks about the cooking, the serving and passing of the food, the arguments, the broken
diets and the sharing of the last piece of cake all give the same

message to my hungry heart: the message that I belong to this people and I am acceptable, as I am here: that this is my home.

Sitting at the breakfast table early one morning, I remarked that I had an important meeting to attend and because there was no car I was worried how I would get there. Several suggestions ensued about borrowing a car, taking the bus, hitching a ride with our farm team, all of which I cancelled with excuses. Dave, munching his cereal and rocking gently back and forth listened, and when everything was quiet, he slapped the table and gave the solution. "Sue, if you really want to go to the meeting, why don't you just ride your broomstick!"

We do try to take time together at the meals. Once again it becomes necessary for us to break from our conditioning of fast foods, of haste and busyness, just to "waste time" at the table. But from this apparent waste, so much can happen as we gradually feel well enough sustained to risk being known.

Jim, who is fifty, had lived with us for three years and we thought we knew him well. But during supper one night, he suddenly began to speak to us about his life in the institution and how, as a little boy of eight, he had tried to run away. Genuinely interested, we questioned and he elaborated on the series of "escapes" between the ages of eight and fifteen and of his failure each time to get away, and then of the punishments upon his return. His words and his expression had a profound effect upon us. He gave us a small portion of his life and of his pain, drawing us into his vulnerability.

After our meal, there is the cleaning up and we try to continue to experience our solidarity by making it a time of singing, working together, splashing water on the others, and fun. But more often than not, we experience the plain drudgery of clearing, washing-up, drying and "Whose turn is it to take out the garbage?"

In most of our communities there is a time of prayer together after the evening meal. It is a wonderful moment, often very quiet, but with occasional verbalization of that which is in the heart. We pray for one another and for our families. Usually there are those among us who remind us of the brokenness of the world, by praying for particular pockets of suffering, strife, war or death.

One may read a short passage from Scripture, and another may start a song. These moments are precious and hold for me many touching memories.

When Frank, who had lived with us for ten years, was dying, Annie, tears streaming down her face, prayed, "Oh God, look after Frankie. I don't want him to die. But look after him, God, look after him for me, because he's my big honey and I don't want him to die. . . ." Or there is Gord, who gives thanks each night for his parents. He talks to God so naturally, but because God does not answer aloud, Gord often winds into a conversation with himself. "Oh Jesus, I thank you for my parents and for the beautiful weekend I had with them. They are a so-precious gift and I thank you for each one of them. My mudder works so hard and my dad is the best dad I ever had. Thank you for my so good family and now that I'm back at Daybreak I just want to say, 'Welcome back, Gord.' "

Then there was Charlie, a very suffering man of thirty-five, who because of a parents' meeting at Daybreak was reminded vividly of the fact that his mother left him when he was five and had never seen him since. "Oh God," he prayed, "help me to find my mother. You know that I am her only son. I'm no good because I can't read or write, but if you help me to find my mother, she'll recognize me as her only son and she'll take me back and she'll say she's sorry she left me."

In front of such simplicity and in front of the pain of an Annie or a Charlie, we often experience our complete inability to heal the wounds so deeply engraved in their hearts. At the same time, their prayer often touches similar wounds in us. But our prayer puts us in touch with the Divine Healer, whose art of healing we need so much, because it touches the pain that otherwise cannot be reached.

Prayer is an element that enters into the daily rhythm of our days, perhaps not for every person, but certainly for a significant number of people who sense that they are "called" by God to live and grow at l'Arche. Just as there is a need for the human contact within the community, so too there is the call to silence and to interaction with the One, who is Father to us all.

In the early mornings when I passed Frank's door. I'd hear him speaking, probably to himself, I thought. One morning I stopped, and because Frank's speech was not clear, I only overheard a few of the words of his prayer, "Jesus . . . happy . . . Jesus . . . Daybreak" and a few of the names of those people in the community whose difficulties at that moment were evident.

When Michael's grandmother died, his mother felt physically and emotionally unable to cope either with her own grief and loss, or with Mike's anticipated reaction, so she decided not to tell him about the death until after the funeral. In general, we would not advise this, because it is important that the handicapped person be allowed to "live" the sorrowful times as well as the joyful ones, but we did also want to respect Mike's mother's position, so we agreed to this suggestion. Mike went home the weekend following the funeral and on the Saturday morning, his father announced the news to him. Mike found his mother resting on her bed and sat beside her, holding her hand, not speaking, but only offering the comfort of his presence. This, he did for almost forty-five minutes, and she remarked to me that it was precisely the thing she needed at that moment. Spotting a silver vase of flowers, he haltingly asked his father to fill the vase with coca cola. An exchange of views ensued and Mike, who stutters and sometimes finds it hard to speak his mind, finally succeeded in convincing his dad that he knew that the vase was for flowers and not for coke, but he still needed his father to fill the vase with coke. Mike, in the meantime, produced a small table and three chairs. He sat his parents on one side and himself on the other, having placed the coke and a piece of bread on the table. "Now," he announced, "we will pray for Grandma." Breaking the bread, he handed a piece to his mother and asked her to pray. He repeated the action with his dad and then he himself took the bread and prayed aloud for his grandmother. He followed through with the "vase" and each in turn prayed for the deceased. Then he finished by announcing to his parents that God would surely look after Grandma from now on, but that they must begin to think of Grandpa, who was now alone and would need their support.

Apart from the scheduled routines, there are all the other hours of our day which carry us from leisure to celebration or rest.

There are the times of simple relaxation where two or three of us are together. Relaxation could be around someone who plays the guitar, or it could be going to the pub for a beer: it could be a goal planning for the things I want to learn, or making a card for someone who is sick or moving house; it could be taking a walk or driving someone to the airport; it might be visiting another of the houses or friends nearby.

After supper one night, Jim called Len, his boss and our farm manager, to see if he could come over to visit and see the renovations that Len was doing on his house. Len told him to come and en route to stop in our egg room and pick up a couple of dozen cracked eggs for cooking. Jim is in charge of the chickens and knows that we save all the cracked eggs for our houses and we sell the good eggs. Len waited and Jim seemed to be a long time coming. When he finally arrived, he wiped his forehead in a gesture of fatigue and remarked to Len. "Whew! That was tough! You see when I went to the egg room there was no cracked eggs so I had to crack two dozen for you!"

Another time, about four of us were sitting around the kitchen table on a winter evening drinking hot chocolate when Gord, who is eighteen, poked his finger into my shoulder and suggested, "Hey, Mosteller, how about you and me getting married?" Having lived twenty years in the convent, the proposal came as something of a shock, but I gathered my senses and replied, "First, I'd like a Cadillac and then a penthouse apartment! When you give me the keys to the car and the apartment, I'll think about marrying you." "Oh no, you don't," he answered quickly, "you'll have a Pontiac and I'll choose the apartment!"

Or another time, driving with Dave, he began his question to me, "Sue, do you ever think of leaving the convent and . . ." I waited expectantly. After a minute or two, moving forward and back as is his habit, he began again, "Sue, do you ever think of leaving the convent and . . ." By this time I was really anxious to know what he had in mind, but I said nothing and waited. No conversation. Dave rocks backward and forward. Finally, he finished his thought, "Sue, do you ever think of leaving the convent and . . . becoming a woman again?"

On another occasion Liz had spent a lot of time with Patsy to help her to learn about money. It was Patsy's wish to be able to go shopping on her own. They worked one day on the similarity between a ten dollar bill and two five dollar bills. At the end Liz gave the final example. "Now, Patsy, if you want to buy a sweater, and the sweater costs ten dollars, you can go to the store and give the lady this ten dollar bill and she'll give you the sweater, or you can give her these two fives and she'll give you the sweater. Is that clear? Any questions?" "Yes," said Patsy, "What colour is the sweater?"

In all our communities there is a great love of celebration, because we experience the need to leave for a time the seriousness of our lives, let our hair down and express ourselves in freedom and rejoicing. For the rejected person or for those who feel inadequate in so many areas of their lives, this time can be one of great spontaneity and joy. Birthdays are special and we prepare the meal and gift together, trying to make it suit the celebrant. Anniversaries too. Gord and I came to Daybreak at the same time and our arrival day becomes a tradition when we make our favourite dessert, cherry cheesecake for the community. We have celebrated the weddings of those who have lived in our communities and, later, the birth and baptism of their children. Hallowe'en and New Year's Eve usually see us celebrating in North America. And around the world we put special emphasis on religious celebrations; Christmas, Easter and Pentecost in the Christian tradition and the Poojas of the Hindu tradition in India. We mark the birthdays of our communities and we have house warmings for the opening of new homes. Once when we had, sadly, to close one of our houses, the group that had lived in the house, in preparation for moving back into existing houses in the community, invited all of us to a "house cooling" party. They met us, wearing sackcloth and ashes, gave us a simple meal, invited all of us to stand outside the house while, amidst speeches and protocol, they picked up the two ends of the ribbon that had been cut when the house was opened and tied them together.

We left then for another house where they gave us the gifts of all their kitchen utensils, coffee jars, and bed linen, wrapped in newspaper and tied with a bow.

One of the many gifts given to our communities is the gift of our friends. Those who do not feel called to live with us, but who want to remain close to us and to support us in whatever way they can. Strangely enough, few of our communities have "volunteers" as such. Rather, we have friends, who come and spend time and gradually see what gift they have that they can offer to the community. For some, it is a certain number of hours spent working for the community with a handicapped person, and for others it is the sharing of their particular skill of typing, or wiring, or painting, or building. For others it is the friendship with someone who may not have a family; it is that person who calls occasionally, goes shopping or out to dinner with their friend, or invites their friend to spend the weekend with him. Others may simply come to the celebrations or to the times of prayer to offer support; others give us money to aid us in our practical projects or vacations. Our friends are invaluable, not only for the practical support they offer but for the new life and the new energy and the new ideas and the fresh air that come in the door each time they come to our communities.

Our friends are those who can take a risk. When they come, they see us as we are and their judgements must be tempered by time. Possibly they have read some of the books and have recognized an ideal that appeals to them, but when they come they enter into a reality that is often far from the ideal.

John, who does not speak too well, has quite a taste for beautiful women and is never slow to show his affection. For the newcomer, this often presents a difficulty, just in knowing how to react when he wants to hold hands or put his arm around her. One new friend managed to get through her first supper sitting beside John, but we could tell that she was pretty uncomfortable, especially when, immediately after supper, she made her excuses to leave. John followed her to her car and as she was speaking to someone through the car window, John went around to the passenger side, leaned in the open window and asked, "Help?", which was interpreted to mean, "Can I help you?" "Oh yes," replied the flustered young lady, thinking quickly, "you can just pull up my aerial there on the outside dashboard, so I can listen to the radio." "OK," answered John happily as he grasped the aerial at its base, pulled it right out of its fixture and handed it to our new friend through the window. Sometimes our ideal gets clouded over by our reality.

We occasionally "live" the amazing gift of the brotherhood that exists between our communities, when we gather for times of meeting and sharing our common concerns and patterns of growth. These meetings call us to tell one another the beauty, the growth, and the wonderful things that God is doing in our homes. At the same time, we try to share the difficulties that arise in our lives to which there are no simple solutions. We might touch on areas of ecumenism, of the sufferings of our people in the area of affectivity and sexuality, of the commitment on the part of each one of us to the community, and on many other things. But with so many different people and with questions that touch deeply our aspirations, these meetings and sharings are important and helpful to give us energy and hope to continue. The "fiesta" on the last night of these get-togethers is now a tradition, be it a small meeting of twelve people from the four communities in India, or be it the two hundred and twenty of us from fifty-four communities around the world, who met together for ten days to share and deepen our vision. Music, magic, skits, dancing, masquerades, refreshments, decorating and the final moment of prayer together are all part of the planning of the fiesta. Usually there is a good take-off either of the director or of someone special in the community who is immediately recognizable. But we depend greatly on the gifts of individuals who, with the help of the organizers, give freely of their talent for music, slapstick comedy, cooking, leading the prayer or whatever. As it all comes together in the fiesta, we sense the brotherhood and we get the energy to work in our own homes to deepen and to grow together.

I have not written much of the difficulties, the resentments and the anger; the differences of opinion, the emotional ties and the "politics" that are also part of our daily life. I have not described the pain and the difficulty of accepting the ambiguities that exist between the professionally oriented, the community motivated and the religiously inclined, all living together and all wishing to be implicated in the decisions of the community. I have not been able to describe the deep disappointment and frustration we live together so often when our dreams of harmony and brotherhood crumble in division and strife. And I have not outlined our individual and communal struggle in the realms of structure, responsibility, power and authority. But they exist and we "live with" that too.

For me the quiet moments spent in God's presence at the beginning and at the end of each day are essential. These moments of silence in the presence of Jesus are necessary in order to try to integrate all the beauty and all the pain. And I feel so small. I am learning, however, that it is essentially in knowledge of my inability to look at the other, in my disappointment at my own reactions in a crisis, in my resentments and my harsh judgments that Jesus, the author of love, can touch me, can teach me, can heal me. In these precious moments I learn to believe more deeply in the essential mystery underlying "Blessed are the poor." I believe it, not because I live with handicapped people, the poor, but because I myself am so poor, so close to my limits, and at the same time so blessed in believing that I am a child of God, called to live with brothers and sisters, who journey together towards the Father.

Ruthanne, our friend from Cleveland, lives in her wheelchair and suffers from cerebral palsy. Her speech is very impaired and only two or three words make her little body shake and jump uncontrollably in the chair, even though at university she studied languages and graduated with the ability to read and haltingly type in five languages. Her gift to this world is her huge smile that fills her face, and a sense of humour that often sends her into a spasm of genuine laughter. At the end of a particularly hard day we had lifted her into the bus that was taking us home and Bill Clarke was sitting beside her, but neither spoke for a long time because both were tired. Finally, Bill remarked to his companion, "Life is tough, isn't it, Ruthanne?" Ruthanne, with a huge smile covering her face and contorting her frail little body, replied with difficulty, "It's hell!"

Somewhere in the midst of all these combinations and dichotomies I have experienced the challenge of "living with" at l'Arche, and I give thanks to Jean Michel and all my other sisters and brothers throughout the world, who have taught me how we live together in truth, joy, pain and in the fullest sense of the word love.

2

THE POOR AT THE HEART
OF OUR COMMUNITIES

Odile Ceyrac

Odile Ceyrac is a French woman who came to l'Arche, Trosly in 1969. She became acquainted with l'Arche through the invitation of a friend, Mira, who was then living in Trosly.

After joining the community, she became head of a small home for six handicapped men, then shared the responsibility for a home for eighteen handicapped men, the Val Fleuri. During that time she completed her studies in special education. In 1976, the community called her to assist Jean Vanier in the overall leadership and then to replace him as community leader.

Odile represents the community of Trosly in the regional council meetings of all Arche communities in France.

We are the Same

"Hey, Odile, I have suffering inside me and it won't come out." Daniel said this to me, pointing to his chest to show where he was suffering. I said: "But you're a bit better now, aren't you?" "Yes, a little bit," he said and then added: "And you, Odile, do you have suffering?" "Yes," I replied, "I have suffering in me too." "Then we are the same," he said with a look of sympathy.

We are all the same, that is one of the discoveries I made at l'Arche – a discovery I made on my very first visit thirteen years ago; a discovery I make over and over again each day I am here. Something happened inside me on that first visit that is very similar to what is happening to me today.

A friend had invited me to come and spend a weekend at l'Arche in Trosly. At that first meal, Claude seemed to touch very deep chords in me; he attracted me mysteriously and seemed to call me forth. His disfigured face and clumsy gestures were such a contrast to his smiling eyes which radiated peace. Claude is a man of thirty who was born into a very poor, difficult family situation. Shortly after birth, it became apparent that he was mentally and physically handicapped. His family could not take care of him and so as a child he was placed in one institution after another. He ended up in a home for old people. From there he came to l'Arche. His family, unable to keep in touch with him, virtually abandoned him. Since, his parents died, he has just one brother left who writes to him occasionally.

Through this encounter with Claude I sensed that I was being called forth to live in this community of the poor, precisely because I was and am "the same". Like Claude I had my fears, my vulnerability, my sensitivity; I had the same desire to love and be loved, the same need to be accepted and recognized. Like Claude, I too had so much difficulty accepting my limits, failures, broken illusions, frustrations, the sufferings of life and my own angers and depression. Yes, basically we are all the same.

It was this discovery of the limitations of our human condition as well as the discovery of our hope, that brought me to live and share my life with handicapped people at l'Arche.

Towards Greater Freedom

But it is not just a question of an acceptance of our limitations. What is more important is that we must all grow together towards greater inner freedom. And it is the poor person at the heart of the community who guides us. To begin with, an assistant who comes to help at l'Arche may marvel at the simplicity and sincerity of the handicapped person. But he must learn how to experience that in the "humdrumness" of daily life, in faithful friendship rooted in time – which for some assistants means the rest of their lives.

The handicapped person needs a warm, friendly, dynamic milieu where he or she can grow and develop. To create this type of atmosphere means essentially to create authentic relationships

Jean and Geneviève, l'Arche, Trosly

which are a source of security. If the handicapped person needs people who can do things for him, if he needs qualified educators, it is also vital for him to have people who are happy just to live and be with him, who are ready to commit themselves to a lasting relationship which becomes a deep friendship and a source of hope. The greatest suffering of the handicapped person does not lie in his handicap but in the feeling of rejection he has known from early childhood. Those who have been truly loved and accepted by their families and surroundings have much less difficulty assuming their handicap. But when a person has felt rejected because of a handicap, it is hard for him to grow and fully develop his personality. Because of these experiences of rejection, it is difficult for him to gain confidence in himself and in those around him; he tends to reject himself and live in a continual dormant state of depression.

The handicapped person is asking something very specific of those who come to live with him at l'Arche. He is asking them to help him, through a relationship of trust, to gain new confidence

in himself, to learn that it is possible to live and to have hope.
Through this authentic relationship, he will discover that he too
can love, that his person is more important than his handicap.

To create an atmosphere where confidence is born is not easy.
Very quickly we can forget what the poor are revealing about us;
we put up a lot of resistance and maintain our masks. Our egoism,
illusions, fears, desire for success and recognition are always there.
But the community reminds us of why we are here: to welcome
the poorest, to open our hearts to them and help them to grow.
In the life we share together, we soon discover that they are our
"teachers"; they give us more than we can ever give them in terms
of acceptance of our human condition, in the discovery of what is
essential in our lives. This is a terribly demanding discovery. Frequently we want to flee from it. We need to be stimulated and
encouraged, on a personal as well as on a communal level, in order
to live it. The first moments of wonder in our encounter with the
handicapped person have to be nourished and deepened.

The poor person needs to be recognized and accepted with all
that is beautiful in him, but also with his difficulties. He needs
someone who can listen attentively, lovingly; who is perceptive
and can decode the message behind his sadness, depression or
aggression. The poor want us to be continually searching to understand their difficulties better and their mental or emotional
blocks, constantly trying to find better ways of adapting to their
needs and potentialities, at work as well as in life in general. The
person who has often been despised, rejected and even oppressed
needs to find a home that is life-giving; a place where he can live,
re-live and dare to try new experiences and create relationships.
This is the goal of l'Arche, to create a milieu of trust. It is really
a matter of taming each other.

Saint-Exupéry says it so well in his book *The Little Prince*[1]:
"Please will you tame me and take me for your friend?" says the
Little Prince. "It takes a long time and it is not easy . . . to begin
with you have to sit far from me . . ." And later: "You are responsible for the one you have tamed and befriended."

[1] *The Little Prince*, Heinemann 1945.

During these years I have spent at l'Arche, I have learnt that I too need to be helped and guided in my approach to the handicapped person. Professional guidance, and the community, have given me help and support in creating relationships that are true. I have learned how to keep a certain distance in order to respect the inner secret of each person and to discover with him the meaning of his life.

The handicapped person has led me often into unsuspected labyrinths, experiences of suffering and rejection that I never even suspected. In so many ways, he has disturbed me in my way of life, my pre-conceived ideas. Penetrating into his world I have penetrated into the wounds and injustices of our society. He has made me discover the deceit and hypocrisy that lie within it and within our own hearts. It will be a long time before Nicolas will be able to smile again, before Pierre can talk again. It will be a while until George will let someone come close to him without running away. And, Philip still has trouble accepting the hand that someone offers him. How difficult it is to accept Philip's refusal; we often take it as a personal offence or rejection. I've had to learn to accept these refusals and aggressions without bitterness, but with hope in my heart, trying to receive them in gentleness and truth. Truth, because I must not be stopped by the handicapped person's emotional difficulties but rather understand the past wounds and rejections which are the cause of his attitudes and reactions. Then, through this better understanding I must try to help him find a way of life where he can discover his own beauty and thus a more positive image of himself.

But in order that the handicapped person can discover that it is possible and good to create and develop bonds of friendship, we must be willing to accept him first with his wounded, broken self-image. The poor challenge us. They challenge us to enter into their world, which is often very chaotic: we are lost in front of incomprehensible words, gestures and attitudes. They challenge us to share our hearts and our lives with them. But it was only when I really agreed to carry this suffering and this chaotic world with them that a new hope was born in me. I discovered that I was called to live a covenant with them. God called me to love the poor with him. He called us to grow together towards greater interior freedom. And it is through that covenant that I have been able to discover the "heart of the poor", in very simple events of our daily lives.

For example: a baby is to be born. This is the great secret and great joy that Roland has in his heart. If you had a chance to visit his home and to sit next to him at table, he would have asked you: "Guess what's going to happen at the end of this month? Something very important." It is up to you to guess. You would probably talk about someone's birthday, or a special visitor or a trip. He would sit there with a wide grin on his face and continue: "Try and guess. Try and guess." You would continue to make a few guesses but without any success. Finally Roland would burst out laughing: "Do you give up? Well, Bridget, she is going to have a baby." I am amazed by the way Roland can find such joy waiting for this birthday which belongs not to him but to Bridget and the baby. What a wonderful heart he has to be able to participate in another person's joy like that. Roland suffers from epilepsy; he is slightly handicapped. His parents have died and he is deeply wounded by the fact that the only remaining members of his family, his two brothers, do not wish to have any contact with him.

Denis wanted to see my new office but I felt it was a pretext in order to tell me something that was important for him. When he came he had a very serious look on his face. He looked all around the office and found everything OK. Then he sat down and looked at me solemnly. "Do you know why I am so often angry?" It is true that he is impulsive and can change moods quickly, becoming very aggressive. His past history gives many reasons for that. But what struck me was his understanding of himself, and his honesty. He was able to tell me, so clearly, how hard it is for him and for others to live with his difficult character. I simply reminded him of the progress he had made, of all we had lived through together and his smile came back. When he said "good-bye", I could see from his eyes that he had found a new hope.

The joy and laughter that Paul, Nicolas and Sylvie communicate are often undescribable. Such good times, intense moments, we have lived together especially on holiday or on pilgrimage.

On our last pilgrimage to Rome, at Christmas 1978, Charles as usual amused us all. He is thirty and some would call him mongoloid. He has been at l'Arche for a long time and is loved by everyone. During the pilgrimage, we visited the Sistine Chapel at the end of very long and grandiose corridors in the Vatican Museum. We walked two by two so we would not lose anyone in the crowd. I was with Charles, hand in hand – which is not always easy because he has his own ideas about where he wants to go and what he wants to do. As we approached the chapel, Charles was pulling me forward; he seemed to be anxious to see something. I only understood afterwards what it was. Once we had entered the very famous Chapel, we were told to keep silent. There were crowds of visitors who were twisting their necks, trying to admire Michelangelo's frescoes on the ceiling. Charles, however, was looking straight ahead. Still pulling my hand, he finally said with a very urgent look: "The stove where they burned the papers for the white smoke, where is it? I want to see it." I began to understand his searching. He had followed very closely the elections of the most recent popes, John Paul I and John Paul II. The crowd and the paintings did not exist for him. He was only interested in seeing this famous stove. It was no use trying to reason with him about the value and the beauty of the paintings; the only thing he wanted to see was that stove. Things were beginning to get a bit loud and indiscreet. People who up till then had been absorbed in the paintings were becoming distracted by this young man who was talking so loudly, and did not seem to be happy. So several of us set out with him in search of the stove. Of course, we never found it. The situation had become so amusing, such a contrast to the rest of the crowd who were so serious and intent, that Charles finally burst out laughing with the rest of us, agreeing that we had been pretty lucky to have already seen the chimney outside.

Towards the Essential

If the poor of our communities can sometimes fill our hearts with joy and wonder, they can also through the simplicity of their lives, lead us on the road of life, as long as we listen to them attentively. In some mysterious way, they bring us back to the essential things in our lives. In our links or covenant with them, they mould us to truth. They guide the direction and decisions of the community, as well as our own personal direction, and they often inspire the right attitudes.

Frequently Stephane refuses to get up in the morning. One day, I just didn't know how to handle the situation. André, his room-mate, saw my incapacity to help Stephane. He looked at me and I knew he understood. He seemed to want to tell me something so I sat down beside him and told him of my concern for Stephane. He asked me if I wanted him to go and see Stephane. I told him how much Stephane needed us and how good it would be if he could help him come out of his sadness and isolation. I realized that André knew him well and was a man of peace. Besides, André had also known that feeling of despair. Perhaps he would find the words, gestures, or attitudes that I had failed to find. These thoughts were still running through my mind when André came back with a sly look on his face: "Stephane says he would like another shirt. He's up now!" André had known how to reach Stephane.

Similar incidents have taught us to allow the handicapped person to have a greater role and participation in the life of the community – in the running of the homes, the workshops and the community as a whole.

The poor in our communities also have a quality of openness and a capacity for welcoming others: welcoming into their homes and hearts visitors, new assistants and new handicapped brothers and sisters. Faith and trust seem natural to them and in this way they welcome God and Jesus Christ. Though they are handicapped in the world of power and efficiency, they have gifts akin to those of the poet and artist, the prophet and mystic – the prophet being one who disturbs, who cries out, who shows the way. They have shown me the way: they have revealed to me the truth of St Paul's words: "God has chosen what is weak in the world in order to confound the strong. God has chosen what is folly in order to confound the wise . . ." (1 Cor. 1:27) Each evening when we are all together at prayer in our home, I am confounded and drawn back to the essential.

Power and rivalry divide, vulnerability and the human heart unite. The poor mould us in the depths of our hearts. They are shaping us. They are creating the unity of our community. Their often disfigured faces and injured bodies are there to tell us, as 'The Little Prince[2]' does: "What is essential is invisible to our eyes; we only see truly with our hearts." Through meeting and sharing daily with the poor, I am gradually discovering the face of Jesus. This "sacrament" of the poor is offered to me day after day, as long as I am open to receive it.

"Your heart is big, Stephane, and open to the dimensions of the world. Yet you are so simple and have touched so many people, simply because with your smiling eyes you say "come," you take us by the hand to show us your bedroom, to share with us your treasures: a photo album, a birthday gift, or a secret. But from this short time spent with you, we come away joyful, with renewed hearts, feeling we have a new friend."

The poor at the heart of our community are a hidden treasure. Better than anyone else they remind us of the essential things and guide us along the way.

Nicolas has often been a guide for me. We have been living in the same house, the Val Fleuri, for nine years. We know and love each other. When Nicolas first arrived he was very unstable and deeply handicapped. He has changed a lot. He has learned to work and to live with others in community; to forgive and to make peace. He can take care of himself in daily activities. He is one of a team of eight who shared responsibility for the house, which means that he was designated by the other members to be responsible for its organization and animation. If there is too much noise in the house or too much disruption at meals, this group tries to

[2] *The Little Prince*, Heinemann 1945.

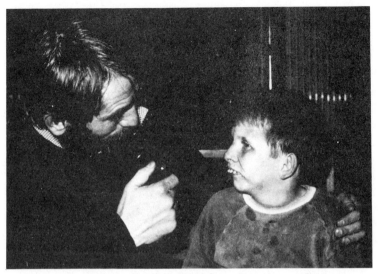

The poor shape our hearts

propose a solution to improve the situation. Nicolas is very conscious of his role and his responsibility. He has also grown a great
deal in his own personal life. He knows and can express his needs
and he can decide and make a choice. For example, given a choice
of ten different small holiday groups, he can indicate the one he
wants and why. Recently he took a very important initiative.
Knowing that there was room in another smaller home, La Nacelle, he asked if he could go there for a trial period, to see what
it was like and if it would be good for him to stay there. We
thought this would be important for him and were very happy
with his initiative. He spent a month at La Nacelle. It was a good
month for him but he chose to come back to the Val.

During that time, something happened which showed me once
again his extraordinary sensitivity and maturity of heart. I met him
in the street one day and he asked to come and talk to me. We
spoke for a while and I asked him how he was. He told me
everything was going well in his new home. But, he said: "How
are you? You're not too sad that I am no longer with you? Why
don't you come and have a meal with us?" Then he proceeded to

ask for news of Xavier, Roland, and each of the others. And, he added: "You know things are going well for me but, if you need me, just let me know and I'll come back. Just let me know." That was Nicolas reacting from the depths of his heart. He was completely free to choose La Nacelle but his fidelity to the people of his original home was such that he had to tell me how much he loved us. I was deeply touched and he knew it. He understood our reciprocal fidelity to that mutual covenant. Above and beyond any material choice of one home or another, Nicolas was simply confirming once again for me that fundamental choice to live and share our lives at l'Arche, being called together by God to be faithful to one another. At that moment something very deep, very essential, was being lived between us. Once again I found myself called by the poor and I touched the fidelity between people which gives meaning to one's whole life. Nicolas was expressing that fidelity with all the warmth and tenderness of his heart.

Many so-called "normal" people come to spend a few days, a few months, a year, or even longer at l'Arche. Most often they are people who have received a lot in life. Some stop and let themselves be touched by the poor. Others avoid really meeting them and do not dare say: "I want to live and share with you," because they are too taken up with their own troubles. Nicolas, who had been abandoned by his mother at birth and placed in various institutions, was able to express his deepest desire: to live the fidelity of friendship, to build together with his friends a community of welcome and trust.

The poor are the cement of our community. They create unity, teach us how to forgive and how to celebrate. They help us find once again the heart of a child so that we can say with Jesus: "I give thanks to you, Father, for you have hidden these things from the wise and prudent and revealed them to the little ones." (Matt 11:25)

The poor bring us to a discovery of our weaknesses, limitations, mental blocks, prejudices and handicaps. When we come to live in community with mentally handicapped people, we often feel we have to prove ourselves and show that we are someone. We need to feel "successful". In fact, we are hiding our fragility behind the barriers of success. It is difficult for us to accept the challenge that our encounter with the handicapped person gives us. We have to pass through many trials before we are able to recognize that it is more often an attitude of domination behind our coming to be with handicapped people, than a desire to listen. The discovery of this truth about ourselves implies a real stripping. The handicapped person has already lived through this stripping. If we cannot accept this, if we cannot accept our fragilities and handicaps as they are revealed to us, then we will probably not be able to live very long in community with our handicapped brothers and sisters. But through genuine friendship, they can help and heal us; they can peel away our illusions and masks and thus they can liberate us. Little by little they can lead us to greater inner freedom. It is important for the handicapped person that we are free in our relationships with him. It is a question of learning to value a loving relationship more than success and prestige, of valuing community more than personal advancement. The handicapped person is frequently well ahead of us in this domain.

If the handicapped person has not been a victim of physical violence, very often he has known more hidden violence. He has been a victim of moral, mental, social and political violence. It is not easy to live this "stripping": not to be heard, recognized nor welcomed. As Christians, we can identify with the crucified Christ if we allow ourselves to be stripped. To live this reality can be liberating for the poor person. If we see him in this way, we recognize him, welcome him, give him the place that belongs to him: at the heart of the community and of society.

In spite of all oppressions life persists in the handicapped person. That always amazes me. The life within him is stronger than all the seeds of death, if we are willing to recognize it. I think of Xavier who is seventeen years old and very severely handicapped. I met him in a psychiatric hospital a few years ago where he had been since he was three. He cannot speak or see. When I first met him, he was unable to walk. Every time he felt someone come near, he would hasten towards them, sliding on the floor, and would grab the person, squeezing him and refusing to let go. He was frantically calling out for a presence, yearning for life. In 1978, we were able to welcome Xavier into a new home we opened. There is such life in him that he can now walk, he can eat practically all by himself and, most important of all, in that frantic search for presence he has found a certain peace. His face is beautiful and radiant, so much so that I never get tired of looking at him and of giving thanks for the life within him.

Our world is so divided; war, oppression, and blatant inequality are found everywhere. Men continue to put up walls of hostility, prejudice, and fear. I discover more each day that mentally handicapped people are among the most oppressed on our earth. So often they have not had the right to express themselves or to have their own desires or their freedom. "Normal people" find them too much of a bother. They want to hide them, get rid of them, even manipulate them or make them become "normal" like themselves.

At l'Arche I have discovered a place where handicapped people can live, express themselves and learn to make their own choices, where they can be themselves, growing at their own rhythm towards greater interior freedom; a place where I can live with them. They have revealed to me how much I am part of a culture that is intolerant and rejecting. But, they have also shown me the path towards the conversion and real liberation of Odile Ceyrac.

3

COMMUNITIES OF THE BEATITUDES

Thomas Philippe, O.P.

Père Thomas Philippe, O.P., with Jean Vanier, is co-founder of l'Arche in Trosly where he makes his home. He has long been committed to living the Gospel in the spirit of poverty and prayer. He was founder and director of a lay community, Eau Vive in France and later chaplain of the Val Fleuri in Trosly.

He is a constant sign of the heart and soul of l'Arche, attentive to the spiritual needs of each member of the community, ministering, writing, and helping the community to live more fully in the Holy Spirit.

The fundamental goal of l'Arche, as it is specified in our charter, is to create communities inspired by the Beatitudes and the spirit of the Gospel, where the "helped" and the "helpers" might live together, assisting one another.

When Jesus gave his sermon on the Mount – his Sermon on the Beatitudes – St Luke mentions that, beyond the twelve that had already been chosen, there was a whole crowd that had gathered there. I believe that this little note of Luke's is very significant. In this speech, the master, Jesus, gives us a marvellous synthesis of all the prophetic writings of the Old Testament, which was already in spirit the proclamation of the New Testament. He gives us something like a seed of the Spirit which is called to grow. This seed is not meant for the apostles only, but for all those who wish to become his disciples.

The Sermon on the Mount is not only the synthesis of all which is most spiritual in the Old Testament; we also discover in it all which inspired the mystics of primitive religions. Is this not the reason why today our Hindu and Moslem friends, and all those who truly believe in the Spirit, are attracted to the Sermon on the Mount?

Poverty: the Foundation of all the Beatitudes

We need to understand how it is that the Beatitudes have such an important position in the charter of l'Arche. Obviously, it is because the poor are at the heart of our community. It is they who make us discover that the Kingdom of God belongs to the poor. It is through the poor, and particularly through the most destitute, that we attain and touch the person of Jesus, and discover that he is the only total incarnation of the Beatitudes.

The first of the Beatitudes is the one on poverty: "Blessed are the poor, the Kingdom of God is theirs." There is no doubt that it is the poor who attract us all to l'Arche. They are the signs that God has used to call us together. From the very beginnings, across all the continents, the two characteristics of l'Arche have been this attraction of the poor, and the desire to become their servants, even their disciples, knowing that the poor can be irreplaceable teachers, and that we have much to receive from them regarding our interior life.

L'Arche seeks to open its doors very wide to all those who seek to serve the poor and who feel that the poor carry a hidden treasure. We come from many places, all very different. And more particularly, we have different mentalities, different ages and diverse spiritual graces. From the very beginning at l'Arche, there have been friends of Jesus that the heavenly Father and the Holy Spirit have prepared to receive the poor. In the earliest days in France, in Belgium, in Canada, in America, there were priests and religious who were attracted to l'Arche in the hope of living out the renewal of the Church which had been announced and called for by Vatican II. But at the same time, they met the young, and not so young, many of whom were struggling in their faith. As if by instinct, these had come to seek among the poor, with the poor, what they believed they had lost, or were on the verge of losing.

Since these early years, through the poor, l'Arche has helped many divided, struggling Catholics to rediscover among themselves a deeper unity, within their own community and within themselves. But since its beginnings, l'Arche has also been a privileged place for the new ecumenical spirit that the Holy Spirit is demanding of all Christians. Without any hesitation, l'Arche welcomes Christians of various denominations who are preoccupied and torn by the separations and divisions of this holy Church which Jesus had wanted united, and whose witness was thus diminished by division. The poor help them discover a renewed friendship and fraternity. During those first years at l'Arche, one found a number of atheists, or at least agnostics, who would feel something profound and mysterious awaken within them in the presence of the poor and in their contacts with them.

We all came to l'Arche for many different reasons. But we all find ourselves gathered in the desire to serve the poor, and, more importantly, to put ourselves under their guidance, to become their disciples. For to be a servant means that one does not come to l'Arche in order to become richer, to make money, to advance in one's social standing, nor even to find there a privileged place to exercise one's talents, or even those gifts which have been granted by God, whether they be abilities to command, to organize, or to lead men. It also means – and this, though it might be subtler, is that much more important – that one does not come to l'Arche in order to gain an experience of the poor, to discover their psychology or sociology. These are attitudes of a master, not those of a servant. The first thing that one learns at l'Arche, and this is a fundamental condition for being able to live there fruitfully, is that one cannot become a true servant of the poor without first becoming their disciple.

When we say that we must be servants and disciples of the poor at l'Arche, we are saying it in the deepest sense. It is not enough to be a servant who tells himself: "I will teach this person a trade", or: "I will cook for that person." Certainly, these are useful services. But if somebody truly wants to be involved in l'Arche in order to grow spiritually, then let him become a servant of the poor. For there are two completely different ways of being an instructor: either one simply wishes to teach someone a trade, or

one does so while trying to awaken this "someone" to his uniqueness. If this is true of trades, how much truer must it be of
community life and community administration. It seems to me
that what characterizes us, even in the administration of material
goods, is the way in which we try to allow those who are
wounded, those who have most often been rejected or considered
as anonymous numbers, to feel that here they are treated as individuals, as people.

We must feel that the poor have something to give us. I am
always struck at Trosly when Jean receives those who wish to
become assistants. He asks them for this inner conviction that they
will receive much more from the poor than they will ever be able
to give. In a way, it is this conviction that is the condition for
being a servant of the poor. The servant knows that in helping at
the level of temporal needs, in giving of his energy and talents, he
still remains only at the level of means. The poor, on the other
hand, will become for him the instruments of Providence and will
help him discover the ultimate ends of his own being, the true
meaning of his life. The poor are our teachers in the school of
wisdom. We can only bring them modest tools.

I believe that this is the primary condition of our unity in
l'Arche. L'Arche is founded on poverty. To be a generous servant,
it is always necessary to be poor, and all the more so if the poor
are to be our teachers. For they receive the message of faith much
more easily than we, and in a way which is almost natural. Given
that there is nothing on earth to which they are truly attached, and
that they have ardent and open hearts, they immediately receive
the Good News when spoken to about God.

The Programme of the Beatitudes

It is important to analyse briefly the programme which is given us
in the Beatitudes. The Beatitudes do not follow a logical order.
Poverty is not a principle from which everything else flows. Poverty is that radical condition which allows us to receive all from
God. But this radical condition takes many names and implies

extremely diverse attitudes, given the multiple facets of human life. The Beatitudes show us that we must be open to the action of the Holy Spirit in all areas of our lives. And if the Beatitudes have been the charter of all Christian communities and of all religious orders since the birth of Christianity, it is because they are difficult to live out on one's own. As soon as we start to want to realize this programme, we feel strongly the need for our brothers' help. What we have not yet realized by ourselves, what we cannot know by ourselves, we realize through our brothers who, in fraternal communion, are with us.

The Triple Depth of Poverty

The first three Beatitudes help us discover what we might call the triple depth of this poverty, this first essential condition which carries us so far.

Blessed are the poor

As Jesus so clearly exemplified, poverty is first of all a detachment from money and all material wealth. This requires at least a detachment of spirit from all that is material comfort, from all which is artificial, and which so easily becomes important in our modern world. In fact all which is material or temporal wealth, all this exterior world, all which is manufactured by man, can be reduced to the money which allows us to acquire these riches. But money can never develop the heart: rather, it clutters up and chokes the heart. And if we become attached to money, it kills the heart. If we want to keep a truly open heart, we must be absolutely detached from money since money carries with it a danger: whenever we own it, we want to own more.

Blessed are the gentle

The second Beatitude – "blessed are the gentle, the weak" – helps us understand that money isn't the only dangerous thing. We understand easily enough that we cannot serve two masters: God and mammon. As soon as money becomes an idol for us, we become capable of all sorts of treason – Judas is such an example. But it isn't sufficient to be detached from money. We all know of teachers, engineers, executives and ministers who are not directly attached to money, and even want to lead a very simple life. But they do so all the better to exercise their power. To be a true servant of the poor, it is also necessary to be detached from power. And this is all the more difficult, given that power is not necessarily temporal. There is a certain spirituality to power. We can truly desire to serve the poor, but we do so by commanding, dominating, being the first, exercising our influence; we want to be a servant, but we want to do it by serving where our talents will be most evidently used. What we need instead is this spirit of Jesus, who wanted his disciples, even in their responsibilities, to be servants who would consider themselves the least, that is to say, detached from the services they would render, so as to be attached only to those they served. This detachment from power is certainly more difficult than detachment from exterior wealth, and it must be continually renewed. Many intelligent people feel that money makes them materialistic and so prefer not to be attached to it in the hope of keeping a greater spiritual freedom. But they remain attracted to those who can be their best collaborators, those who appear as the élite of intelligence and of mind. They are very rare who truly love, and are attached to those whose only wealth is in the heart.

Blessed are those who mourn

The third Beatitude, "blessed are those who mourn", shows that there is yet a more difficult detachment, if we truly wish to be poor as the Gospel would have us. An artist or a dilettante can live a bohemian life, wanting neither money nor power as such, so that he may be freer and more objective. A philosopher who loves speculative thought, a scientist who delights in research, an artist whose sole effort is to reach the symbolic value of things and beings; all these seek to be detached from a world of power in order to better give themselves to their task. But to be a true servant of the poor, we need to feel that the poor bring us something. Otherwise, there cannot be the reciprocity which is essential to all friendship. But this demands that suffering and tears purify our interior being, our ideas, our ways of seeing, feeling, reacting; all this extremely subtle inner world that inhabits each of us. This inner detachment of the spirit can only be attained through suffering. The heart cannot be purified unless it has been moulded by God himself through many tears. And this is necessary if we are to become these poor servants, attracted to what is invisible in the poor; servants who are able to find the least signs of hope and so establish a dialogue free from aggression and bitterness with those who are violent, critical and revolutionary. Only tears can allow one to become gentle, so as to be able not only to be attracted to the distress of the poor, but to discover this distress when it hides itself behind such an aggressive front. Our hearts need to have been purified through suffering if we are to be able to spontaneously discover that all violence, all confrontation, most often hides a great pain. This is a mystery. Only God can purify us and conform us to it. And it remains a fact that those who have not suffered much, or who have not been open in all humility to the suffering of others, are lost before certain attitudes they find among the poor, and therefore cannot be servants to the end.

Spiritual poverty thus implies a triple detachment: the detachment from wealth, the detachment from power, and the detachment from one's own spirit, or, in other words, from this individual who dwells in the depths of each of us and constitutes a kind of spiritual, nearly metaphysical, selfishness. Spiritual poverty requires of us that we discover, beyond this living individual, our truer self whose essential characteristic is that it is made to be in relationship with others. Yet, this truer self that is in each of us can only come to our awareness through God's work, through his giving of himself to us. God alone can teach us to love by loving us himself. Through this alone can we become that person who is the deepest mystery of our being. If we are not firstly open to God, we will never be able to be open to what is most ineffable and mysterious in others.

Blessed are the pure in heart;
Blessed are those who hunger and thirst for justice

"Blessed are the pure in heart" and "blessed are those who hunger and thirst for justice." It is very important to see that these two new Beatitudes are complementary in their relationship to the others. Interior and exterior poverty and detachment do not necessarily awaken hunger and thirst for justice. Or, to put it in a more correct way, true and total detachment from all that constitutes our living individuality does indeed call forth this hunger and thirst for justice and this purity of heart.

A pure heart is not only a detached heart. There is something more positive in a pure heart. That is why our Lord says that the pure of heart will "see God". A pure heart is not a naïve heart, for there is light in a pure heart. A heart can never be empty. But in order that it be completely detached from immediate pleasure, in order that it be free from jealousy and bitterness, some kind of interior fullness must be given it and must abide in it. To attain a total detachment from ourselves, we must necessarily have a heart filled with God. And, let us add, filled with the God of love. God cannot give himself directly and immediately but gives himself in and through his love. It is not enough that we be poor. God's superabundance must fortify our heart's interior, so that we might be attracted to all the miseries which usually accompany poverty. We need to have experienced the fullness of God.

The Beatitude on hunger and thirst for justice is also an important one. At l'Arche, we do not seek only to help the poor discover what can be developed in the depth of their person, but we also try to provide a milieu and conditions of life conducive to their growth. This requires that we be hungry and thirsty for justice. Certainly, this Beatitude is first of all concerned with the justice of God: that we respect nature just as God has made it in his loving art; that all things be in the order, in the harmony that God wants for them. This hunger and thirst for justice implies that our heart is pure, but also that it be strong, not with a desire rooted in the nature of this will, which is to say in love. Our heart must become hunger and thirst.

To help the poor, it is certainly necessary that we understand their suffering and, in a special way, their anxieties. But when we ourselves are anguished, it is impossible to help another in the same state, for we let ourselves be drawn along in the other's anxiety: this situation is contagious. To help an anguished person, we must have come to the point where we have integrated our own anxiety, not by ourselves, but thanks to a stronger love and a greater hope than our own. We need a pure heart, a heart able to forget itself, even when it is tormented. God must come from inside us to give us his love so that, even when we are anxious, we will still be present to whoever might come to us. This is a pure heart: a heart detached from itself, that can hunger and thirst for the justice due to others. This hunger and thirst for justice is neither violent nor revolutionary: rather, it bathes our aggression in a greater love which unites in us both deep feelings of love and deep aggression. This can only be the work of the infinite love of God. That is why these Beatitudes are gifts which only God can grant to us.

Blessed are the merciful;
Blessed are the peace-makers

The programme of the Beatitudes does not stop with a pure heart and a search for justice. What is mysterious about our human condition is that we must be detached from all our realizations, knowing that God will judge us, not on our successes, but rather on the deepest, and sometimes most hidden, motivations that lie within us; and yet we must *do* something. We cannot be content with good intentions. We must throw ourselves into the realm of action, with all the risks that this entails. Action is necessary: "blessed are those who *do* mercy", "blessed are the peace-*makers*." Here are two essential deeds that require of us complete spiritual poverty, and that allow hunger and thirst for justice as well as purity of heart to realize works of purity in the world.

If the Holy Spirit does not dwell in us, then we can be neither truly merciful, nor makers of peace. True mercy is quite different from a kind of human pity that ultimately does not respect the poor. Through its gentle and tender actions, true mercy speaks of

their worth to the poor. Mercy implies the divine love which
uplifts the poor from within, that does away with the distance
which can exist between the misery of the poor and the help which
is offered them. What is true of mercy is even more so of peace.
If the Holy Spirit, the Spirit of peace, does not dwell in us, we
cannot be makers of peace. Peace is not only of an exterior order.
Peace is firstly concerned with the interior order of the heart. Peace
is the full ultimate gift which might be found in each of our hearts.
An impeccable exterior order can exist which all the while hides
terrible suffering and injustice. There are psychiatric hospitals that
are very well ordered, where each heart is nevertheless walled-in
by anguish and incoherence. We know that peace is first of all a
gift of the heart that God alone can give.

To try in all possible ways to banish injustice is quite wonderful.
All men of good will must strive for this ideal. But we also know
that, in a special way, the poor require more than justice. True
peace can only come from love. We are not able to give this peace
to mankind on our own, for in each person there is a thirst for the
absolute. Only God can give such peace. In the works of peace as
in the works of mercy, we are but the instruments of God. This
implies a gift from God – the kingdom of heaven belongs to the
poor.

Blessed are the persecuted

The programme of the Beatitudes culminates with this last one:
"blessed are the persecuted." We have not had many occasions to
live out this Beatitude at l'Arche, but should we not prepare ourselves to do so? Is not our community a challenge for those who
live according to the spirit of the world? This last Beatitude was
foreshadowed in the Beatitude on tears. In each of these two
Beatitudes, there is something of grace which, thanks to the Holy
Spirit and his love, adds a new fullness to all the others. We do
not have to seek for tears and suffering, sorrow and persecution
for their own sake. But when they are granted by God, they should
be accepted and seen as signs of the special love he has for us.
Saints understand that when, after everything else, they are also
persecuted, they are in fact being given a divine means of adding

to their love of God. Persecution becomes a Beatitude when it is accompanied with forgiveness, total pardon, helping us to truly love our enemies. "Father, forgive them, they know not what they do." Through suffering and the grace of forgiveness which transforms it, the poor sinner can most resemble his infinitely merciful Father.

Persecution carries with it a kind of new, totally inner consecration of all that the Holy Spirit has done in us. Tears and persecutions give us a new inner poverty. Both of them complete the detachment from our ego, and the creation of a new inner person who derives his being from a loving relationship with the divine Persons.

The Beatitudes and the Life of Jesus

Who would dare say, when confronted with the programme of the Beatitudes, that he fulfills it completely? We realize how much we need a teacher: not only a lecturer who will proclaim it from the top of a mountain, but a gentle and humble teacher who will come down with us into the daily valley of tears which is the stuff of our days. Through his birth in the poor, humble stable of Bethlehem, through his hidden life at Nazareth, through the humility and gentleness of his apostolic life, Jesus is the gentle and humble teacher who has made himself the compassionate friend who shares the life of the poor with its tears, its miseries and its rejections.

The Son of God, having become the Son of Man, and filled with the Holy Spirit, lives out all these Beatitudes in his concrete, personal existence. He lives them out in a new way, a way which is both more dignified and yet more simple. Living them in such a divine way, he gives to each of these Beatitudes a new dimension of humility and interiority: he makes them more divine, for they will henceforth be in the very image of the loving God, Father, Son and Holy Spirit. And in this itself, he makes them more human, for he lives them out firstly in his relationships as Son of

Man, with Mary his mother and our mother, in his hidden and sorrowful life.

The Beatitudes can no longer be the heroic characteristics of some prophet who cuts himself off from his family and his people by his extraordinary works and marvels. Instead, they become the gentle, humble characteristics of a new family, the Holy Family, which, with its apostolic life, becomes a new people of brothers and friends. Are not the Beatitudes of the Gospel then like a precious key, like a nearly invisible watermark that allows us to discover the secret of love in the life of Jesus, to follow him during all the various steps of his earthly existence, to understand those hidden ties that bind the Saviour's life as a child to those of Mary and Joseph, and to the life which he led in public with the apostles and the disciples?

The Beatitudes and the Church of the Holy Spirit

The Beatitudes have another dimension: a prophetic one. They help us to understand the continuity and progression in the life of the Church, inaugurated at Pentecost by the Holy Spirit, and inspired and animated by saints of all times and places. The Beatitudes help us to grasp the fundamental spirit which unites so many different vocations in the Church of Christ; to be its contemplatives who, in their hearts, live anew with Mary the joyous, sorrowful and glorious mysteries of the rosary, to live as apostles who proclaim these mysteries through the word of God; or to be men and women who testify to them through their lives, by works of mercy and peace in their families and cities.

In a sense, we must go beyond the first two dimensions: that of the past – of prophets in the Old Testament and primitive religions – and that of Jesus' hidden life with Mary and Joseph at Nazareth, and of his public life with the apostles and the disciples in the midst of his people, ending with the mystery of the passion and of the cross. For a third dimension adds a new facet to the first two: it is that of the Holy Spirit. Did not Jesus tell his disciples: "It is good that I should leave, so that I might send you the Holy Spirit"

Père Thomas Philippe and Jean Vanier

and "When the Holy Spirit will be given to you, you will do things even more wonderful than those I did when I was in your midst." The new religion founded by Christ through the cross is the religion of Jesus and the Spirit. Through his sacrifice, Jesus won us a new grace, a new state of grace which helps us inwardly to relive the mystery of his life and death in each of our own lives. But it also institutes a new economy of salvation and holiness which is granted to all of renewed humanity through this divine sacrifice; it will henceforth be applied to all through these humble signs of love that we call the sacraments.

The sacraments institute a visible, social structure that nevertheless, because of their divine founder, remain at the interior level of the theological virtues: faith, hope and charity. Thus they can give both a temporal, exterior help and an eternal, interior grace. Through these signs of love, so humble and so poor, Jesus continues the work of his Incarnation through the church, in time and space. That is how he evangelizes the poorest: by giving them

proportioned and efficacious means that will allow each and every
one of us to be united to him in the deepest and most concrete
way, thereby constituting one family, one people, totally inspired
and bathed in the spirit of the Beatitudes.

The Beatitudes and l'Arche

In order to understand both the great diversity of vocations and
the profound unity that is found in the Arche communities both
among the helped and the helpers, it will be necessary to consider
them from the perspective of the Beatitudes and their triple dimension. Would not this be the secret that would allow our communities to be stable, and yet be dynamic as they should be? At
l'Arche, there might be some who seek Jesus without yet knowing
him, perhaps without being conscious of their own seeking (just
as so many men of good will have done throughout the ages and
in all places). In our communities, these men of good will can
already be assigned temporal responsibilities: they can effectively
serve the poor. Others already know the secret of our fellowship
and friendship. They have already met Jesus and want to live his
spirit in an explicit way. Whatever might be their functions, both
helpers and helped are the true animators of our communities.

Finally, the poorest of our brothers and our friends, through the
detachment effected by the Holy Spirit or through their severest
handicaps, will choose to root themselves in our communities by
taking on the most difficult and obscure of duties. These are the
true inspiration of the new Christian communities that l'Arche
seeks to found. In this divided world, l'Arche's vocation is ultimately to bring together, through the Beatitudes, all Christians
who recognize Jesus as their only Saviour – even if they have yet
to find the ways and the visible structures that will allow the
ultimate and enduring realization of his plan. L'Arche also brings
together all people of good will, whatever their country, their age,
their race or their culture: For without knowing his name, they
also sincerely and loyally seek the Saviour.

4

A PLACE FOR HUMAN GROWTH

Hubert Allier

Hubert Allier, from Grenoble, France, completed his studies in business administration and it was during the Faith and Light pilgrimage to Lourdes in 1971 that he first met Jean Vanier and l'Arche. In 1972 Hubert joined the community in Trosly. At first he was head of the pottery workshop and lived in a home with ten handicapped men in the town of Compiègne. After his marriage to Françoise in 1973, they took a flat in Compiègne and Hubert became head of the whole work programme in l'Arche, Trosly.

In 1978, Hubert, Françoise and their two children moved to the Arche community in Ambleteuse, northern France, where he now leads the community of some 120 people spread out in six different homes and several workshops.

At the same time, he was called upon to co-ordinate all l'Arche communities in France and in this capacity to represent them at the International Council meetings. In 1982 he was voted vice-co-ordinator of l'Arche International. As such he seconds and supports Sue Mosteller, the international co-ordinator.

Each person should be able to find within l'Arche a space in which to develop, a soil from which to grow. It would be dreadful if this community were only a community of tenderness and love but made no demands on our capacity to grow. Would it then be a community of genuine love? Surely not. There is no love where no demands are made.

Others in this book will tell of what the poor can give us and talk about sharing their life. This is indeed at the heart of l'Arche. But this "living with" must spur each person forward to a greater fullness of being. It must urge us to grow at every level so as to become more clearsighted, to attain inner freedom, to grow in openness to others and in the capacity to give freely of ourselves and to become independent. Isn't there sometimes a danger at l'Arche of existing in a world of affection and feelings, forgetting the demands made by personal growth? Obviously, growth in this sense must be different for each person and the most important aspect of growth must always be that of the heart. How wonderful to see Peter, after spending twelve years of his life in an institution, begin to smile. When he arrived, he was so full of frustrations and aggressiveness that his face seemed dead. It is obvious that this growth towards peace and inner joy is not self-willed; it comes from knowing we are deeply loved and accepted and that we have found our place. Only then is it possible for us to exist.

In this chapter, I am not going to consider the healing of the heart and the opening up of the person which comes with it. Nor am I going to talk about the place of psychiatrists and psychologists in human growth. We all know how important their role is when there is a serious blockage of the personality.

Rather, I would like to consider that aspect of growth which involves an effort by the person himself if he wants to make something of his life. As I have been in charge of work at l'Arche, Trosly, many of the examples I use come from that experience. I have seen such happiness in the eyes of men and women discovering that they are capable of making something beautiful or useful. Other examples are drawn from the time before my marriage when I lived in the Tremplin, an Arche home for eight men, in the town of Compiègne. There it was a matter of helping some of them to make and give effect to clearly defined choices and so to find meaning and direction to their lives. To help someone grow, you don't need to be on his back all the time. Each person must always have the freedom to grow, but also the freedom not to grow. Wanting to grow and develop doesn't happen to order; it comes from the depths of our being. The one who accompanies is there to help us discover that it is possible.

Yvan and Hughes, l'Arche, Trosly

Does l'Arche Provide
the Conditions for Human Growth?

As I put this question, there comes to mind a whole series of examples, memories, experiences, crises, failures and successes. Faces and encounters come to life again in my memory. I relive those difficult but at the same time wonderful moments when I saw individuals in a group or the group as a whole moving forward, beginning to grow.

Living together, working together and weaving relationships which should be fraternal and educational at the same time, all this involves growth. Not only for the handicapped people who are progressing and making their way towards their own independence and therefore need a guide, a framework for development, sure points of reference and well-defined stages; but also, and especially, for those who are there to help and support the handicapped people in their projects. We cannot talk about growth without adding to it the word "reciprocal." Helping someone come through the various stages of life or work means that whoever provides guidance and accompaniment must be ready to grow just as much. He must be able to "tune in" to the other, to adjust his receptiveness, to exercise patience and question his own attitudes and demands, if he really wants to live a truthful and growing relationship with the other person.

All those who come into our community – whether they be assistants or handicapped people – find a soil in which they can grow and the means for such growth: being able to wash and get dressed on one's own, to arrive on time for work, to take charge of an activity implies growth. Becoming responsible for one's friends in a helping relationship or progressing towards social integration means growth. Giving a meaning to one's life, learning to accept oneself as one is, living out our differences in harmony with the group, accepting one's limits: all this is growth. Giving oneself rules for living, allowing oneself to be challenged, developing one's power of listening, of tolerating others, knowing how to forgive: this too is growth. Knowing how to stop and admit one's failures and to draw lessons from them is just as much a matter of growth as being able to cross new thresholds of knowledge and skill.

We must not limit the word "growth" to simply acquiring, becoming capable of . . . No, community life makes us believe in moral growth in its full sense of living and believing in one's life. The kind of relationships we establish with one another, our faith in man, in each person's uniqueness, whatever his wounds, weaknesses or limits, leads us to this one reality which is fundamental, the only one which gives the acquiring of knowledge its proper place. What's the point of being able to live alone and earn money if we cannot give a meaning however humble to our life. In the not so long run, we are in danger of creating one more marginal person. Morality, in this sense, is a dimension of life where every one of us has room to evolve and progress if we really want to live with another person, with the other as starting point. Because that other is different, he lives differently and he challenges us to transcend ourselves if we are to meet him, be with him and live a relationship with him.

While the handicapped person can be expected to grow in his capacity for independence and the acquisition of skills, the assistant is more often called on to change his way of thinking and to let go his convictions and preconceived ideas.

Some Examples

Having left the community, Jean decided of his own free will to come back and ask for help in taking the few remaining steps that will bring him to a certain degree of autonomy. Every time he felt that he was crossing over to the side of those who can "be responsible for themselves", he fell back into the position of being assisted. Again and again we had to go and look for him because he had run away, fleeing the contract between us although we had worked it out together. He dreaded the possibility of independence and at the same time longed for it. Each time we had to pick up the threads again, explain the situation once more, define the different steps to be taken, renew our mutual trust and confidence and reaffirm one to another that it was worthwhile and that he was capable. Each time a tiny step forward was taken, part of his fear was overcome and new hope opened out before us. From the assistants he demanded even more trust and support, putting them to the test to see how far they would really go with him. It is this mutual trust and support that have enabled Jean to pull himself out of his dependence and set forth on a new course.

Marie lived in the land of make-believe. To hear her talk, she could do anything: hold down a regular and satisfying job, keep a budget, and not give in to that treacherous friend, alcohol. Miles away from reality. Thanks to the help of assistants who prevented her from building castles in the air she was able to move towards her own project in short, well-defined stages which were within her reach, and didn't make her feel underestimated. This required the assistants to be creative, not to impose their own will too strongly on her, to grow with her. Today Marie is married to Philip.

Georges used to try to make himself heard by throwing fits,

exploding with anger and shouting. He was unable to control himself when he felt insecure, judged and trapped. Violence was his language because of such a difficult past history and such an uncertain future. All that was hard for him to bear – could anyone bear it? But thanks to a long-term relationship with the people who lived with him and a milieu that restored his self-confidence and was open to his problems, he was able little by little to express himself by other means than violence.

It was months before Henri agreed to take part in sports with the others. Through watching the group without participating, then putting shorts on over his trousers, and running alongside he finally joined in with the whole group. What an achievement, and what a pleasure to see him afterwards. The assistant, not under-standing what all this meant, found it hard to accept that his whole project was upset because one person would not bend to the rule. However, it was Henri's attitude that helped him to accept the other person better, with his differences, and to understand that each one has a different road to travel.

In the pottery workshop, Danielle's difficulty lay in mastering the clay, which kept collapsing just when the goal was in sight, leaving her discouraged and defenceless. When she finally mastered it, what frenzied achievement she displayed. From this the assistant learned that well-defined methods do not necessarily achieve their goal and that above all the rhythm of each person must be respected.

Jean-Marc had just come out of a psychiatric hospital; he lived in one of the homes, then in an apartment with other handicapped people, gradually moving towards complete independence and living alone. But he had to find a meaning for his "living alone" and was not happy until his own home became in turn a place of welcome. The assistant did not have to teach him techniques any more but help him find a true meaning to his life. It isn't easy. It requires us to be clear about the meaning of our own lives, to confide our deepest beliefs and values.

We could extend the list of all these little events, these tiny steps forward, perhaps insignificant in themselves but which are signs of hope. To succeed in repeating the same gesture a hundred times is stupid only for those who already know what success is. At every stage, from the first step forward at one end, to social integration and normalization at the other, one need remains constant: a person must have been able to express his desires and find an environment and friends to help and support him, he must agree to set himself certain requirements in order to achieve his goal.

We could have chosen examples where the goal would seem, provisionally at least, to have been missed, cases of failure on the path of progress. In our communities we often pass through such times of despair, times when it becomes very hard to maintain the other's confidence in what we have built. Such situations help us become more sharply aware of a certain number of pre-requisites to the undertaking of a relationship of growth, however minimal the progress may be.

Pre-requisites for Growth

To accept having to make an effort

A person cannot grow unless he has within him the desire to move onward, to build something. Surely Marie's experience would be impossible to imagine if she had not agreed to enter into a relationship of trust with the assistant and to live through certain demands with him. Could she have accepted such constant challenging and goading, such repeated corrections, if she had not expressed the desire to grow and change? We must be capable of perceiving this will, which is not always expressed in words; sometimes it can be perceived through attitudes, crises or sudden depressions. We must be capable of understanding these, for the other person hasn't the means, nor even the wish to do so himself. The environment of a person can play an important part in fostering this perception. We will talk about this at length later on.

Subsequently we must see to it that this "will to grow" is held on to, sustained, always making sure that it is there, present at the heart of the person's desire. For this, there must be special times of meeting, moments when the person knows we are there for him and him alone, to listen to what he has to say, to dream with him and bring him back into the line of his original desire. We are not respecting people if we claim to be listening to them without giving proper attention to the time and place and conditions in which we do so.

This concept of "will" seems to me to be fundamental because it is at the root of any possible growth of people and implies two ways of working with people. First, there is a need for people who will commit themselves to being alongside the person who wishes to grow, doubting with the person, suffering alongside him, accepting his regression and encouraging him.

Secondly, there is the guarantor. It seems desirable to make a distinction between the permanent accompaniment of the assistants in the home and workshop and another, equally important accompaniment provided by whoever is helping the person to retain a vision of his project. The greater a person's potential for growth, the harder it is for him to hold to that vision of himself if whoever lives or works with him is also guardian of his personal project. Of necessity, the day to day relations of work or home entail tensions, conflicts and challenges which can strain a relationship and at times undermine the mutual trust which each must give the other. Someone who only intervenes from time to time with regard to the handicapped person and his day to day companions will appear more impartial and therefore better able to embody the long-term hopes expressed by him.

A true appreciation of the person's capacities

In order to support and help a person in his growth, we need to know him very well. This requires a relationship other than educational, allowing an evaluation which is broader and therefore less technical. All this allows us to begin working with the person "where he is at," not setting goals too far off which will only discourage him. Indeed, all our initial energies and support are directed towards affirmation. Someone who has never had the opportunity to do things on his own will succeed better with a simple repetitive kind of work than with something complicated. In this way he gains confidence in himself. Too often we have caused despair and frustration because we have been impatient, inattentive and over-ambitious. It is true that when we love someone we want him to succeed, to aim high. We project ourselves onto the other person and that's only natural; it proves our interest in and hope for that person. The assistant must therefore aim to reconcile these two parameters – his ambition for the person, and that person's potential. This is the hardest thing of all and it demands a great deal of humility, because again and again it is ourselves we have to re-examine.

Accepting the risks of failure

All growth implies the risk of failure. Stating that risk is even a proof of honesty on the part of the one who accompanies. It is a result of two wills coming face to face: "You can, you are capable" and "I can't; I'm afraid." Out of confidence and a true relationship is born the desire to try, to stretch out beyond our known limits. The risk of failure has to be thought of beforehand because if failure does come it must be put into its place, in the perspective of the whole, and re-examined as a positive contribution to the person's project. We have already mentioned the example of Jean, who illustrates this point very well. He almost carried it to extremes since he himself provoked failures without warning, so that he wouldn't have to progress any further. In this case failure becomes an integral part of the project because it defines part of the person's basic problem. This possibility of failure teaches us to be prudent and realistic. We need to present one by one the new elements that must enter into the project, as well as the different stages that must be gone through. Thus, if someone's ambition is, for example, integration into society, all the elements needed to prepare for this must be brought into play progressively. Then, when the time comes, a trial period should be arranged which will allow the person a more realistic appraisal of his situation since it will be firmly rooted in practical experience.

Gilles thought that once he was outside, everything would go better, and it was only the assistants who were holding him back. But he would have to be confronted with the reality of the work-a-day world, and this would need preparation. Before his trial run at the factory, each one of his mistakes was pinpointed, so that any comments made during the trial run might arouse some echo in his mind. The try-out was not a success. But because it had been well prepared, a new start could be made from more solid foundations and with a clearer vision of the way forward.

The Proper Conditions for Growth

All these prerequisites; the handicapped person's resolve and the attitudes of those around him, must be lived out under certain conditions. In fact three things are needed: the right environment, a well-formulated project, and agreed requirements.

Environment

L'Arche is a community of life and relationship before being an educational community. It is the intersection of a place for simply living and a place where we believe healing is possible, giving therapeutic value to our communities. If we have set up homes of human dimensions where participation is demanded from everybody, it is because of a certain conviction. If, in these homes, assistants and handicapped people live together, eat at the same table and join in celebrating important occasions, it is because we are convinced that for someone to be able to grow, he must have a place to live that gives warmth and security.

How often people have come to our communities from psychiatric hospitals and institutions completely blocked in their relationships. Imprisoned within themselves, they sought protection by shutting themselves off from others or by being aggressive. In reality, the wounds they had suffered in their emotional life and in their capacity for human contact were deeper than those of mind or body. Every assistant living at l'Arche could bear witness to the time – sometimes so long and thankless – during which he must approach the person with the utmost delicacy if he is to win him over. The assistant must earn the other's acceptance of him, lead him to discover and believe that he has a friend who wants a living relationship with him. During this time, the person so welcomed tests us to find out if it is true that we are committed to him, or if yet again promises made will be followed by another let down. What is needed is some shared ground of being which will give birth to relationship and friendship. This ground is everyday life in all its apparent triviality: washing, getting dressed, eating and having fun together. Only when someone has realized that we are not going to let him down and that within the home there are assistants ready to love and support him (while still making certain demands), only then can a traumatized person accept letting anybody penetrate his defences. This whole climate of living, which we try to infuse with warmth, trust, tolerance and patience, will enable the person, once he has been accepted with his capacities and his limits, to let down his barriers. It allows him to open the doors of his being, to reveal the depths of his person, to discover the self which he has never allowed anyone to know.

Once he understands that the assistant has freely chosen to put himself at his service, the handicapped person can prepare himself for growth. And the assistant must prepare himself to accompany him. Some will skip this phase of self awakening (they have no need of it), and demand straightaway an accompaniment that will enable them to move forward. Therefore, we must offer them a programme and situations where growth is possible.

This is where work comes in, as a complementary situation that offers the promise of growth, work being the activity which, by its very nature, fosters the consciousness of one's capacities. The various stages which one must pass through are clear and precise, and constitute an established organized framework, subject to the usual rules of work. It is a situation which allows a positive recognition of the self, since people around can recognize what has been done and see that it is useful, beautiful or good. What is more, progress is always possible in working attitudes – team life and other forms of work – as well as in the work itself with increasing responsibility and more difficult tasks.

The fact that the place where people live complements the place where they work allows us to live with and guide them in a more unified and concerted way. It also helps to resolve the tensions which sometimes arise around the project we have for someone, when the various people who accompany him are not in agreement. Some Arche communities which have associated workshops can avoid this snag. Organization meetings between home and workshop offer a real opportunity to set up a project and make a success of it.

However, this possibility of unified action requires us to watch out for several things. At some point on the road to autonomy a person may need to feel that the two places are independent of each other, especially if he is relatively free in his relationships and thus has greater capabilities. We must take care that this unity doesn't become a prison or a limitation of freedom. We must let a person have his work-scene to himself, where people do not necessarily know what happens in the home, and vice versa. Therefore, we must learn to adjust the help we give, so that it does not get in the way.

Jean-Paul was unable to come to work for months and months. Was it because of laziness, lack of interest, despair, fear? Both the home and the workshop were convinced that staying in his bedroom all day was bad for him. A well thought-out support system was needed over a long period of time in order to motivate him. When he began to find an interest in his work, when we realized that what he wanted was to live happily and not become incapable before his time, he began to take himself in hand. He had learned that our wishes coincided with his own interests. At that moment, we had to make a greater distinction between supporting him at work and at home so that he could feel freer.

When an Arche community has its own workshops, it does offer this possibility of unity. However, it can also appear to be a sort of ghetto. We are always seeing the same faces, encountering the same problems; all our talk is about community life. This danger of shutting out what is beyond the place in which we live could

be contrary to people's growth, if it does not allow a real choice
of life and work. This is why it is important that in the various
Arche communities there should be people committed to the community but who do not live the daily life in the homes. Such is the
case of the professional who comes to l'Arche as his place of work
while adhering to the basic aims and values of the community.
Besides his particular skill – horticulture, carpentry, accounting –
he brings with him an opening on to the town or district where
he and his family live. This dimension allows the community to
keep in touch with the world that surrounds it, and offers something other than the home itself to the handicapped people. This
is also one of the roles of the specialists – psychiatrists, psychologists, social workers. Because of the particular service we ask them
to provide, they can challenge us in our support since they have
other reference points and have had other experiences. They force
us to not turn in on ourselves and not to forget that other sources
of inspiration exist. They can also remind us, (if we tend to forget
it), that while the assistant has come to live at l'Arche by choice,
the handicapped person is usually placed here – a fact we must bear
in mind as we support him.

This is also where the friends of the community come in. Within
the town of Compiègne there are several Arche communities
where we try to create local contacts through cultural and sporting
activities, and through the efforts of couples or families who have
become real friends to the handicapped people. These friends are
totally outside the community and do not have to refer to the
assistants. They bring emotional and spiritual support and help our
reintegration into society; they create a sort of bridge. This brings
us to consider the place of the 'volunteer' in our communities.
This role has sometimes been questioned by social workers but,
in the light of the important place held by friends, we can assert
that volunteers are indispensable. The relationship such people can
have, the very meaning of the friendship they offer handicapped
people, is of a very different order to that which is expected of the
professional, or of the person who lives and works each day with
the handicapped person and therefore has an educational relationship with him. If what we want is ultimately the 'demarginaliza-

tion' of the handicapped person, it is fundamental that people from outside the milieu of specialized education should have their place in it.

L'Arche aims to offer a place to live which is warm, brotherly and demanding, in order to give security and, when necessary, protection against the kind of attacks the handicapped person cannot endure, but l'Arche must also be open to the village, the town and the world. If there is to be reintegration or progress, and thus partial or total participation in "normal life," our acquaintance with the preoccupations of those who do not live with society's outcasts, and their participation in some of our activities will help the transition, when it comes, to be a less brutal an experience.

A Project

If the environment is truly what we have just described, everyone will be called upon, and will call upon each other, to grow and to want to live more fully. This desire to change, to put one's talents to use, and to become responsible for oneself, comes from the atmosphere in which one lives and must be defined in a project. A sense of responsibility, however small it may be must be fostered.

There is Jacques, who never used to get to work on time, but who, after months and months, is now not only there when he should be but has even taken charge of opening up his workshop.

Michel, who always waited to be served by the assistants because 'that's what they're paid for', is now the one who makes and serves the breakfast coffee.

Pierre, who always needed someone at his side in his work and any other activities – otherwise he disappeared the moment our backs were turned – has succeeded in doing things on his own, out of sight of the assistants, and in doing them well.

Jean-Marc, who was classified "irretrievable" because of his IQ now lives on his own, manages his own budget, invites his friends in and radiates a real sense of welcome.

All these people have progressed, have been able to fulfill themselves, not only because they lived in a milieu which accepted and stimulated them but, also, because they were able to express their project to other people who were there with them and who believed in them.

A project means simply setting objectives so that each person can know where he is going and why, and how he will get there. We must make the words "responsibility," "capability," "autonomy," intelligible to everyone. A project means making specific and concrete what is general and abstract.

Defining a project is not so simple because it depends, apart from the described pre-requisites, on being able to communicate the project or being able to stick to a project designed and adapted for you. Thus, attentiveness, patience, and commitment are necessary on the part of the one who provides the accompaniment. Not in terms of minutes or hours, but in terms of days, weeks, months, even years. Therefore, the permanence of some assistants is more than desirable if there is to be continuity.

David and Pierre were unable to build a project for themselves. For a long time it was the assistant who was the driving force for the project. They stuck to it because they discovered that each day their project helped them in their growth. Much time was needed before they could put into words their desire to take more direct control and responsibility for it.

The concept of an assistant who accompanies and the commitment demanded of him points to one of the dangers facing our communities. Because of the importance we give to relationship, there can be an unconscious tendency towards fusion between the two people, the assistant and the handicapped person. In this case, there is no longer the necessary distance between the accompanying person and the one he accompanies. If the assistant sees the project as his own business, if he no longer leaves the person any freedom, if he can no longer question his own motives, if he no longer wants to stand back and take a good look at the relationship, then we are no longer dealing with an open relationship for growth. We are faced with the phenomenon of the projection and satisfaction of the assistant's instincts. When the day comes for the

assistant to leave, this may provoke a serious collapse. The relationship is egotistical.

To keep this distance in the relationship which alone can guarantee a certain objectivity, the assistant needs help from a third
person who is less involved – the "guardian" I mentioned earlier.
This person can see more easily the snares in the relationship. He
can analyse more clearly and therefore correct and warn. Here we
find the possible role of a specialist or simply someone ready to be
a competent "outside eye."

Agreed Requirements

Very early in his life at l'Arche, Maurice formulated in a very
concrete way his desire to live independently and to work on his
own. We tried to check out with him what this desire signified:
was it real, was he capable of it, was it not too early, what would
he need in order to move closer to his goal? In the course of several
meetings with him and the assistants from his home and workshop
whom he had asked to be present, we sorted out the list of points
he would need to improve if he was to succeed in holding down
a job in a normal environment and live in an apartment. At work,
he mustn't "blow his top" and walk out whenever someone makes
a remark; he must be able to carry out correctly the job given him
and to judge if it has been done well. In everyday situations, he
must be able to assume responsibility for all the daily actions of
independent living and find or ask for help, thus acquiring a degree
of socialization. Afterwards we determined which way of proceeding was the easiest and therefore the most rewarding for him
and we fixed the priorities with him. Should he begin with independent living or with the demands of a job? He chose to put
his main effort into working. The home would therefore be more
discreet in its demands without, however, abandoning all
stimulation.

Establishing a priority in this way is fundamental because it
prevents the person from caving in under too many demands and
thus provides times of respite and room to breathe. Once this had

been made clear, the work sector, with Maurice's co-operation, sorted out the stages that must be gone through and the rhythm of meetings and check points which would steer Maurice's training towards increased autonomy.

This detailed example will convey what is meant by setting out agreed demands. This kind of procedure, I believe, should be adopted for any project that demands an effort. But what I have said does not necessarily apply in every case. Some will need the proper environment and nothing else; others will need someone to accompany them and be exacting towards them. So we cannot make generalizations.

My life at l'Arche has strengthened my conviction that every handicapped person is unique, that each one can move forward. For someone who is very handicapped, the project often takes shape in the assistant's mind on the basis of the person's need. In this respect the example of Bernard is significant. He was labelled "deeply backward" and had lived for many years in a wing of a psychiatric hospital where he could not be recognized as unique and capable, because he was lost in the crowd. Having been welcomed into the community, it needed only a few months of living together, receiving attention and also meeting demands made on him, for him to start learning how to walk by himself. For me this is one of the most wonderful proofs that every man is called upon to grow, and that few things are needed for this growth to begin. In Bernard's case, what was important was that he be recognized and loved. For the handicapped person who is capable of dialogue, the project is one he expresses and which is taken up by the assistants. This desire to offer life to all, this belief in man, takes on substance in our community life and in the kind of relationships we live. We want to give to all growth its moral, human dimension. For us, the most important thing is not that a person should be able to walk or live on his own. It is that he should discover that the world needs him (perhaps merely his smile, but how important a smile can sometimes be in our lives); that he is its hope.

There is Frank who lives in a home, lying on his bed all day. How many people he must have upheld with such a beautiful smile, so radiant, so trusting, while his body is torn and forever struggling.

Nonetheless, I think back on all those people for whom no project, however well-adjusted to their personalities, could incite them to keep to it; for a Michèle or a Paul we have still not been able to find this tiny hope for growth. They put whatever I have written in context. There are no certainties, there is no one truth . . ., we must always be searching, challenging our methods and our means. For this we must remain open to other experiences which may bring us new light. My text aims simply to share the discoveries we have so far made.

5

GROWTH TOWARDS COVENANT

Claire de Miribel

Claire de Miribel, from south-east France, has been with l'Arche, Trosly for ten years. She came to know l'Arche while she was studying and working for a voluntary organization for mentally handicapped people. After completing her studies in political science, she came to l'Arche in 1972 and was asked to begin a new home for ten handicapped women, Massabielle, where she still makes her home.

However, the community has called her to other responsibilities: first, to co-ordinate community activities (holidays, celebrations, recreational activities, etc.), and also to welcome and guide new assistants and to assist those who are putting their roots down in the community.

I am a child of a rich nation. The family I was born into was a happy one and comfortably off. I grew up knowing that I could take up whatever studies I might choose, confident they would not be cut short by the need to earn a living. I was very much aware, nevertheless, of being a member of a small and privileged group. That the overwhelming majority of humanity, plagued as they are by hunger, poverty and war, could never pretend to such opportunities, was a realization which gave me acute feelings of guilt but provided no way out. Whether or not I went along with the system, there would always be some people I would be condemned to reject and exclude. I felt trapped. When I first heard about l'Arche it was like discovering a third choice, a possible solution to my dilemma. No point wasting any more time feeling guilty that so much had been given me. "Never mind what you've got, start sharing it with others and we'll be able to build a better world." This was the trigger which brought me to l'Arche, the answer I had long been groping for in the dark.

That, briefly, is my story. The political dimension of this community, the urge to build a better world, is one of the motives which bring people here. In l'Arche we live alongside handicapped men and women, but the same motive can impel people to live with outcasts of other kinds – society's rejects – to build with them a community where sharing means, above all, sharing our true selves.

There are others here whose primary purpose is to share the lives of handicapped people. Often they are professional people, trained as specialist teachers, social workers and so on. Being dissatisfied with their experience of hospitals and institutions they have been searching for an alternative way. There was a girl called France, for example, a social worker, who had found it increasingly difficult to come to terms with a career which brought her quiet and comfortable evenings at the end of a day spent among people whose living conditions were, on the contrary, often very precarious. She came one day, for professional reasons, to visit one of the Arche communities. To her surprise, she was shown round by the odd-job man, who was evidently quite at ease and only too glad to introduce her to his home and to the people with whom he shared it. Later she came back, this time for good.

Others come in answer to God's call. They are travelling blind, so to speak, convinced that l'Arche is the place where they are being invited to live, for a while at least, in order to become better acquainted with this God who is calling them. Sometimes they have only recently discovered him, or they've reached a stage in life where they feel the next step they have to take is to let go the rudder. For them, the discovery of community living and of the handicapped comes later.

There are also quite a number who come to l'Arche in search of "something different", because of personal or family difficulties, or because they have no job. Some of them discover the essence of l'Arche and decide to stay.

All these motives are rarely so clearcut at the outset and are even less likely to remain so. Whatever the aspect of l'Arche people first encounter, by living here they eventually come to discover all its

Work as a means of personal growth, l'Arche, Trosly

other dimensions: a community of life among handicapped people who are trying together to build a Christian community.

The Difficulties of Commitment

Whatever the motives which first bring you to l'Arche, whatever the length of time you intend to stay, whether it is for a limited period before pursuing your studies or some other project, or for a longer term, the first months are tough. You step into a world whose values are the opposite of those current in the society where you have been living. You move from a world of efficiency and productivity into a world where the essential values are people's relationships and personal presence one to another. From a world where everything is to be had here and now, you enter a world where the essential element is time: the time required to create personal ties, to win each other's trust, to grow. Leaving a society based on individualism and personal success, often won at other people's cost, you discover a community where no one does anything alone. And coming from a world whose essential motive and important yardstick is money, you find yourself in a world where what is essential can only be given free, where money is no more than a means in the service of the community. That other world expects you to be big and strong, and to hide any weakness as something to be ashamed of, whereas here each person's weaknesses are brought to light and shared, and this sharing is the foundation of unity.

Such a culture-shock, requiring total reorientation, is a painful experience. Inevitably it produces a certain loss of balance which will last for as long as it takes you to adapt. And, if you resume normal life after spending a while in l'Arche, the same problem of adaptation arises in the reverse direction. This initial difficulty is increased by a number of other factors which may arise.

It often happens that an assistant's family disapproves of his or her coming to l'Arche, because they had other plans for their future, because life at l'Arche gives no security, because they see their children's choice as so different from their own as to constitute a personal challenge. It is not easy for an assistant who loves his parents to face the fact that the choice he is making will cause them pain, however certain he may be that this is the right path for him.

When you come to l'Arche you soon find yourself moving away from the friends you had before. At first the move is often a matter of geography. Many of your friends promise to pay a visit, but few do so and rarely more than once. Then again your lifestyle will have changed, your interests no longer coincide. Inside l'Arche, assistants often experience relationships which are deeper than any they have so far known, and earlier ones begin to seem superficial. "We don't have anything in common any more" is a frequently heard comment. This break with your former milieu is inevitable and can be frightening. You are afraid of being out on a limb, of losing your place, frightened of insecurity.

But the essential difficulty derives from the fact that the new assistant is immediately plunged in at the deep end. There is no preparatory training to teach him what to do, how to react, how to avoid getting hurt. He will be living with people who are quick to show him his limitations, when he would rather they were left hidden. Communication goes far beyond words, so it is impossible to cheat. We are very soon shown up for what we are. For some people this is unbearable. Madeleine, who had come to live in l'Arche, left three days later at dawn, leaving no address, and was never seen again. Rare, but such things do happen. Others feel nothing but pain on being faced with their own weaknesses, a burden which they find impossible to carry alone and yet can no longer ignore. Armelle taunted me three months after her arrival with the remark, "You're good at stripping people bare, but then what happens?" In that respect the community is dangerous, it's true. No one comes through unscathed.

Some people indulge in the dream of a community which would accept everybody and refuse no one. Such dreams are naive. A community has no right to invite people to risk embarking on community life unless it has the will and the means to stand by them all the way.

There is no model of the ideal assistant. L'Arche is a place of growth where each member of the community should be able to realize himself and develop his potential to the full. The freedom given is extraordinary, and demands a concomitant sense of re-sponsibility. It is up to each person to determine the life he wants to lead and to take whatever steps that choice entails. This is no easy matter, especially as many come to l'Arche fairly young. Often they have just completed their studies or have only very limited experience of a job. Not only do they have to discover community life and adapt to it but at the same time they have to become adult and acquire a certain maturity. No more living in a state of expectation, which is the attitude of adolescence; they have to get down to the nitty-gritty of daily life with all its banality, and establish their priorities. Take the example of spiritual life and prayer. Each person must learn what his needs are, for they vary from one to another, and then organize his time accordingly. Assistants are sometimes heard to say "There's no time for me to pray" but what they are really saying is "I don't have the will to

pray". For it is easier to hide behind lack of time or the unsatis-
factory organization of the community. It has always struck me
that those for whom prayer is vital do in fact find time to pray,
even if it means getting up a little earlier.

A new assistant will find it much easier to discover his needs
and how to satisfy them if he can talk things over with someone
more experienced in community life, who can act as a companion
and help him to formulate the important questions. Some weeks
ago Jo, who is responsible with her husband for the Arche community in Calgary, was explaining to us how she meets each new
assistant regularly every week for two or three months. Her first
question is "What are you hoping for from the community?"
Then, "What are you prepared to give to the community?", "What
are you willing to do to achieve that aim?" Dialogue of this kind
is essential. Besides, it helps the newly arrived assistant to feel he
is accepted as a person with his own story, his own aspirations,
and is not just being used. It is also important for him to enter
into personal relationship with someone who is further ahead on
the path of community living. It too often happens that young
assistants can only share their questioning with others who are as
inexperienced as themselves. No wonder they feel they are going
round in circles.

We must become aware of our responsibility as communities
with respect to young assistants so as to help them clarify their
aims and progress towards self-commitment. This point is vitally
important and is bound to be more difficult to deal with in the
larger communities and in those where the fully committed assistants are few in number. But the future of l'Arche depends on it.

This passage to maturity is made both easier and more complicated by the fact that young assistants are very soon called upon
to shoulder considerable responsibilities, such as a house or a workshop. Hubert often says, "L'Arche doesn't leave you time to be
young." To be entrusted with such a responsibility can bring some
people to give of their best and to commit themselves because they
can see the magnitude of the task. But others can be frightened
and crushed by it.

If people are to feel attracted to community life they must have examples before them of persons who have been living this life for a long time and who can be witnesses that such a life is possible, that it is worthwhile, and that it can bring fulfilment and happiness. This is where those who are further on in this way of life have an important responsibility. If they go around always looking tired, always under stress, in a hurry, or worn and blasé, they are unlikely to incite young people to follow their path. Life at l'Arche is attractive to many young people and they love it. But they are afraid that with time their enthusiasm may fade and they will become frustrated old maids or crusty old bachelors. We have to show them the opposite is true and to foster in them the wish to commit themselves. This came home to me one day in an old Benedictine monastery which a group of us from l'Arche were visiting. I realized how valuable it was for the young novices to see the old monks around them, men who had been living that life for forty or fifty years, who were completely integrated into it and at peace with themselves.

L'Arche is young, it was founded in 1964. No one can say what thirty or forty years of life in l'Arche will bring us; it's up to us to find out. That is our challenge and, like any challenge, it implies risk. This is what David was saying, after two years in l'Arche: "We're all in the same boat. We don't know where we're going. Perhaps we shall sink, but at least we'll sink together." It is hard for the young assistant to know, in those moments when everything seems hollow or dark and the life he is leading seems no longer to make sense, whether this is just a transition period, a stage in the deepening of his commitment, or if it is a sign that l'Arche is not his place, that life is leading him elsewhere. Is his desire to leave, to engage in some other experience a good thing, or is it an escape? There again, it is important that he should be helped by someone more experienced who can explain the different stages he is living through, can share his own experience, the difficulties he himself has met, and so help the young assistant in discerning where his true path lies.

For myself, I have often thought that the day when I no longer feel like doing a hundred other things will be the time to leave. To remain cocooned in the community can be an escape. You don't

Regular work and a sense of responsibility are important factors in growth

have to face up to society, to struggle for your place in the sun. You're living a nice cosy life in a warm atmosphere where there is no competitiveness and you can gently sink into infantilism.

Commitment

"Whom am I committed to? The community? The handicapped people I am living with, the house or the assistants?" In this question of Elizabeth's, I recognized the different stages of my own commitment. When the house where I live was opened, I felt very committed to the handicapped women we had just taken in, and to the assistants, the house and the community. As time passed these various commitments had to be re-examined, sometimes very painfully, but on each occasion it was a step towards a deeper commitment.

After a year or two several assistants who had started the house with me moved on to follow other paths, one to a monastery, another to resume his studies and get married, a third to start an

Arche house in a Third World country. This gave me the unpleasant impression that each of them was taking up a much more beautiful project (the grass is greener . . .) and I was being left behind – not a very energizing feeling. But once I had got over my depression I was brought to realize that staying put could be a project in itself, my project, and that this was the place where I must find my source of energy, and not keep dreaming of some "otherwhere" but begin to put down roots and grow. Now I still felt committed to the ten women we had welcomed, many of whom had nowhere else to go. One evening one of them, who was going through a deep regression, was in such a bad way that I spoke to the head of the community. What he then said left me dumbfounded, "Today is perhaps, because of her, the day of your commitment." It was the truth, and it goes, I think, for many of us. We have stayed because at some point a handicapped person has called us to a deep commitment to him or her. However, some of the women with whom I had strong ties progressed so far that the time came when they needed something else. They left the house for a more autonomous life. What then became of my commitment? I remained for them a point of constancy, a faithful though distant friend. But when other women arrived, I discovered how hard it was to implicate myself anew in the process of commitment to them.

While the commitment I feel is strongly tied to certain people it nevertheless goes beyond them. It can become a double commitment. You commit yourself day by day to the people you live with. That is the basic commitment. But for it to endure it must be supported by another commitment which reaches beyond the person, whether it is spiritual, political or professional. And so the various motives which have brought you to l'Arche reassert themselves.

Most people who come to l'Arche spend some time before discovering bit by bit that their commitment is deepening. They may spend several heart-searching years, setting date-lines for themselves, until the day comes when they take the step of accepting that l'Arche is the community where they are being called to live. For some, the path to this acceptance is a long one as though they were resisting themselves, holding off from this sense of commitment they can feel taking root in their heart. Their timing must be respected.

There are other people, who know almost before they have even arrived, that this is the place where they are called to live. They have no idea what they will be doing and it doesn't matter. Their certainty is an interior one, which spares them much heart-searching and questioning, such as "Should I stay? or go? and if so when?" But that doesn't make things any easier. All the stages that the others have experienced during their years of questing, they too must go through one by one, and this inevitably entails suffering.

A few major stages are the common experience of everyone. First of all, though it may seem too obvious to mention, you have to accept the risk of commitment. This cannot be done unless you can see the dynamic of the community. Society's dynamic is easily perceived; that of l'Arche is harder to recognize. It is not a matter of earning more, or having more responsibility, a more comfortable life, and dreaming of running the place one day. It is a matter of discovering each day what it is you are required to live, and to live that to the full. Young assistants recently arrived in the community often say how hard it is not to have their work recognized. Once the step has been taken towards commitment, this ceases to be a problem. I do what I am expected to do, not in order to gain recognition but because it is my way of building the community, my way of belonging to it.

We are not in a position to choose community life until we have learnt to bear with our solitude, the solitude that is the lot of every one of us. It is no use expecting to get everything from personal relationships, however cordial they may be. We must understand that each of us has his burden of solitude which nothing can dispel.

One of the great temptations if you live in a large community is to dream of a smaller, more exotic one, where of course everything would be simpler and more beautiful. You would be master of the ship and the only problems would be your own, and you wouldn't have to be putting up with the choices made, in their weakness, by the others. I have discovered, from talking with a number of people committed to l'Arche in Trosly, that many of them, like myself, had not intended on first coming here to stay in such a large community, and had planned to move on elsewhere. I fancy the reverse temptation haunts those who live in small communities – everything would be so much simpler and more beautiful in a large one.

To accept to remain in the place where one is needed is one of the major steps towards commitment. Another important question revolves around marriage and celibacy. In order to be truly committed one must have made one's choice, in the knowledge that this will in no way put an end to challenges or temptations.

In recent years we have come to discover the commitment that married couples can give to Arche communities, and to understand the forms such a commitment takes and how enriching it can be. While our society still recognizes fairly well the commitment of marriage, for all its present-day fragility, the world's view of celibacy is not so clear.

For some people in l'Arche, choosing celibacy is one way of sharing the life of the handicapped, who must in most cases bear with a celibacy which they have not chosen. Others have opted to live in a home with handicapped people and celibacy follows on from this choice, while for others, celibacy is their response to a specific call from God. Here again there are those to whom this choice comes as a matter of course at a specific point in time. In Claude's words: "The first night I spent at l'Arche I knew that this was the place where I was going to live and this naturally entailed remaining celibate." There are yet others for whom this choice becomes possible only with the passage of time.

It would help us all, I think, if we were more willing to share one with another the way we live out our marriage or our celibacy, the difficulties each of us has to face and the stages we go through. Far too often young assistants leave for all kinds of valid reasons, when their real motive is the fear that committing themselves to l'Arche will entail their accepting the celibate life.

It seems to be an imperative requirement that each person should take his stand at some point on each of these different issues – accepting the risk of self-commitment, putting oneself at the ser-

vice of the community, choosing between marriage and celibacy
– if he is to live in fullness and joy the life that is given him and
not wake up one day feeling trapped in a life he would never have
deliberately chosen. And this point is no less important if we are
to witness, without loss of serenity, the choices made by others,
and not feel turned inside out each time someone leaves or gets
married or enters a monastery.

These essential decisions are not made easier by the fact that at
l'Arche there is no one occasion on which we can officially make
them. That is one of our strengths. It is part of that freedom I
mentioned earlier which is not easy to live by. Each person ad-
vances at his own rhythm and the community has a responsibility
to help young assistants make their decision when the time comes.

In our communities the word "commitment" has never been
very popular. Another word which has become current lately and
has won wider acceptance is "covenant". It probably corresponds
more closely to the life we are called to lead. We are being asked
to enter into a covenant and the decision is ours. A number of
people from different communities, who had gathered for a retreat,
testified that they had been invited to enter into a covenant in this
sense: "You are invited to live, in l'Arche, a covenant with Jesus
and with your brothers and sisters, in particular those who are the
poorest. Do you want this?"

We are only beginning to discover what riches lie within such
a covenant, without knowing where it is taking us.

Growing Towards Covenant

Once the vital step has been taken, everything remains to be done.
Each one of us is responsible for his commitment so that it shall
grow deeper and remain authentic. This is a task for every day that
comes. A covenant needs to be nourished and sources of nourishment must be found. This requires you to know yourself, to know
what is needed for your progress and with this knowledge, to
make the relevant choices. If you are committed to your community, you are responsible to that community for the way you

organize your day and your free time. Nadine says for example: "I have no right to sit up talking half the night; otherwise, tomorrow I'll be inflicting my foul mood on all the people in the house."

The will to grow in commitment demands a great deal of honesty with yourself and the life you wish to lead, and honesty towards those whose life you share. This is often a source of friction in a house or a community, and it is easy to see why. No team of assistants is ever homogeneous, and is much the richer for it. Each member is at a different stage. Some are there to gain a few months' experience; others are on the way to commitment; others again have already taken that step and have begun to fulfil their commitment. Often it is none too easy for someone strongly committed to a community, and who may well carry important responsibilities, to accept that others should still be at the discovery stage, and equally difficult for those who have just arrived in a community to understand the demands made by the more committed members.

Differences of motivation can also bring suffering into the life of a team. Many communities, for example, experience a unity of life in their common commitment to the handicapped yet are divided in their profession of faith, either because their members belong to different Churches or because they are at different stages on their spiritual path. This is how Louise explained to the other assistants of her house what was to her a cause of suffering: "When you come together in the morning to pray, for you that is a way of making a good start to the day. For me it means a bad start, because I feel excluded." Likewise those who are married should not feel frustrated because they can't put themselves so freely at the disposal of others as the unmarried. And those who live the celibate life must come to understand how enriching is the contribution made by married couples who commit themselves to the community.

It is therefore important to create occasions where one and all can come together so that each one can declare what he desires to live and others can be witnesses and help him be true to his aim. On one occasion, when various Arche communities were gathered together, a community of Jesuits shared their experience with us. They used to meet together once a week for an hour, when each would tell the others "where my heart is". They explained: "When we talk of sharing and community life, we tend to think of the externals. We spend time together; we pool the contributions that each can make in terms of reflection and action, but often we overlook the essential, which is to share the life that is within each one and goes to make up our life together." It is not easy to do but it's worth trying, remembering that it won't be done in a day, that it will take time for the necessary trust to grow among all of us, that some will leave and new people come, and yet, to hold to the conviction that through all these changes the community will continue to grow. It is important to find time to talk not about the people entrusted to us, nor about matters of organization, but about the things we live for.

If we can share one with another the heart and purpose of our lives, then we can all help each other persevere in fidelity, and the beauty and diversity of our intertwining covenants will fill us all with amazement and wonder.

It is up to each one of us to discover within his commitment to the community what is his personal commitment, what is his role, his peculiar calling and who are the people entrusted to him. Otherwise it is easy to lose oneself inside the community, especially if it is a large one, and to use the community atmosphere for one's own benefit without making any personal choices or implicating oneself in concrete terms to anyone in particular. Without this day-to-day commitment to people, with all the demands it makes and the fidelity it requires, everything else is just wind. One cannot be committed to "community-as-idea".

We can sometimes be tempted by the desire to be heroic. This is another danger to real commitment. Instead of trying to discover in what way the community needs me, and where I can give of my best, I start looking for what I think is the tough spot. This is another way of escaping real commitment and turning in on myself.

Once the step has been taken and we have lived a few years in our community, bearing with our increasing vulnerability, it may happen one day that we are assailed by fear, the fear of having gone too far, of being unable to turn back. This is the fear of St. Peter, suddenly realizing he is in the water and beginning to sink. It's easy to commit oneself in a flush of enthusiasm at twenty, aware of the other doors that still remain open. Let a few years roll by and the choice you made then will have to be reaffirmed, all the more humbly now because you know not only what you are turning your back on, but also how great are the demands and how little the security you can expect on the path you have chosen.

Such fears are human, deriving from our recurrent temptations to say: "I must be mad. This life is impossible. The insecurity is unbearable. I ought to look for something else. I ought to be doing my own thing." We must recognize these temptations for what they are. As they grow familiar we will be able to put them in perspective, and no longer feel alarmed when they bear down on us like waves. And so we shall live out our covenant like a love story, its roots growing deeper with each successive wave.

We like to say that l'Arche is a gift that has been given us, a gift which, like an iceberg, reveals only the little bit that emerges while the greater part, the essential, lies hidden, waiting to be discovered. This discovering is our daily task, if only we will allow each fresh discovery to challenge us anew and never cease to marvel. Let each one of us keep faith by remaining true to our daily life, true to the poorest of the poor, true to the covenant which is offered to us. That fidelity is our path.

6

A PLACE FOR A FAMILY

Pat and Jo Lenon

Pat Lenon and his wife Jo are both from Edmonton, Alberta, Canada. They tell the story of their growth and commitment in l'Arche. They had met Jean Vanier at a Faith and Sharing retreat and, touched by grace, they felt called to create a community. Thus in 1973 Marymount was opened in Calgary, Alberta. There are now two homes and two apartments with a total community of twenty-five. Pat, Jo and their three children live together with five handicapped people in a semi-detached house.

For four years, Pat was called to serve as regional co-ordinator for the Arche homes in the Western region of North America. Now he and Jo put their energies and time into building and deepening their own family and community roots at Marymount.

The first four months Jo and I and our three children began living in community were long and tiring. By December many of our illusions about living as brothers and sisters in Christ had been shattered. Any thoughts we had about building community on our own strength were disappearing. People we had counted on were no longer with us, partly because of their own inner struggle, and partly because we had little sense of what it means to be shepherds. The old house we were living in was taking more time and money to repair than we had anticipated. And every night, Suzanne, our daughter then aged seven, was crying herself to sleep. During her prayers she would ask with a quivering voice: "Why did we have to sell our house in Edmonton?"[1] Our hearts were pierced by the question. We felt challenged in our call to community. How were we to reconcile the sharing of our lives with mentally handicapped

[1]Marymount community is in Calgary, 190 miles south of Edmonton.

adults, and yet tend to the very obvious needs of our own natural family?

Since making our decision to live in community in 1973, Jo and I have had a long struggle. By the grace of God we are discovering what it means to live in community and to be shepherds. We are discovering the great joy of community, and we are discovering also that it is community life that supports our marriage.

Our decision to live in community was the result of many years of searching: searching for a vocation in which both our head and heart could be united. Jo and I had been raised as Catholics and loved our religion. But we were always confronted with the gap between the words of the Sunday Gospel and how we lived during the rest of the week. There seemed to be no place for a married couple to serve within the Church other than in the traditional roles of men's or women's clubs, or other such activities, which did not speak to our hearts. The suburban parish appeared to be a place of complacency supporting, rather than challenging, our comfortable suburban life style. The struggle of our married life was a struggle between serving ourselves and serving others; within our parish framework we could not find the way to serve others.

The ideal of service had nevertheless been in our hearts. Jo had spent three years training and then serving as a nurse. From the age of nine I had been groomed to take over a thriving family business. We were married in 1965, and essentially the first five years were years of "getting ahead". All my energies went into the business. The fruits of my labours were a beautiful suburban bungalow, an expensive foreign car, a well stocked wine cellar, two young daughters, and a wife I rarely communicated with. In the last three years of working in the family business I had discovered the beauty of the marginal person when our company became involved in employing emotionally disturbed students.

Jo and I had been aware of God's hand upon us at an earlier time in our life. As young children we were aware that a loving Father would uphold us, and save us from many disasters. But as we grew up and eventually married, our awareness centred upon the fulfilment of our own egos. The child inside each of us, the place where we were dependent and trusting, was becoming remote. An eager heart of childhood was being replaced by the saddened heart of adulthood; a responsive spirit of early marriage was being stifled by too much material wealth and a dependency upon our own devices. To fill the void of sadness we began to press outward. Our life was filled with participating in adult education courses, material goods, people, and all of this was directed towards the fulfilment of self.

By 1970, after being married for five years, we discovered that our life was shallow and meaningless. Our marriage had begun to collapse. We were confronted with the emptiness of our existence. Conversation was idle, people were used. We saw all this but didn't know what to do. This realization that our life was empty brought no change, only an awareness of the pain of being lonely.

For several years I had a strong desire to leave the family business. No sooner had I informed my father of my decision to leave than Jo and I became sick with hepatitis. During the recovery period we could be only with each other, simply lying in bed, sharing our hearts about what was happening to our marriage. We saw that the busy-ness of our lives had prevented us from getting to know each other.

During the recovery period we discovered that one of our needs was community. Community had always been an intellectual topic of conversation over coffee and liqueurs. We had shared many weekend and holiday experiences with friends, and our church community provided numerous close relationships. But we had always searched for community outside ourselves: the right building, the right grouping of people. Our search for community always began from a false premise, the premise being that all the conditions had to be perfect before we could begin. In other words if we had the correctly designed building, the right grouping of people, community would work. We did not understand that community begins at the point of our own imperfections. As our hearts healed we began to see that our family was a community, that what we were seeking we were already living, but it had to become more concrete, more explicit. Could we allow someone to share in this?

John: the Turning Point

Soon after the birth of our third daughter, Natasha, we made contact with a workshop for mentally handicapped adults. We were struck by the need people had for places to live. Our visits brought us in touch with John who had been virtually abandoned by his family. Originally from a small town in northern Alberta, John had been through a succession of living situations in the city. Unable to cope with the pressures that were upon him, he became aggressive and then depressed. The welfare agency was about to send John back to his family. Because of our contact with the workshop, we were asked if we could take John into our home.

John was the gift we yearned for. He helped us to see that, in order for our little family community to flourish, we needed to be open to an outside influence. We had no knowledge of mental handicap and very little support from our friends. Most of the time we had no idea of how to be with John. What we discovered was that John brought Jo and me closer together: in trying to discover John's heart, we were discovering our own.

John taught us that we could not change people to fit our preconceived notions of what they should be. We are still discovering that it is much more difficult to accept people as they are, than to enter a person's life as his saviour. We thought we could save John. He taught Jo and me how to accept and eventually love him. John did not reciprocate with gentleness or a thank you. Rather he was aggressive, sullen, with a strong dash of humour. John lived with us for nine months. He eventually left after he called the police, claiming he was being kept a prisoner. John's phoning the police was his protest against our trying to change his life. We were beginning to discover that all of us are at particular stages of growth and that it is important that these stages be recognized and accepted. We were not called to force people to grow, no matter how good our intentions. Rather we were called to accept people, allowing them to begin to believe in themselves. We discovered in our time with John that some type of structure is needed for growth, not only for the handicapped people, but also for ourselves. In living with other people we need to know the boundaries of our relationships, for it is within well-defined boundaries that we can authentically be ourselves. John showed us that if we were to live with wounded people we would need to look deeply into our hearts for the gifts of compassion and acceptance.

Marriage and Community

We have received a fundamental understanding of our concept of marriage and family life: an understanding that our marriage and family are gifts that we share and give away. We have learned that we cannot invite people to participate in our family life as other Lenons. All we can do is share our family life with other people, allowing them to shape and mould us, rather than being shaped by our own needs and egos.

How did this change occur in our marriage? Our starting point was an awareness that by always catering for our own needs and egos, our marriage would die. This awareness was enhanced by our meeting Jean Vanier through several retreats that he gave. He

Pat and Jo Lenon in community: l'Arche, Calgary

encouraged us to become close to handicapped people and to pray. Jean's suggestion that we become close to handicapped people was the springboard for our welcoming John into our home. It was more difficult to follow his suggestion to pray. Slowly we began to learn how to wait and to listen. It was in prayer that we risked living with John, and it was in prayer that we were able to wait for our hearts to become one with each other.

In order for our life in community to work, Pat and I each needed to make a choice. It wasn't a question of one of us desiring community and the other following. Rather we came to l'Arche as a couple. Pat was the first to discover the yearning for community. It was essential that he wait for my heart to be opened. The reality of our choice, the day-to-day living in community, implicates our marriage. We know that if we had responded to community, with widely differing degrees of commitment, the experience would have been disastrous for ourselves, our children, and for the community.

In the beginning Marymount was a single family dwelling, located in a semi-rural area. By the end of the first year there were eleven of us living together, three of whom were handicapped. Eighteen months after the community was founded our second house opened. After living in the single family dwelling for two years we moved to a semi-detached house.

Marymount is now an urban community made up of twenty-one people in two houses. In our part of the house, there are five men who are handicapped and two assistants. The men had each spent over ten years in an institution north of the city. They work during the day in various workshops. One of the assistants carries out maintenance within the two homes or works as a caretaker with one of the handicapped men; the other assistant helps me in the house. The second house is a twenty minute walk away. There nine people live together, six of whom are handicapped.

When we look more deeply, we find that we bring hope to people who have no hope, no options. Those of us with intellectual training have many options available. Our society offers us a myriad of choices. But the people we welcome and are committed to have few if any choices. In many instances they cannot choose where they are going to live. Many were placed in institutions against their will; and many, as a requirement for living in the institution, were sterilized. Most were placed in our homes with no choice. What we live is a commitment to a group of people who are virtually abandoned. And what Jo and I have learned about commitment to each other and to our children, we share with the people we welcome.

Our life in community is both simple and complex. Simple, because people come first. We go to work, clean the house, prepare meals, pray together, laugh a lot, cry sometimes. Yet it is in this simple commitment to people that complexity arises. When to accept someone, when to challenge? When to start a teaching process, when to allow the person to discover on his own? And beneath all this there is inevitably anger, fear, insecurity, compassion, empathy. Many of the handicapped people we welcome, come with deep frustrations and anger. This can cause fear in those of us who assist. How do we deal with our own tensions and yet be present to the people we live with? There are no easy answers, but two things are important: team work, and the need to be in touch with our own emotions.

Our life in community also means we welcome into our houses men and women who desire to serve. Many of the assistants who come are young and filled with a deep desire to serve. Yet it is their very gifts of youth and this desire to serve that sometimes cause a struggle. Living with handicapped people can be a confrontation. For many of the assistants, it is the first time they have had to look at themselves. There can be the discovery that there is not much difference between the person who is helping and the person who is helped. This can cause fear. The fear is not so much a fear of the handicapped person, although this can be projected; rather it is the discovery of one's own limitations. The acceptance of one's limitations can be difficult but if the assistant does not accept these limitations, he or she will usually leave. Because many assistants come with good will, and give of themselves freely, it is important for the community to support its members during difficult times of growth.

We are discovering is that it is important for all of us to grow in the trust and acceptance of our feelings and of each other. If the movement to trust does not occur, assistants may find themselves in an either/or situation: either the desire to serve can lead to busy-ness, and then the assistant doesn't have to look at himself; or the assistant becomes so involved with himself that the handicapped person is missed out. At Marymount we struggle with how to balance our own needs with the very real needs of the handicapped people we welcome.

A real struggle we face is the coming and going of assistants. Because most assistants are young (in their early twenties) their time in community life is short. It is not yet time to put down roots. For Jo and me l'Arche was the end of a search; for many who come to serve it is the beginning. Most assistants stay an average of fifteen to eighteen months. This causes our community to be transitory; yet at the same time there is a vitality that new people always bring. Jo and I have our relationship with each other that helps to sustain us, but for the assistant a primary relationship, close at hand, is not always available. I feel that we have much to learn in the care and nurturing of our assistants.

The Source of Community: Sacramental Relationship

During the past six years our life in community has caused our relationship with each other to deepen. We are more acutely aware of the goodness that is in each other; yet at the same time we are much more conscious of our own weakness. In the past we were threatened by the other's limitations. Now we see that our limitations help us to depend upon each other.

In welcoming handicapped people to share in our family life, our marriage has become richer, far beyond our expectations. But there is a paradox to our life in community. As we put our roots deeper down into community life, we are constantly confronted with the lack of time we have for each other. This can be a deep source of tension. We have tried to set aside times of the day to be with each other, but always the needs of other people appear. What has helped us to live through the moments of tension is the awareness that our marriage is a sacrament, and that for this sacrament to bear fruit we must give our marriage away to others in a life of service.

Our understanding of the sacrament of marriage is that we have formed a covenant between ourselves and with God the father. This covenant is lived out in our faithfulness to each other, to our children, and to the men and women we live with. This understanding that our marriage is a sacrament developed from the fact that our relationship was almost broken, and we recognized this. At the point of our breaking we became aware that we loved each other, but that much of our love was self-seeking, rather than self-giving. There was a death and resurrection within our marriage. The resurrection created within us a desire to open up our marriage.

In our culture today the emphasis is on the indulgence of self. There is very little that supports relationships, particularly the relationship between husband and wife. We see that much of what is supposed to give security and happiness is false. The desire for comfort is a pretence that leads us away from the real needs of people. Our marriage is not something we can cling to. Rather we see that we have been given to each other by God so that we can more deeply serve our children and the men and women we live with.

The deepening unity of our relationship as husband and wife is the gift that has been given to Pat and me by those we live with. Often what happens is that this very gift of our marriage and family causes deep and painful areas of others' hearts to be touched. These painful areas are recognized and gently healed in the day-to-day living faithfulness of one to another.

Another source of tension is that we become substitute parents for the other people in the community. It is important for us not to fall into the trap of unconsciously assuming parental roles.

For the handicapped there is a great security in placing Pat and me in parental roles. For a time we may have to allow ourselves to be viewed as substitute parents. We are conscious of assuming parental roles and the danger of the handicapped people becoming jealous of the children. What we are coming to see is that the deepest desire in people is for relationship. It is the unity that we find with each other that enables us to call people forth in relationships beyond the parental model.

Children and Community

We have three children, Suzanne now thirteen, Shelagh, eleven and Natasha, seven. The gift our children bring to community is their "naturalness". Their relationship with the people who are handicapped is unique for each one. Sometimes there is fear, sometimes frustration, sometimes gentleness, sometimes presence, sometimes play and teasing, sometimes testing and sometimes tears.

Shelagh walks down the street with John who has Downs Syndrome. They accept each other. Suzanne while she is washing up teases Dan who is making lunches. Dan teases her back. There is friendship. Natasha allows Basil to trap her, then calls for John to be her hero and rescue her. There is trust. Manipulation does not exist in these relationships, "What can I get? Who will I offend?": They just are.

The children are also leavening agents in the larger community of the neighbourhood. Many of the children's friends participate in various community activities. Because other children come into the home, there is contact with parents in the area. There is acceptance on the part of the children's friends of the community life they live. A danger that we see for our children is that they might not grow in responsibility. By the very fact that the household is made up primarily of adults who participate in the daily chores, the children could conceivably expect everything to be done for them. Because we see them as ever growing vital members of the community, the two eldest girls set the table for each evening meal, wash up, empty the rubbish and make picnic lunches once a week. They clean their play area and bedrooms. The community welcomes their presence at our Monday night meetings. Suzanne and Shelagh now actively participate in community decision making, and offer suggestions for various activities on which the community often acts.

The children's perception of what they live is perhaps illustrated in this encounter. They were talking together one evening and Shelagh asked Natasha if she liked living in l'Arche. Natasha said, "What's that? Have we been there?" Suzanne and Shelagh broke into gales of laughter. They understood that Natasha accepted and loved, without question, what she was living. Suzanne and Shelagh can feel more acutely the difference between a single family unit and the family living in community; and they seem to flower within community life.

Making it Work

To ensure that our choice of community life deepens, and that at the same time we nurture our marriage and family life we have, over the past six years, formulated some principles. We find they work in our situation with our personalities.

The first principle is that of *homemaker*. My attitude is one of creating a home for people to live in. I do not work for the community in any particular capacity. Rather I clean the house, do the shopping and the family laundry, mend clothes and am available to everyone. Implied in this principle, is the role of mother to the children. It is very important that I remain a strong reference point for our children. In other words, the needs of the children are foremost in my daily activities. Even though there are many activities that I could attend to, it is most important that I do not let a substitute mother emerge to allow me more involvement in the community. It is a difficult balance between the needs of our children and the needs of the community.

The second principle is that of maintaining the *natural family identity*. There are twelve of us who live together in one household, five being our own natural family. To ensure this identity, we ask that no one except ourselves discipline the children. This has always been respected. We eat breakfast as a family each morning except Sunday. After breakfast we pray together. With prayer we are able to identify ourselves as a family to each other. One day a week and one weekend a month we take together as a family. During the children's Christmas holidays we take ten days together, away from the community. During the summer we have always taken a month's holiday with our children. This holiday has always amazed us. The fruits of our community life are evident at this time. It is peaceful, communication is open and a great concern is shown for one another. To enhance further the unity of our natural family, the five of us are grouped together during the community evening meal. This helps both ourselves and the other members of our household to see us as a family.

A third principle is that of *space*. What we understand by this is that there is space to accommodate a natural family in a semi-detached house. One side is the community dining room with a small sitting area; the other side is the community living room. Our family bedrooms are clustered on the living room side. One day a week we use the dining room side for our day away. A door connects the two sides and we simply close the door. Also the children have their playroom on this side, and this area is off limits to everyone else in the community. This means that the children do not always have to compete for space with people bigger than themselves.

A fourth principle is that of *clarity*. It is necessary that Pat and I constantly review together needs and expectations, not only in our own relationship, but in all other areas of community life. We believe that we are not to make any assumptions with regard to ourselves, or to any other community member. Hopefully then, there is no split between us. Because handicapped people have a history, for the most part, of broken relationships, they are acutely perceptive of any division and can play on these divisions.

The Ache and Joy of Family Life:
No Illusions

We are certain that our family is at the core of the household. Because the family is at the centre, it enables us to share with great intimacy the rhythms of our family life. Though this intimacy leaves us vulnerable in our own relationship and in the parenting of our children, it creates an atmosphere of warmth and caring.

The handicapped people and the assistants we live with are a great gift to our family life. By the very fact that we live so closely together, many situations arise that have to do with relationship. These moments need to be lived through, not denied or suppressed. The children ask piercing questions, and we discover that there are no answers, just acceptance. When a young assistant left with very little warning, many hearts were broken. Natasha cried and it took a long time to comfort her. Suzanne was able to put into words what all of us felt: "She left without even saying goodbye."

In l'Arche the majority of those who live with the handicapped people are not married. Now there are more and more families living in l'Arche, seeking their place, asking questions. The questions that are before Pat and me are: how do we develop and support unmarried assistants, and how can we help other families find their place within the community. As l'Arche grows and develops, families and single people will discover together that they can create a safe place not just for the handicapped people but for the assistants.

Our hope is that families will commit themselves to a life of service and discover, as we have, the beauty of living with handicapped people. In sharing our life a gift has been given to us. Because of our very weaknesses, we need community, we need our brothers and sisters of l'Arche. Our selfishness is still present, and we know that without community we could easily slip back to old patterns that certainly would lead to death. So each day is a "yes" to our life together.

7

RHYTHMS OF LIFE

Chris Sadler

Chris Sadler, an English woman, lived and worked with harijans in South India for seven years. In 1971, she met Jean Vanier and l'Arche at a retreat given in Bangalore. A few years later she felt called to start a community in Kerala, South India, on ten acres of land, beautifully situated on the side of a hill overlooking the Arabian Sea. The land had been given to l'Arche and she and a number of Indian assistants built a home and welcomed seven handicapped men. Together they live and share the daily tasks of drawing water, watering the plants, picking cashews, taking care of the cows, cooking and trying to become financially self-sufficient, as well as welcoming, praying and creating together a community of hope.

Building a community in Christ is a work of eternity in each little moment but a work which must pass through long periods of time. Our community in Nandi Bazaar is very young, very new. We can only point to some tiny shoots, a few flowers, and remember in gratitude the thorns which also mark our way. Many seeds are still hidden in the unspoken vision of our own hearts and God's plans are always beyond and greater than any of our visions. I sense that we are being called to find in the risen Christ new harmonies of the inner and outer, of solitude and communion, of secret and revelation, of creation and celebration, of light and darkness, of life and death. We are blessed to live in a culture and climate which makes it possible to discover some of these harmonies in a very simple, natural way; but the more deeply we realize them, the more the universal dimension of what we live becomes clear. Yet, in our work and in our prayer and in our being together, we fail many times to respect the unique rhythms of each other, to reconcile the apparent clashing of our many calls. We must look constantly to God manifested in the divine artist of nature and human nature, the divine clown, and above all, the divine lover who gives and forgives, in order to live creatively in the tension between what we are and what we hope.

The beauty and unceasing creativity of the universe are a source of wonder, of inspiration, but also of wisdom. Here, we live on a hill always exposed to the great skies with their infinitely varied forms, often calling each other to witness the clouds, the setting sun, the appearance of a new moon. We are often surprised by extraordinary creatures or plants we have never seen before, continually discovering marvellous signs of God's glory, signs of his love for us. There are some who help us to see anew the miracle of life, the daily gift of grace even in the things which happen all the time. Mitran is amazed each time it rains or a cashew fruit falls to the ground. We are invited to look afresh at this frog which he calls a chicken or this lizard which he names a mongoose, at this banana which he insists is laughing. In Calcutta I remember the delight of Barun in the extraordinary redness of chillies in the market; his astonishment at the sizzling of oil in a pan; his eye for some little plant 'defiantly' growing out of a crevice in a dark alley, opening my own eyes. Yet we are confronted with an inescapable paradox, because to be truly sensitive to beauty one must at the same time be deeply sensitive to suffering. A community, whether in the city or the desert, cannot live without wonder, but neither can it grow without being pierced.

Unlike the rest of India, a country of villages, each house in Kerala stands alone in its compound, a solid fortress against the heavy rains. Our house is not too solid, though following a year of experimentation, it survives the rain. It is true that our compound is larger than most – ten acres – but being isolated has become a source of openness. A house without doors is a sign of our welcome and trust, a willingness to have our life exposed to anyone who cares to climb up the hill, or to our neighbour's children who leap over the wall. The places where we eat or sleep or pray are only demarcated by different levels connected by steps or a small bridge, and the inside is not separated from the outside.

The simplicity of sharing, Nandi Bazaar

In the summer even the walls, made of split bamboos through which we can see all the time, are rolled up. There is always a great sense of expansion, looking out at the vast skies, the thousands of coconut trees and the sea beyond.

Viswanathan spent ten years since the age of sixteen in a mental asylum that is notorious even in India. Happily, he was not confined in one of the "lion-cages" there, built more than a hundred years ago with no toilet or bed, just a floor and bars, where men or women, sometimes naked, are still confined. He was in an enclosed ward for long-term patients and almost never went out except for his "electric shocks", which until recently always haunted his daily conversation. When he first came here to Nandi Bazaar he was astonished to be free; for months there was no greater joy than just to sit out under the open skies, even in the heat of the sun when others were resting. Gradually, he came to sense that the house is also free, that the outer flows into the inner, and to be inside is not confining.

Some of us helped to build the house: we know what is under

the floor! We all share in remaking the roof of woven coconut palms each year before the monsoon, reinforcing the sense of continuity with the world around us. The simple structure of the house in which we can always see or hear one another also enables us to find harmony within, in our being together as a community. It seems important that people can freely gravitate to the kitchen, a perching place, but also a "way" in constant use. It is a distraction but not a disturbance that everyone is around while I try to write our accounts or letters, Ramesh telling me again and again that he wants to marry "tomorrow itself", Viswanathan imitating an elephant, and Lanci just sitting silently but catching my eye. If I am annoyed by Prasanna's obsessive meddling or irritated by Mitran's latest mood, it is never to the point of regretting the design of the house, or questioning the deeper joy of being together. This being together means in fact the willingness to be disturbed by our own deep fears and lack of love, to be continually questioned and often painfully bewildered by the anguished heart of Aravind or the distrustful eyes of Selvaraj.

Each person finds the rhythm of his need for privacy or solitude elsewhere – in the woods, or higher up on the hill, or in the yogalaya, a circular place of prayer unseen from the house, which everyone uses at different times, or, for Ramesh and Haneefa especially, down in the village tea-shops. Our men would be deeply unhappy if they were given individual rooms – not at all in the Indian tradition – but this also reflects something about our life, that we are not afraid to be together, to know each other and be revealed in our nights as well as our days.

It is in our culture, and in our indigenous medicine, that we are nourished and healed by the five elements: earth, water, air, fire and the great Akash, the Unseen element. The sun is fire but it is also light and rules our day in many ways. We rise before dawn, rolling up our mats, gathering around a candle, to sing three times:

Lokah samasthah sukhino bhavantu
(May all the world be happy, at peace.)

and then the great Upanishadic verse, Asato ma Sat gamaya:

From untruth lead me to truth.
From darkness lead me to light.
From death lead me to everlasting life.

Out of the darkness and the silence, the day emerges. Mitran
leaps to the well to give us water and Ramesh with his broom
returns our dust to the earth; Mani or I go to kindle the fire, while
Viswanathan breathes the joy of existence into a song. We work
for more than an hour until breakfast, watering the plants before
the shrivelling heat of the day, and then for a few hours digging
or collecting cashews. When it gets too hot, we move inside,
making rope out of coconut fibre or paper bags out of old newspaper, cleaning the cashews for marketing. In the monsoon we
follow a different pattern, hopping out of the workshop window
as soon as the rain becomes lighter. When it starts again, Mitran
gleefully points to the heavens, knowing that Subbaiyan, responsible for the work, is no longer the authority. Each evening, once
more at the meeting of day and night, we gather together in
thanksgiving, leading into the meal as the morning prayer led into
work.

We may bring to our prayer the fruits of nature and the fruits
of our work – the harvest of yams or a bunch of bananas, giving
thanks to the One who has given the seed containing life, which
we have only planted and tended, to the One who has prospered
the work of our hands, as he prospers the work of our hearts. It
seems quite natural to bring back the beautiful shells we find on
the beach, or to share the pattern in the beetroot we have just cut
for the curry, to speak of the healing mysteries of plants and
flowers, to give thanks also for the oddities and freaks of nature
– the tiniest cashew nut, the double mango.

Sometimes our morning prayer is clear and strong, but sometimes we all start off on a different note and we trail off feebly,
out of tune but still precious in the eyes of God. And precious in
his eyes are the spontaneous songs of our evening prayer: "Oh,
oh, oh, Iswara (Lord), we went out in a bus, we went down the
river in a boat, a booooooat. And Viswanathan is singing a song,
a little song is singing Viswanathan". We will not easily forget the

exuberance of his red-fire song, in the weeks when we gave thanks for different colours – all the blue gifts, for example, or all the green hopes of our lives. Several times, a sign of deep healing has been manifested in the community prayer itself, for example, Aravind singing with us after so many months of angry separation or the day Lanci (who would not sit down for a meal or even go to the toilet unless specifically asked) himself got up to receive for the first time the body of Jesus at Mass.

In India the reality of symbols – of water, light, the seed – is vividly close, helping us in our prayer to make visible, but not necessarily verbal, the deeper meanings of life. We see the dry brown earth "which mourns and withers" at the end of the summer almost instantly sprouting with shoots and green growth after the very first monsoon rain. Digging the well, chipping away at rock in the belief that within is the water of life, was in a sense the foundation of the house and remains at its centre. It is really a mystery for each one of us, staring down into the depths at the hidden spring which becomes a never-ending fountain. And if we only knew the gift of God! Drawing water from the well was the first work that gave Mitran security, a sense of being needed, and even now, if he has been "naughty", his way of saying sorry is "Do you need water?" During our evening prayer recently, we drank the first sweet water from our third well, built with great difficulty, and Viswanathan sang our thanks: "New water in the new well, pure water is given in the new well, new water is given."

Every day is full of gifts and offerings, but there are special days and special feasts: Deepavali, the festival of lights, celebrating the victory over darkness; the harvest festival of Onam; other festivals of cows, of new cooking pots, of coconuts and the nine grains. There is an Indian feast of thanksgiving for all the instruments by which we accomplish our work. In the days before this feast, each person in turn brought a favourite implement to the prayer, trying to imagine how it would be without Viswanathan's pick-axe to dig the land, or Mitran's bucket to take water from the well, giving thanks for each one's work, and for the tools which make it possible.

When we left for our first holiday, our first pilgrimage, each of us had a small cloth shoulder bag, just enough for a spare shirt and dhoti, or another sari, a towel, a sheet to lie on, and a few other things like our cymbals and tambourines. The bags we would carry were placed around the lamp, as we prayed that God would guide us, carry us, before setting off joyfully in the dark, taking a bus (going north!), to the furthermost tip of India. It was a great pilgrimage of laughter, a witness of our constant celebration of being children of God. Yet we carried silently in our hearts the brother who was forced by his own mental agony to stay behind.

We are blessed to have no electricity and so we become very conscious also of the lesser lights which rule the night, the cycle of the moon and its meanings, the stars which are like friends and yet remind us of the vast universe of which we are part. On full moon nights we go down to the sea with our supper, and bathe and pray there in the rhythm of the waves.

We are Moslem, Hindu, Christian – both Catholic and Protestant. Viswanathan was once asked: "To which God do you pray?" "I don't know to *which* God," he exclaimed. "Can that be *known*? There is a little light, and in that we pray, that's all." Personally it is a lonely pain to live with people who do not know Jesus, "light from light", to feel one's poverty in making him known, even though his presence is already so visible in the wounds and the hearts, certainly more loving than mine, of each one. Without desiring a superficial syncretic oneness, we can speak of a unity which grows, through the meeting of our hearts in the little moments of each day, through our shared experience of the beauty and mercy of God, by which we are forgiven and learn to forgive and respect each other. We begin to discover the power that is released in a community when we allow ourselves to be embraced by the other, the one who is different and pierced by our separations. The simplicity of Prasana penetrates with a certain innocence to a truth beyond the barriers that remain so crucial to others. It is a gift that becomes at the same time a revelation, breaking new ground, revealing a new dimension of the pilgrim church, of the deepening presence of the resurrection in our vast and diverse world.

In our work we spend much time clearing the tangled, thorny undergrowth, moving earth to form terraces or bunds; Subbaiyan prefers to call it "soil conversation" rather than soil conservation. The earth calls us forth like a mother and imparts its secret wisdom. In it we see the fruit of death becoming the seed of life – often growing out of the rubbish heap. Everything is a parable. When Lanci, who is not usually very articulate, was asked why we spend so much time shifting earth from one place to another, he said "to feed the roots, to give them space". "And what's the point of that?" He did not answer but gazed upward into the tall palms just beginning to form new coconuts, surely seeing the hidden flow from root to fruit. His relatives, bringing Lanci for the first time, had said cheerfully: "No need to worry about *him* – he has no feeling." Very slowly, the healing sap of life and his so many wounded feelings are rising through the hard knots of his own winter tree.

In nature we discover how profoundly everything is inter-related, everything has its place, nothing is useless or irrelevant. We know more deeply than ever that among us too, if anyone is discarded we break the chain of life, we reject their essential and unique contribution to the development of the whole. We know also that in the garden there must always be a balance between growth from the earth, nourished by water or compost, and the growth that comes from above, from light and warmth. Too much compost or water stunts rather than promotes growth. And so it is with man: it is a delicate balance in our attention to body, mind and spirit that leads to wholeness. Being close to nature, to its rhythms and processes, being close to that which harmoniously, absolutely and spontaneously conforms to the will of God, calls us deeply to conform to the same harmony, the same will. And the more we enter into the secrets of the earth, the more we are enabled to enter the hidden movements in the gardens – or the prisons – of the heart of each one.

It is a great gift to have our work determined by the seasons and the needs of plants, giving a dynamic and meaning to each day that calls us forth. If we do not water the seedlings to enable them to put down roots in the heat of May, they will be unable to withstand the force of the monsoons in June. If we do not shift the cow-dung into the tank to make gas, we will be unable to cook, and the dung will overflow down the path. Such exigencies often push us to our limits and to the discovery of unsuspected capacities – and often unsuspected humour. This work also generates a sense of belonging, of unity, of needing each other – so evident in the human chain of water-carriers passing buckets up and down the hill-slopes. In such shared activity, relationships are deepened without and beyond words. We are revealed to ourselves and to each other in an extraordinary transparency through our way of working together, through our respect for the earth, desiring neither to exploit nor pollute, and through our reverence for one another (and saying sorry when we fail). Above all it is the very simplicity of our life and our dependence on earth and sky, sun and rain, in meeting the fundamental necessities of eating and drinking, bathing and cleaning, which has helped to make us whole and to make us relate more fully to the reality of matter, to one another, and to the source of life itself.

In l'Arche the need to distinguish "work" and "home" and the corresponding division of authority and responsibility has been rightly emphasized. In an Indian village, however, there is never a clear distinction. It is one continuous process from the transplanting of seedlings to the eating of rice, involving the whole community, including the children who weed and sing and the blind, old grandmother who winnows. Growing out of this we search for a deeper wholeness, not so much a balance of work and leisure, but another meaning of work in which there is a rhythm of many different elements including play. I had already learnt this in the workshop in Calcutta with Barun, who is mongoloid and has such a creative imagination and spontaneous sense of fun when handling the rather boring wires for Philips radios. There is always time in our work for singing and laughter, just as there is time to stop our digging to gaze in delight at a kingfisher, or in respect at the deadly scorpion Tayyib has found.

It will not be killed but carried carefully on a leaf to another tree by Kanaran who believes that it absorbs the poison of the earth into itself so that we may live. And so we speak of the Indian myth of Shiva who drank the all-pervading poison to save the world, (and in my heart I rejoice in Christ prefigured and now risen).

We are certainly poor in developing those creative potentialities which are always uniquely personal. But we find that even the inevitable element of repetition in work can be positive, if it is shared and if it is never the only kind of work a person has to do. If we are fortunate to have scope and variety in our work, we are also fortunate to have variety in our people. We try to respect and welcome the delicacy of Ramesh or the fastidious meticulousness of Aravind – who gives a little order to the chaotic "office" table – but we encourage them to go beyond the limits of sterile habit. Both have developed, through physical labour, a degree of health and inner balance beyond all expectations. On the other hand, it is the security of the daily routine that has opened the way to peace and fulfilment for Mitran, who spent his adolescent years in throwing stones at people and in other wild and unappreciated diversions, as it has contained Viswanathan's blind but vital energy, released after so many years confined in sedated idleness. There is a link here with the community prayer. The beauty of simple Indian bhajans ("Iswara, Iswara, have mercy", "Jesu, Jesu, Jesu, Jesu, your name be praised") repeated over and over again often lead to a deep silence, a source of peace and unity, even to the most restless among us, inspiring us to enter new dimensions of life.

If we seek in our community to attain a degree of autonomy, it is only a means, a part of attaining the autonomy of each person. It is not easy to discern true needs, needs that relate to the truth of one's being, but in deciding together the distribution of the work or the utilization of the land – (whether to plant cocoa for profit or beans – for lunch), there are obviously fundamental principles involved. Human beings must always be ends in themselves; money must never be an end in itself. It is true that we may get impatient when our work is spoiled or wasted – when Koyassan, for example, impetuously pulls out a young tree that has been tended for a year. It is true that some of us are tempted to do things alone when it is quicker and surer than working with others. We never succeed in the struggle to balance the demands of the work by which we will eat and live, and the demands of those of us whose natural limitations or interior pains sometimes have consequences that would certainly be judged harshly by the criteria of rationality and efficiency. When Viswanathan arrives from his bath with his banian inside-out and back-to-front, he simply laughs and his dance becomes a somersault, reminding us that our serious, ordered, grasping world is all upside down, that life is often very funny and we should enjoy it. Certainly, we can laugh at our foolishness, but it is also important to know that the integral development of the person and of the community comes precisely through, and not in spite of, the points of our greatest weakness.

In our work we have tried to discover a truer relation to ourselves, to each other, to matter, to the cycles of nature, and to time, which means to make the "present" meaningful, to enter into the dimension that is of eternity. It is good to feel that the work we do is so close to our life and our needs, to sense the creative process in which we are involved, believing in the seed even though we may never see the fruits of the trees that we plant. In our other work too, in the healing of inner wounds, we must have faith that the seeds of love, perhaps only after many years, perhaps not in "our time" at all, but in the heart of God, will bear fruit.

Jesus Christ is the centre and the circumference of my own poor little life which he redeems constantly. We speak much of the rhythms of life, but for me personally it is to discover there an echo of the deeper rhythm of the cosmos, knowing that here on this insignificant little hill in an obscure village, with Viswanathan and Ramesh, one can attain the whole universe in the heart of Jesus.

Sometimes I feel alone but in a solitude that compels me to communion in the whole Christian community; being called through feasts and fasts, through the seven seasons of the church; called to live in all that flows from the daily, but often interior, celebration of the Eucharist and of the Word; called into the hidden life of Jesus, the life of Nazareth in all its simplicity and trustful waiting, and the life of the One who continued to go to the mountains before dawn; all carried in the immaculate heart of Mary.

Slowly I discovered how deeply I carry in my own yearning for God, the yearning of each one here, and as we become more and more one body, I sense a little bit the great groaning of the universe. It seemed that the freedom which is one of the gifts of a life of simplicity, was given to me precisely to become more aware in my heart of those who live oppressed by complexities and anguish in our world. I know that I live this very poorly, but it nevertheless binds me to the city, to the West, to the many pains of riches, to the great struggles that are lived there in hope.

Yet, for all of us, our life here would be lacking in meaning if we did not feel ourselves to be part of the body of l'Arche, through which we are nourished and supported in a thousand ways, but above all through the prayers and the interior presence of those who carry our little community in their hearts given to God. And it is in l'Arche that I am called by Jesus in his mercy, called by the poor in his heart to a covenant sealed with his blood.

The rhythms of life and work, of prayer and pain in all times and seasons and hours and moments of the days of our life are the rhythm of the wounded heart of Jesus which is the source of Life, forever calling us to adoration and to the life of the resurrection, the life of the Holy Trinity.

8

A MEETING OF CULTURES

Dawn Follett

Dawn Follett from Calgary, Alberta, completed her studies in 1971 at Queen's University, Kingston, Ontario. She came to l'Arche, Trosly, that same year. After a trip to several African countries with Françoise Cambier, she decided to found a community in the Ivory Coast in conjunction with the Ministry of Health and Social Affairs in Abidjan. L'Arche, Bouaké was founded in 1974, and has grown into a community of thirty people.

Dawn also helped in the foundation of a small community in Ouagadougou, Upper Volta, in 1977. She co-ordinates both of these homes, representing them on the International Council of l'Arche.

Introduction

We who come to live and work at l'Arche come with many different motivations, but most of them are born from a certain idealism. Some of us desire to help handicapped people grow by providing an atmosphere of love and security; some search for an experience in community living; others desire to live in Christian community. Many visitors and new assistants speak of their first impression of l'Arche as one marked by an atmosphere of joy and unity, and by the quality of the relationships within the community.

The charter shared by Arche communities throughout the world speaks of the goals held by all: creation of one community with respect and love for each person; breaking down of barriers that too often exist between "assistants" and "handicapped" members; creation of a place where there is mutual trust and love, where there is a unity which allows for the growth of all members, especially those who have been very wounded.

After the initial period in any Arche community, one discovers, sometimes with a certain disillusionment, that living in community involves a certain struggle. Divisions do exist despite first impressions of joy and of unity, and differences exist despite our shared goals.

In our Arche communities in the Ivory Coast and in Upper Volta, we are faced with this reality. On the one hand is our ideal, our desire to create a unified home where Amouin, Poyé and Karim may live and grow, and on the other hand are the differences that do exist and that can be sources of division.

How can we live in deep communion, "handicapped" and "non-handicapped", "blacks" and "whites" together? How do we create this unity necessary for growth?

Birth of a Community

In 1974, after living in the community of Trosly, and encouraged by the fact that the Arche community in India seemed to be growing quietly, meeting the needs of a small number of very destitute handicapped men, a team of three set out to begin the first community of l'Arche in West Africa, in the city of Bouaké, Ivory Coast.

The first few months of preparation were spent finding local interest and support, finding Ivory Coast friends who were convinced of the value of the project and ready to work with us in our integration in such a new country. We then welcomed our first handicapped man from the local mental hospital. Seydou was referred to us by the psychiatrist who diagnosed him as "schizophrenic". His condition, after one year of intensified treatment of electro-convulsive therapy and psychotropic drugs, had shown little improvement. He was considered to be mute (they called him "Saturday" because that was the day of his arrival at the psychiatric centre), and his only activity was to leave his room each morning to lie outside on the ground, wrapped from head to toe in a cotton sheet. "Saturday", a man perhaps in his late forties, came to live with us.

Saturday seemed to want to participate in some of our daily activities and from the first day was willing to help us wash up after meals and work with growing regularity in the garden. Although there was no verbal communication, we sensed his desire to be with us and express certain things to us.

At the weekend, we planned an outing and went to the local market place. There, to our astonishment, in one section of the very large market, Saturday was recognized by the salesmen who spoke to him in Aoussa, a language of Nigeria. He became very excited, answering back verbally to them. We were able to discover many things about Seydou from these old friends. They told us of his previous work as a jewellery trader who travelled extensively between the Ivory Coast and Ghana. When Seydou showed distinct signs of mental illness, his wife took their young son and left with another man to go back to Nigeria. This sickness had lasted almost twelve years before it became so acute that he was confined to the psychiatric centre. It was during this long period that Seydou slept at the market place and was given food by these men.

Within a few weeks, Seydou's drug treatment was completely stopped and over a five-year period in the community it has not been necessary to reintroduce it. Although he is quite independent in the group and rather solitary, we sense the importance of the community for him; it gives him a deep sense of security and a sense of family. Although in many domains, Seydou would be capable of going on to something else, there remains a deep fragility resulting from long years of physical and psychological hardship. The actual "stepping out" of the community seems unlikely at this stage in Seydou's life.

Seydou needs a family, a place of security where he may live and work, recognized as an aged person with the respect that this holds in the many traditional cultures of African societies. Outside our community this family does not exist for Seydou. Having friends who give him food and a place to sleep in the market place is something, but this is not enough to ensure his growth and his dignity as a person who needs, as each of us does, the warmth of a home and family.

Within a number of months, we welcomed N'Goran into the

community, referred to us from the same psychiatric centre. N'Goran, a man in his early thirties, had been admitted four times previously to this centre, but each time had escaped to continue his life as a wanderer in the streets of the city. He became one of the "crazy people" who wandered about almost naked, often mentally tormented by hallucinations, eating food from the garbage pails, or given by sympathetic passers-by.

N'Goran's integration into the life of the community was gradual. His mental state meant that he was often "far away", talking with, or even fighting against, imaginary people. Medical treatment was, and is still, necessary although greatly diminished in strength. N'Goran has discovered over the five-year period a real home in the community, and we, in turn, have discovered his many beautiful gifts as a person. The structure of the daily life, the existence of community tradition and the stability of relationships, especially with some of the other handicapped members, have helped N'Goran become more grounded in reality. He has his daily work (which he does extremely well), meals which are important moments together and free time which he spends as he chooses. He often participates in other leisuretime group activities (especially the cinema, when he is more than happy to join us all, although he invariably sleeps through the film!).

In August 1975, we discovered a small girl of about eight years of age in the psychiatric centre. Found alone in the market place, obviously abandoned there, the police had taken her to the centre. She was visibly handicapped, hemiplegic, and suffered from epileptic seizures. Although unable to speak intelligibly, she seemed to understand one of the local languages and seemed to respond to the name of "Amouin", a common baoulé name.

Amouin was almost savage in her behaviour, running excitedly from person to person, eating from the plates of the other patients, looking for attention in a disordered, almost frenzied way. We often came to the centre to visit N'Goran who had been admitted for a short stay for necessary and more specialized psychiatric treatment. We were touched by Amouin and especially by the beautiful relationship which was growing between her and N'Goran. She spent more and more time near him, and he was extremely gentle with her even when she became excited and sometimes aggressive.

The social worker's search for her family was of no avail, so when N'Goran came back to the community after his treatment, Amouin came also to live with us. A beautiful little girl, very much at the heart of the community, Amouin's whole being cried out for love, for touch, for relationship. Obviously she had been very frustrated at early and important stages in her development. She was much like a child who needed to be held, who needed to find the gentle, but firm love of a mother figure, which was to be balanced also by N'Goran's relationship with her. One sensed so strongly the depth of her thirst for love and affection, and this was sometimes a source of frustration for us because of our own inadequacy in the face of the intensity and never-ending expression of this need.

The community has now grown to include ten handicapped people who live within the home, three handicapped adults who are day workers, and five young handicapped children who come daily to participate in the school programme. These people who have come to live with us share this need for a place of growth. This family must give security, there must be love and unity between its members. This is Amouin's need, and to create this community is our desire and our struggle.

Need for Community Tradition

In any country, in any racial group or family group, there is an accepted way of doing things. The women in the village know their responsibilities; expectations of them are clearly defined. A very young girl already begins to prepare herself to fulfil these duties of cooking, cleaning and child tending. The old person in the village has a special place and others show him important signs of recognition and respect. The men have certain rituals that only they may participate in. All know what religious rites are necessary during harvest time or at the time of death or what sacrifice should be made when the anger of the ancestors is to be appeased after

N'Goran has found a true home at l'Arche, Bouaké

the transgression of some common law. These aspects of community living are defined and assure a certain security, a peace and a way of coping with the realities of death, sexuality and authority.

Our life together must have a structure which replaces, in some way, the family or village tradition. What, for instance, is the place of the child in the community? Amouin needs to know her rights, her responsibilities and the limits on her behaviour if she is to live and grow in security. What is expected of her as she grows older? In traditional African societies these things are clearly defined.

L'Arche cannot simply adopt local village traditions. This, in some ways, would be the easier solution and would ensure a certain unity. Our communities are situated in more heterogeneous urban settings and have been created during a time of rapid cultural change. They are composed of people of many different nationalities, ethnic groups and religions. And more important, the person who in other situations is marginal to the accepted way of life, is at the heart of the Arche community and the accepted tradition must answer his need.

The difference between the traditional culture and our way of life can be seen easily at meal times. In the local African family, the meal together, as it is known in the West, does not exist. Men eat separately from women, and children from adults. In the community, however, we take our meals together. Other realities in the home may be quite different from the normal local family patterns.

To create this community tradition, we look to the needs of Amouin who is called to grow within the community which has become her family, and within her own culture and her own country to which she also belongs.

Diversity within the Community

To say that our communities are composed of "whites" and "blacks" does not give an entirely accurate picture. The teams within our homes are formed of people of many different countries including the Ivory Coast, France, Upper Volta, Canada, England, Ireland and Belgium. This, although a source of richness, is not as easy as it may sound.

These differences are often expressed in small ways but they become sources of tension in a day to day living situation. For example, one's sense of humour cannot always be understood by the others. Leisuretime activities which should bring us all together are spent in very different ways. Assistants from the Ivory Coast or Upper Volta like to work in the field or prepare a good sauce on the open fire during their free time; Canadians would head straight to the local store for a beer and the French would sit and discuss important issues. Kuadio and N'Goran might go to the neighbours to watch television; Seydou would stay in his room to listen to the radio; N'Dabla might choose to visit friends in the neighbourhood.

Obviously these individual choices of leisure activities are important and satisfy the need of each person. We try to respect these. But together we try to discover the moments that help us to deepen the friendships, deepen the unity that must exist if we are to be at home within the community.

As well as the differences of nationality and race, there is the obvious and related one of language. Within our Bouaké home there are people of eight different language groups. Which one of these should be spoken during meals and during meetings? How do we help each person retain his own language if this is not the one usually spoken within the community? We try to help Seydou feel as much at home as the others even though his dialect is the one from the north and is not as common within the Ivory Coast. How do we help our children who have speech problems when, in the home itself, they regularly hear three different spoken languages? And Binta, who was abandoned at the age of eighteen months, what language should she learn in order to feel that she belongs, both to the community and to her country? L'Arche, a Christian community, is open to people of all religions. Although up until the present time our assistants have been mainly of the Christian faith, our handicapped people are largely from an animist background, a very common and deeply rooted religion within the local traditional culture. Seydou, Bakari and two of our day workers are of the Moslem faith. Here again we are faced with many questions. How do we help Seydou deepen his Moslem faith and not abandon it because of our lack of understanding or our lack of support? Bakari, an eight-year-old boy, has been with us for two years. His father is of the Moslem faith and when we speak to Bakari of "going to pray", he makes the gesture of Moslem prayer. It is important that we try to give him a formation within his own faith.

L'Arche is very much Amouin's family. We feel it important to raise Amouin within a religious tradition. Should Amouin be baptized within the Christian Church? Her gradual integration into the larger community of the local parish would be an important factor in her growth.

What religious festivals do we celebrate within the community?

Do we celebrate Christian, Moslem or animistic sacrificial rites? A large diversity in this domain is perhaps only confusing to the handicapped person. What does he know and understand of God, of life and of death, of prayer? We need to speak to him of these things – so important for his inner growth and peace – in simple and meaningful terms.

Many of our assistants have chosen to live in Christian community. Some are of Protestant background, others are Catholic. Together we yearn for deeper respect and understanding. In such a diversified setting, our witness here as Christians is meaningless unless it is one of unity.

Creating Unity

In spite of this diversity, in spite of our many questions, Seydou and N'Goran have shown such growth over these last five years. They have found a home within the community. N'Goran, who lived as a wanderer, and who later escaped numerous times from the psychiatric centre, has found a new peace and security within the structure of our life together. What aspects of the community have helped Seydou and N'Goran to grow?

Deepening of Relationships

An Arche community is based on relationship. In our life and our work together, we try to be attentive to individual needs. This means spending time with each person informally. But we also have meetings where we try to listen to each person's desires and difficulties. Together we try to discover how best to answer these needs.

These meetings can involve much listening, for some of our people have lived in situations of deep suffering. Gilbert, who is twenty-five, needs to tell us over and over again the story of his father's death, and how he was close to him at that moment. After his death, the house where he had died and where Gilbert had always lived as a child was "burned to the ground – nothing was left". He went to live with his uncle, an alcoholic, who rejected Gilbert very violently because of his epileptic seizures. Gilbert spent the night at the market place, unable to sleep because of his fear of the dogs who roamed there in search of scraps of food. These experiences have marked Gilbert very deeply, and he needs to speak of them. We in turn can help Gilbert at these meetings to see how he is growing within the community. We do make definite demands of him. Our caring for him must often be shown by our firmness. We express our confidence in him – our confidence in his capacity to grow. The dialogue is important – our listening, and his listening, for we are called to live and to grow together. Not all of our people have the same facility for expressing themselves verbally. We try to be attentive to them, for they communicate their needs in other ways.

Although it is non-verbal, Amouin expresses to us her need for relationship, for affection. We sense the importance of strong references who help her to set limits on her otherwise somewhat frantic behaviour. Privileged moments with Amouin have been during times of sickness when we have been able to care for her physical needs, to stay near her bedside, to take her into our arms as a tiny child, holding her firmly in warmth and in tenderness. These are important moments for her. She knows more deeply that she is loved and that she is cared for. There is a gradual deepening of her feeling of security and peace.

Some of our people will try to see if these new relationships are trustworthy. Do we *really* care? Can we support them in their instability and aggression? Will they, in their sometimes destructive behaviour, succeed in dividing the community?

During the first few months in the community, Bakari, then a six-year-old boy, seemed very quiet and well-behaved. We wondered how he could have experienced rejection by his mother when very young and yet not manifest this more openly in his behaviour. But only when Bakari felt secure in his new environment was he able to express his aggression. Bakari needed a mother figure who could help him in the gradual healing of his wounds and disappointments. But Bakari could not accept this relationship without being sure that he would not be hurt again. His aggression was often expressed against the mother figure. He wanted to know if this person would continue to be firm and yet loving. Could he trust? It is the deepening of these relationships over time that gives security, brings healing and calls forth growth.

The relationships between the handicapped members of the community can be sources of security and growth. N'Goran has been able to absorb Amouin's aggression in a firm but gentle way. Every day he shows his concern for her. At meals he makes sure she has water to drink, and all that she needs to eat. When Amouin needs something, she may call to N'Goran even if he is sitting at the opposite end of the table. He then communicates this to us. When he comes in at night, he checks on her to ensure that she is sleeping peacefully. When she is sick, he is concerned and stays by her bedside. This relationship has been a source of healing for both Amouin and N'Goran.

N'Goran is, in some special way, a source of unity in the community through the relationships he has with each person. His qualities of patience, gentleness and attentiveness to Seydou, Amouin, N'Dabla, and the others, are sources of peace and unity within the group.

Structures

The structure of our day-to-day life is an important source of security. The diversity of age within the community means we need a variety of daily activities suited to each individual.

Our earliest work activity was the garden. We grow a wide variety of vegetables and cultivate some of the crops which are the staples of the local diet such as *yams*, corn and sweet potatoes. There is always work to be done, and each person participates according to his capacity.

N'Dabla, a man about twenty-two years of age, has much difficulty in fixing his attention or in carrying out a task from the beginning to the end. We asked N'Dabla to take the wheelbarrow, go to a specific place, fill it up with straw and bring it back to the garden. Each row of plants was to be covered with this to prevent

Gabriel and his sense of life, l'Arche, Bouaké

it from being scorched by the hot sun. N'Dabla was delighted to use the wheelbarrow and to have a specific job for himself. The task was an active one and involved going directly from "A" to "B" and back again, all with very simple clear movements.

We then began a small chicken farm and now have about 1,600 laying hens. Seydou is responsible for two of the chicken coops and waters and feeds the hens daily, as well as collecting the eggs. N'Goran, who is so gentle in all that he does, cares for the small chicks. Some of the other members of our community were involved in the building of the chicken coops, and others in the sale of hens or eggs to neighbours who come regularly to buy them. Each person knows his task and knows that he must be regular and faithful to it if the hens are to live and produce the number of eggs necessary to satisfy the demands of our customers. As in the work of the garden, there is the satisfaction of bringing to the whole community the produce, resulting from the efforts of each person.

As in the local culture, Poyé and Madina, two girls of about sixteen years of age, work in the home. They help to wash the children's clothes and clean the house and courtyard. Madina, who lives with her family and comes into the community as a day worker, loves especially to help prepare the meals. In time, she will be able to cook a meal with little guidance or supervision.

The children in the community, accompanied by Marcelline, an Ivory Coast assistant, leave each morning for our small school which is about a ten minute walk. Other children, some of whom are also labelled "handicapped" but who live with their own families, come as well. This small school welcomes ten or twelve children.

The daily routine is important: leaving the house each morning with Marcelline; finding at school a certain rhythm, clear expectations of behaviour, relationships with the other children and with the assistants who work there, and coming back home each evening, again finding peace and security within its relationships and structures.

Meals

Meals are important times of sharing and of listening. If each person comes only to eat, and is in a hurry to finish and to begin his siesta, then this moment, important to unity, will be lost. If we let Mamadou talk throughout the meal because we are too tired to enter into any meaningful conversation with him, or if we are not attentive enough to bring others into the sharing, we have done nothing to deepen the bonds that exist. If Seydou comes and eats and leaves the table to go back to his room without saying a word, or without anyone asking him about his day, then we have done nothing to increase his sense of belonging to the group.

But if each of us comes ready to participate in the sharing of the meal, this deepens the level of meaningful communication. Not all of this communication must be verbal, of course; some very deep sharing is of a more non-verbal nature. Our attentiveness to Seydou may be to respect his silence but to assure him, by other gestures or by a look, that his presence is important.

The evening meal brings us together after having been dispersed during the day and is a good moment for us all. We are much more relaxed since it is cooler and there is no rush to go back to work. Our day workers have gone home to their own families, so the group is smaller. We take more time just to be together and to enjoy the presence of the children. It is already dark, and there is something more peaceful and intimate about this moment; we feel very much at home together.

Meetings

All members of the community meet together each Saturday afternoon. There is time first to chat, to drink coffee, to wake up from our siesta, and then we begin. Everything is translated into three languages to ensure that each person will understand. There is an information period when we speak of the programme for the next week, the visitors who are to come, or special events. We often have news of friends to share or letters to read. Then there is the opportunity for each person to speak, knowing that others will listen. Mamadou inevitably repeats all the points that we have just gone over; it is important for him to show to himself and to all of us that he has understood. N'Dabla may ask if he can spend the weekend with his older brother who lives in the city, and so we decide that with him. We speak of aspects of our community living, the small day-to-day things, rules that need to be known, understood and respected by all. Perhaps the person responsible for feeding Bandit, our dog, has not been faithful to his task. Occasionally we need to remind the older people in the community to be a bit more understanding with the children who can be, as in any family, a source of disturbance in the group. Perhaps food has been missing from the pantry! We then decide together who will do the household chores; each person chooses to wash, to rinse or to dry the dishes, and he knows he must be faithful to his task until the next Saturday meeting. And so another week begins.

Prayer

Our evening prayer is a precious moment in our life together. Even though not all members of the community participate, all know that there is this special time of prayer in our chapel.

Each evening after the washing up, Amouin lights the candles in the chapel and waits there for us. When we are all present she and Bakari clap their hands in rhythm for our "Arche prayer"; they are ready to begin. At the end of the prayer, which usually lasts for about twenty minutes, Amouin gives each candle one by one to the younger children to blow out. All this she does with such enthusiasm! She receives such joy from observing and knowing how she can participate, and in this way gives something special of herself. The evening prayer is an important moment of quiet and peace which unifies us, especially if Binta has managed to fall asleep, a frequent and much appreciated occurrence.

I have mentioned the diversity of religious faiths within our community and the many questions that we ask ourselves. These are questions that we live and struggle with. But they do not prevent us from praying together, yearning for a deeper unity in our day-to-day life.

Friends

Our desire to create a unified community cannot mean isolation from the people around us. N'Goran, Amouin, Gilbert, belong to the community of l'Arche, but also to the larger community around them. These relationships of friends outside l'Arche are essential for their growth, and especially in our country where the sense of relationships and solidarity is so deep. The security and the unity within the community should permit and encourage this outward movement, going towards other people and welcoming friends into our home. We have many regular visitors who come to buy eggs and chickens from us, and who in many cases become friends of the community. Our small school welcomes some handicapped children from the nearby area, as well as young women

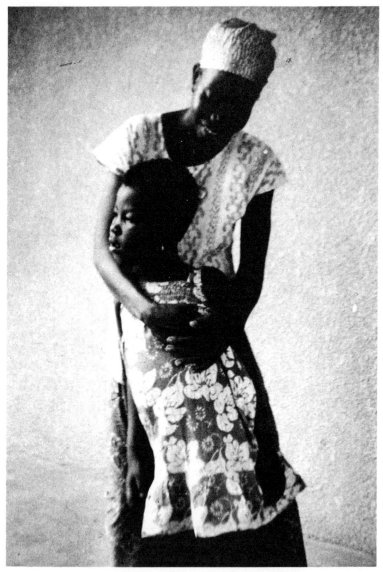

Binta cries out her need for love, l'Arche, Bouaké

who come to work with us. This also helps us to deepen our integration within the neighbourhood.

The Needs of Assistants

The assistants in our communities need additional times of meeting and of sharing. It is essential for us to plan and to organize our day-to-day living together so that things run smoothly.

There is a consistent therapeutic approach for each of our handicapped people, and this is looked at regularly by the group of assistants, taking into consideration new growth or new difficulties. Each assistant feels free to relate to Amouin in his or her own way, but in certain areas of behaviour, Amouin needs to feel a unity around her, a common attitude. We need to be clear in our expectations of her or she will be confused.

We need time together to come to a common understanding of the needs of each person. We are sometimes confronted with difficult situations and called to make decisions which will affect the growth and the future of someone in the community. For an assistant to feel at home within the community, he needs to feel that his own presence is important, and that his own needs can be expressed. In many ways he needs to feel that the community is a place of growth for himself. We have regular times of sharing when we look at the place of each assistant within the community, his work, responsibilities, needs and difficulties.

At other moments of deeper sharing we try to look together at situations of tension that might exist within the group – misunderstandings, or feelings of mistrust or anger. We try to learn to verbalize these difficulties and to do so in an atmosphere of listening and of respect, for it is through this that we eventually come to a better knowledge of each person, to a deeper understanding of our cultural differences. Working through these tensions together can result in a gradual deepening of mutual trust and can be a source of growth and of unity.

Celebration

I described leisure activities as events that tended to separate people rather than bring them together. Times of prayer are important moments, but do not include everyone. More and more within our communities, we discover the importance of celebration as a source of unity.

Each celebration is a special occasion, something that takes us all out of our daily routine. We can be lifted out of our fatigue, out of tensions or daily worries. Together we plan and prepare, for it is important that each celebration be meaningful and a source of joy for each person.

There are many local fiestas during the year that mark religious holidays, or Independence Day, or the New Year, and we join the crowds to participate in the religious ceremonies, or to watch the parades and traditional dances that are held. The people of the Ivory Coast have a very deep sense of celebration and there is electricity in the air created by the drums, the rhythmic music, the excitement and the joy expressed in dance!

On 18 June, we celebrate the day that Seydou came to live with us. It is his day, and with a special meal and a gift from everyone, we celebrate his presence with us, expressing our joy and our thankfulness. We do this for each person and Mamadou talks about *his* day all year long. We talk about how the person came to the community, and perhaps tell a few stories of important moments during his time with us. Sometimes we act these out in a short play after the meal. And always afterwards is a time of dancing, for this expression of joy is so much a part of the culture and a part of each person.

Other important moments of celebration are departures. We become deeply linked to people who live with us and it is not easy to see someone leave. But we can express our thankfulness for all that we have received from his presence and our joy in having had him with us, and we can express our love and support for this new step in his life. Sometimes the person will share what he has received from the community and from each one. This is a meaningful moment for us and for the person who is leaving, a moment that deepens the bonds that exist. We learn that our community is not limited only to those within its physical boundaries, but is much larger. Fidelity to these friendships is important.

Celebrations do bring us together. We express our joy and we receive the joy that is expressed by all those around us. We celebrate our being together, deeply aware that our life together has meaning. These moments of unity are precious and give new hope, new energy to work for a deeper unity in the daily life of the community.

Conclusion

Amouin's presence at the heart of the community is an important source of unity. If we are faithful to her needs, if we are committed to her growth, we will go beyond our differences to create a home where she will find security and peace. Her presence renews daily our desire to work for this unity and reminds us that our efforts are important. We receive much joy from Amouin, Seydou, N'Goran and from each person, and we see that they have found a home within the community. We are committed, one to another, and so we continue to deepen our life together in our mutual covenant.

9

A STRUGGLE FOR UNITY

Thérèse Vanier

Thérèse Vanier, sister of Jean Vanier, is a doctor in London. Before joining l'Arche she was a clinical haematologist on the staff of St Thomas's Hospital. After taking part in the Faith and Light pilgrimage to Lourdes in 1971, she decided to work with l'Arche and to this end resigned from St Thomas's Hospital, taking up part-time work at St Christopher's Hospice.

Early in 1973, Little Ewell, the first Arche community in England, opened at Barfrestone in Kent. There are now three other communities in England and one in Scotland. These, together with the communities in Denmark, Norway[1] and Ireland make up the Northern Europe region of l'Arche. From the start, members have come from different Christian traditions, and the communities have lived with the pain of division and the desire for unity.

Thérèse has co-ordinated the region since 1975 and was leader of the London community until January 1981, while continuing to work part time at St Christopher's Hospice.

L'Arche seeks to develop communities where mentally handicapped men and women can find security and love, a home and a sense of belonging to a family, a community where they can grow to greater inner freedom.

The charter of l'Arche states that handicapped men and women are "at the very heart of the community" and are "welcomed without distinction of religion, race or social class, though priority is given to the most rejected". In addition, at present, l'Arche makes no demands of its assistants regarding religious beliefs or

[1]Mariahuset, the Arche community in Norway, left the Federation in 1981, but close links still exist with it.

religious commitment. Therefore, in all our communities, regardless of whether they be in France where the majority are Roman Catholic, or in India where the majority are Hindu, there is a great diversity in religious beliefs and depths of belief. Each person who comes may bring his own tradition, or that of his family; he brings his apathy or enthusiasm, his prejudices; he may come with an openness to God or deep feelings of anger towards Him.

Our charter says that we are Christian communities[2] but this must be understood in a very open sense. Our communities are not Christian in the same way as a parish where all come together because of their belief. Although this brings a richness to our lives, it also makes for very complex situations. Handicapped men and women are frequently very open to religious beliefs and practices. Their simplicity leads them to believe and to trust. At the same time, each one gradually discovers that he is free, and the degree to which he can be open to the religious side of life varies greatly. Each person carries his own particular wounds and the barriers that have grown from these.

We do not seek to impose a belief, even were this possible; and of course religious practice is not obligatory. We do try to help each one find inner peace and union with God according to his own tradition, if he has one. We try to give each one the opportunity to discover the special love God has for him, to discover too that death is not the end of our existence but that God has promised us a new life, an eternal life. We try together to discover that love, welcome and forgiveness can eventually triumph over selfishness, rejection and guilt.

Our communities are anything but homogeneous, when it comes to matters of religious belief, even if most members belong nominally to the same religion or Church. When many religions or denominations are represented among the members, very specific questions and problems emerge. We are well aware of the prejudice and hatred that may exist among Christians of different denominations and of the many wounds and unwieldy structures that are a legacy of history. We are aware of the divisions and

[2]The charter of the communities of India does not use this term.

mistrust that separate Christians, Hindus and Moslems; we are aware of the gulf that exists between believers and those who are searching and those who have no faith; those who are antagonistic towards belief because at some time they have been hurt by official religious leaders.

Religious, philosophical and theological reflection and discussion take second place in our communities to the actual business of trying to live together. This order of priorities is not necessarily something to be proud of but it is a fact and, I believe, a fact on which we can build. This is our challenge. Maybe it is the love that gradually must bind a community together if it is to survive, that can be the bridge; maybe, through this living together, we can play our part in the healing of some wounds and in deepening truth.

In setting about the writing of this chapter. I am conscious that it is a very personal account and an interpretation of the ecumenical situation of our communities in northern Europe, although I am able to draw on reflections of each community as they were written, for the most part in 1977. I am in no position to touch upon the much wider area of the relationship of Christians and members of other religions in our communities in India and elsewhere.

L'Arche started in France. Its links from the start were with the Roman Catholic Church. The expression of the spiritual life of its members has therefore developed and deepened mainly within that communion. Without seeking it, communities in Northern Europe bring together Christians of Anglican, Lutheran, Presbyterian, Roman Catholic and other Churches. As one might expect, the handicapped people belong mainly to the Church which predominates in a particular country. Unlike many ecumenical communities, therefore, we have found ourselves living something that was not a deliberate choice. This is undoubtedly a gift of God and, like many of his gifts, it is hard to handle.

Along the way, he has sent us signs on how to handle his gift. Frequently, we have seen the sign only long after it was given. Those of us, Anglican and Roman Catholic, who began the first Arche house in England at Little Ewell near Canterbury, well remember the strange set of circumstances which began with a

Frenchwoman living in Paris offering us a house she owned near Canterbury. At the same time she said that anything we did in that area should be brought quickly to the attention of the Archbishop of Canterbury. The house was not suitable, but we obeyed the second injunction. Our meeting with Archbishop Michael Ramsay led to numerous contacts and consultations within the Anglican Church as it did to the purchase of an old rectory to serve as our first house.

Another sign which marks the beginnings of our region is the existence of Niels Steensens Hus in Denmark. The founders, among whom is a Roman Catholic priest, were all Catholics, and because of the attitude of the Danish government towards voluntary organizations, there are few mentally handicapped residents in the community. Most of the latter are members of the Lutheran Church. The house is anchored and nourished in the Roman Catholic tradition. It is a sign of faithfulness to one's Church. Because it has had more than its share of difficulties in surviving as a community, it is also a sign that unity of belief is no guarantee of unity between people.

Yet another sign has been the presence in the one Irish community of an assistant who belongs to the United Church of Canada. Who would have expected, in a tiny village of the Irish Republic, this reminder of diversity?

I think we first became conscious of our ecumenical situation just as Little Ewell was due to open in 1974. A Roman Catholic priest from Canada asked to spend his sabbatical year with us. His presence meant that we had the possibility of daily Mass in the house and providentially brought to a head the whole question of how we were to live our lives as Christians within the community. At first we wondered about asking special permission for Anglicans to receive communion at Mass. Such permission is often granted in France, for instance, where Christians of other denominations may have difficulty in reaching their own Churches. Obviously the situation is different in England but our case was to rest on the fact that Anglican members of the community who wished to receive daily communion would have to travel ten miles into Canterbury early in the morning. After more consideration and seeking advice from a Catholic priest who knew the ecumenical scene, we realized that the matter was not clearcut at all. If Mass were celebrated daily as part of community life, those Anglicans who wished to participate in the Eucharist would have no choice in the matter of attending their own Church and their own rite, even if they had the choice of coming or not coming to Mass. It could be seen as, and would indeed be, a Roman Catholic takeover. What would the families of our handicapped members have felt?

We had to face certain basic issues, the first of which was the needs of our mentally handicapped members, all of whom were Anglican. We must provide for them, we must ensure that they be recognized as full members of their own Church. Secondly, we had to realize that divisions interwoven into four hundred years of the history of these islands could not be swept away. The divisions are there, deeply etched into the being of each person and tangibly expressed in the Anglican church and Catholic church standing alongside each other in towns and villages, with Anglican and Roman Catholic bishops and priests living in the same area.

We therefore reached certain decisions although not everyone was in agreement, and how could this be otherwise, since we were so different in age, formation, background and culture as well as religious denomination? The Anglican rector from a nearby village agreed to celebrate the Eucharist once a week and the Roman Catholic priest celebrated Mass once a week during the community working day. On other days he said Mass very early so that only those assistants came who were courageous enough to get up early. Thus the Mass was not a sign of division. On Sundays we each went to our own church and on remaining weekdays we agreed to have special times of prayer together for healing and reconciliation. This arrangement did not in any way solve our problems but it contained them in a structure that tried to respect people and respect reality. We still had to live the irreconcilable rules of the different Churches relating to intercommunion. The community lived through and continues to live with many tensions, but realizes more and more that tensions due to difficulty in relationships in community life may be focussed on the eucharistic division, but

John Grist and Thérèse Vanier near Little Ewell

again how could this be otherwise? Jesus in the Eucharist is the scapegoat just as he was on Calvary.

L'Arche sprang from commitment to Christ and a particular response to his invitation to live certain contradictions which he expressed in the Sermon on the Mount. If we believe that the poor (the weak, the powerless) are blessed, then it becomes a question of listening to them. One of the tenets of our communities is that individuals and society as a whole have much to learn from those who are called mentally handicapped. This must suppose a profound respect for the handicapped person and for other individuals and for the society in which we live. Much has been written on this aspect and here I wish only to mention its significance where Christians of different traditions, handicapped and "normal" are living together in a very demanding community situation, desperately needing the nourishment which comes from shared faith and in a special way from sharing together in the sacrament of the body and blood of Christ.

At the level of theology and of Church law, necessary and patient discussions are taking place: men of good will are finding so many points of contact alongside insurmountable barriers. In St Luke 10:21 we read: "In that hour Jesus rejoiced in the Holy Spirit and said: I thank you Father, Lord of heaven and earth, that you have hidden these things from the wise and understanding and revealed them to babes; yes, Father, for such is your gracious will." Each man can be reached by God, and those who are mentally handicapped set up fewer barriers than the rest of us. We know from experience the capacity of the mentally handicapped for helping us to break down barriers which separate us at so many levels and we know that God reveals secrets to little ones that are hidden from the wise. We simply do not know how Christian unity will come about but if we believe that the Spirit acts through the poor, the powerless, then they too must live in the *real* world and not in an isolated and comfortable "unity". Their sensitivity will soon discover the sadness at the point where unity is broken, and they will help us to yearn and pray together for healing and reconciliation. If we seek to heal and break down barriers, we must assume into ourselves some of the sickness, some of the harshness and pain.

Principles were comparatively easy to enunciate. It was more difficult to consider and apply all that they contained. Quite likely we simply felt unable to do this and, looking back, I hesitate to say that we were wrong although we were certainly inconsistent and imprudent. We did not, for instance, explain the situation fully to the mentally handicapped people and made no attempt to prevent them from receiving communion at both Eucharists in the house if they wished, and many did so receive. This meant great hurt and confusion for some of them who of course failed to recognize the different situation and were refused communion in a Roman Catholic church where they were known not to be Catholics.

Two years after the house opened, one of our objectives was achieved in that Anglican members of the community were confirmed by the Anglican Bishop of Dover in the twelfth-century parish church. They were now full members of their own communion.

Because of the larger proportion of Roman Catholics in the city of Liverpool, the Anchorage community there has more Catholic members. On average, Mass is celebrated once a week in the house by a visiting priest. They have had to face the particular situation of Colin who is quite severely mentally handicapped. I quote from their report: "He is baptized into the Church of England but attends the Baptist Church with his mother. He likes to come to Mass and follows it very closely. This prompted his parents to ask that he be considered for reception into the Roman Catholic Church. We have not encouraged him or indeed allowed him to receive communion at Mass. This is mainly because the priest is not normally permitted to give him this, but even where individual priests like to include Protestants in communion (and indeed some do) we have not allowed this in Colin's case and also in the case of another boy who is not a Catholic. For Colin's sake it seemed very important not to confuse him. If he were allowed communion in the community Mass and not in the parish Mass which he sometimes attends and where it is known that he is not a Roman

Catholic, then, because he is who he is, he would not only be confused but it would be entirely in character for him to create a commotion at the altar rails. If we took his Church of England baptism seriously and made greater efforts for him to attend and receive communion in the Anglican Church (and this would in any case require the normal preparation) he could be received into full communion of that Church. If he were to receive communion in the Church of England, however, then refusal in the community would bring out the confusion and anger there. All this is to say that so far we have been obliged to follow the ruling of the Roman Catholic Church, not necessarily because that is what we set out to do, but because of the very vulnerable and uninhibited personality of someone who could not cope easily with such discrepancies in religious practice."

At the Lambeth house in London, most handicapped people are Anglican and most assistants Roman Catholic. The assistant who was first in charge of the house was Anglican and spent a year at Trosly in France where permission was given to receive communion, there being no possibility of regular attendance at an Anglican Church. Such a reason cannot be invoked in London. Many of the assistants, whether Anglican or Roman Catholic, would welcome the opportunity to participate in the Eucharist daily. Frequently this presents difficulties since the times that their presence is needed in the house may be the very times that there is celebration of the Eucharist in a local church. It would be easy, in London, to invite priests and ministers to celebrate the Eucharist in the house on weekdays, and we do feel the need to draw together for this nourishment. As director, at that time, and a Roman Catholic I would not take the initiative in issuing such an invitation because it would have put each one into a difficult situation. Anglicans would not be able to receive communion at a Roman Catholic Eucharist, contrary to their experience in France. Celebration of the Anglican Eucharist would produce an equally hurtful situation in that either Roman Catholics abstain from communion or break the rules of their Church.

Zacchaeus House in Bognor Regis, perhaps because it opened more recently and has drawn on the experience of older communities and also perhaps because its handicapped members may be more intellectually able, is clear in its approach. All the handicapped people are Anglican, most of the assistants Roman Catholic. Each is very clear about which Church he or she belongs to and worships in. Appropriate religious instruction is taking place to lead to confirmation. One handicapped woman helps with the local Anglican church's Sunday school and another hopes to join the church choir. Each person goes to his or her own church and on the rare occasions when Anglican or Roman Catholic Eucharist is celebrated in their little oratory the rules regarding intercommunion are respected. The whole community prays together each day and the unity they feel at such times seems painfully broken when they go their separate ways to worship in their churches.

At Braerannoch in Inverness, the majority of handicapped people belong to the Church of Scotland, although other denominations are represented in the community. Those who wish to go to church on Sundays attend their own church. Some of the handicapped people choose to attend a Roman Catholic Eucharist in addition to going to their own church. At times one of them will express the wish to receive communion and, although this is not encouraged, the wish is respected because in their own simple way they recognize God's special presence in communion. Visiting priests and ministers are invited to celebrate the Eucharist or hold a service in the house if they wish, and the local bishop of the Episcopal Church in particular comes several times a year to celebrate the Eucharist.

At Mariahuset in Oslo three young women, two Roman Catholics and one Lutheran, live with four severely handicapped autistic children. On alternate weeks the Eucharist of the Roman Catholic and of the Lutheran Churches is celebrated. The rules of the Roman Catholic Church regarding intercommunion are fully respected. The Blessed Sacrament is reserved and Jesus's presence adored there by Catholic and Lutheran alike while each remains entirely faithful to her own church.

Numerous people from outside the community come to the eucharistic celebrations. Among them are many who do not dare to enter an "ordinary" church for fear of having to be "good" or socially acceptable. The presence of Lutherans, Catholics and of those outside the institutional churches has wide implications for the little group in the house. They carry within themselves a deep longing for unity, for one Church, for "one people" groping for the truth. They feel deeply the divisions among Christian Churches, many of which seem linked to spiritual and material "possessions", ultimately separating them not only from one another but from the Heart of God. At these celebrations of the presence of God in their chapel, matters of dogma and liturgy become a luxury and fall away in the presence of the profoundly handicapped children and the "marginal" young people in desperate search of truth.

The community has faced a complicated situation regarding Laila, a severely handicapped girl in her teens. They discovered that she was not baptized and hoped she might be baptized into the Roman Catholic Church. Then began a long and legalistic process during which they discovered that, as she was a minor, she could not be received into the Catholic Church unless her mother who is officially a member of the Norwegian (Lutheran) Church left that Church. The law was definite on this point despite the fact that Laila's mother had in practice, if not legally, abandoned her and in addition was perfectly willing for Laila to be baptized into the Catholic Church. The mother clearly could not be asked to leave her Church, and so Laila was baptized into the Lutheran Church.

My own reaction to this situation, which may or may not be shared by the community, is that it is probably right for Laila to be a member of the Lutheran Church, one reason being that she, at present, seems much more able to cope emotionally with the more formal ritual of the latter.

The examples quoted from Little Ewell and The Anchorage in particular illustrate the difficulties with which we are grappling, the inconsistencies of which we are capable but also the concern for individuals and the trust we have in just living through situations. It is obvious that we need to reflect more on what we are doing or not doing.

To illustrate another principle we hold, that of consultation with our Pastors, I quote the report from Niels Steensens Hus. It also spells out some of the fundamental attitudes towards mentally handicapped people and their participation in the Eucharist.

"The priest may under certain circumstances permit a Protestant Christian to receive communion if he shares the Catholic belief of Christ's real presence in the Eucharist (not only at the moment of receiving communion) and the belief that the Eucharist is a sacrifice. However, the local bishop must be in agreement with this practice. This practice was followed by Cardinal Willebrands when he visited Lutheran friends in Denmark. During celebration of Mass in their home he permitted them to receive communion.

"With mentally handicapped people one must distinguish between the faith they have and the faith they are able to express. A large number of mentally handicapped people will be able to distinguish between ordinary bread and the Eucharist; they may also have some understanding of the real presence of Christ and of the Eucharist as being in some way connected with the sacrifice of the cross.

"The mentally handicapped person may reach out for God but he cannot grasp the difference between Catholics and Protestants. His longing for God should be respected and kept intact and it should be fostered. Christians, whether Anglicans, Lutherans or Catholics should first of all help the mentally handicapped person to grow in faith and in his longing for Christ. If he wants to receive communion, he should be helped to do so; if he wants to receive communion in both the Anglican/Lutheran and Catholic Church, he should be allowed to do so. He should be supported in his inclination towards one or the other Church or towards both Churches when this is the case. The guiding principle must be his longing and reaching out for God. However, it is not enough to let him receive communion; he must be taught and given the opportunity to develop faith and knowledge.

"In Niels Steensens Hus, where we have both Lutherans and Catholics, but only Catholic Mass in the house, we permit

Lutheran handicapped people to receive communion if they really want it and if they have received some basic catechetical instruction.

"The above suggestions should only be carried out in collaboration with the local bishops as it is of primary importance to live and to grow with the Church."

In all of this we feel hope, pain, confusion, exasperation and frustration. We do not always find that our Pastors understand what we are trying to live and maybe this is because we are not too clear ourselves. At our Regional meeting in 1977 we made an attempt to define what we should do:

1. We should become better informed about our own tradition and history and those of others by asking people to come to talk to us.

2. We should inform our Churches and their leaders of our situation; that is, that we are trying to live the Christian Gospel in a demanding way without the nourishment that sharing in Christ's body and blood can give.

3. More and more we must deepen our prayer together, particularly as it expresses that mysterious phrase of St Paul where he talks of completing what is lacking in the sufferings of Christ (1 Col: 24).

4. L'Arche has a part to play in reconciliation among Christians and we need to think, pray and understand what this is. It is linked to the teaching of the Sermon on the Mount and to the paradox of suffering that is joy.

5. In all this we have much to seek forgiveness for and much to forgive each other.

At the international meeting of the Federation of l'Arche in 1978 we expressed our position as a region during the time of common prayer as follows:

"Communities in our region bring together Christians of Anglican, Church of Scotland, Lutheran, Roman Catholic and other

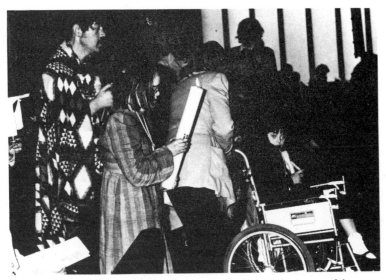

Members of the community of Little Ewell share in the events of the Easter Vigil

traditions. For many of us, the Eucharist is a vital source of healing, nourishment and focus of our adoration of God and fellowship with our brothers. Irreconcilable rules regarding intercommunion exist in each of our Churches, and lead to confusion and hurt.

"The intellectual content of our differences is meaningless for many in our communities. Such people may lead us to truth providing we deeply respect them, seek to understand their needs, and never make use of them to achieve what we want. This will mean concern for freedom and clarity. It will mean avoiding inconsistency between what is allowed inside the community and what is allowed in the parish. It may mean the seeking of special permissions in some cases. It will always mean painstaking search for ways of communication and understanding with our Pastors and with our disabled people.

"We must try to understand why Jesus washed the feet of his disciples and exactly what happened that night. Eucharist means to give thanks. Jesus, on the night he was to be betrayed by a companion and to cry out for release and then assume his pain totally, gave thanks – Eucharist. He gave Eucharist for all that had been, all that was and all that would be. He gave his body up to death in thanksgiving. Lord, teach us the meaning of Eucharist, of giving thanks for each other in the washing of the feet. As we come closer to the true meaning of this, so will we come to sharing Eucharist – thanksgiving."

Despite our plans and good intentions there has been little systematic attempt to deepen our understanding of the ecumenical situation in most communities, although for many of us it remains a burning question. Perhaps it is too painful; maybe we are lacking in hope. It is certainly part of the difficulty many of us experience in reflecting together on what is being lived at all levels in our communities. I feel we must now take up this challenge which is also a gift and really move forward along the lines we have set ourselves. We must not try to avoid this but neither must we belittle the first place which is given to the struggle to live together, with all that this implies. I am becoming more and more convinced that our different Churches will only drink from the same chalice when all have learned to drink from the chalice of suffering of those who are poor and oppressed. The Blood of Christ leads us necessarily to their wounds. Maybe in living with handicapped people we are learning in some way to drink together from this chalice of suffering.

10

L'ARCHE: A HOUSE THAT WELCOMES

André Roberti, s.j.

André Roberti is a Jesuit priest from Brussels who, in 1970, began a home called Le Toît for physically handicapped people. After the Faith And Light pilgrimage to Lourdes in 1971, he came in contact with l'Arche and asked that his home become part of the large family of l'Arche. This was realized in 1974.

Since then, six other Arche homes have been opened in Brussels and five communities have begun in other parts of Belgium.

In 1980, Father Roberti stepped down as director of the Brussels community and is now the community priest.

Le Toît was opened in Brussels in 1971. The idea behind this house came from a little group of handicapped people with whom I had close ties. It was to be a place of welcome and meeting. But it quickly became home for people suffering from difficulties such as physical or mental handicap, and a number of other people, ranging from social outcasts to foreign students searching for a place to live. Later, other people of various ages came to join them because they wished to share in the life of the home.

Once Le Toît was established, other homes were founded in Belgium on similar lines, so that today there are sixteen of them grouped into six communities; only one of the sixteen is government funded.

Some months after the opening of Le Toît, I met Jean Vanier and discovered that what we were living there was the life people had been leading within l'Arche for the past seven years. And so it came about that links between l'Arche and Le Toît eventually became so strong as to make us into a new community of l'Arche.

I have briefly described the genesis of our community because it explains its peculiar nature among the various communities of l'Arche. The variety of people who have been welcomed there, the special place reserved for friends of the house and the wide-ranging hospitality we continue to give, all derive from the initial founding spirit. The many friends who regularly come to visit us have now become integral members of the house; a house which is full of gaiety – and sometimes noise – but which is always open. A distinctive trait of l'Arche in Belgium has been, from the beginning, the presence of physically handicapped people, principally those with cerebral palsy.

They are rich in their emotional life and in their intelligence, but very limited in their capacity for movement; some totally paralysed, others unable to speak. Helen, for example, remains indelibly engraved on the memory of those who have met her and who remember that vibrant "Alleluia" she threw out at the close of a television broadcast in which she declared: "I wouldn't wish for any other life. Alleluia!" Although life since then seems to have taken her on to a different path, she remains true to herself, full of courage and daring.

Then there is Denis; who could forget him? This young man who was born prematurely knows better than anyone what it means to be handicapped. He talks very little but has the art of condensing what he is feeling into a single telling phrase. He was asked one day, for a forthcoming press article, to say what he thought of abortion and asserted: "A child coming into the world is even more beautiful than a flower unfolding." And yet every part of him is paralysed and therefore dependent on others.

If I am to describe Patrick I must describe goodness itself, an unconquerable goodness, always ready to dispel tensions; but with that goodness is a quality of anxiousness which never leaves him for long. Nevertheless, during a pilgrimage to Lourdes, he was able to declare in front of 3,000 people: "It makes me so happy when people no longer think of me as handicapped. It's difficult. It takes time maybe, but afterwards it feels really good." And he went on: "But the handicapped people must understand that normal people are afraid to come close to them. There are fears on both sides, we must learn to wait in patience."

Many people ask themselves: "What do physically handicapped people do all day, when they can't work, or be helpful, and are so clumsy in expressing themselves?" Helen's answer is: "I am alive."

A community of l'Arche which has taken root in the city will naturally give such people pride of place, because their peculiar gift for welcoming is so truly in line with our vocation. Some will offer that welcome in a single smile, others by a mischievous glance, others again through the acuteness (and sometimes imper-tinence) of their questions. And there are those whose welcome rests in the strength of their prayer, bringing the Lord to all who come.

By its very origin, then, Le Toît set out to be a place of meeting, friendship and welcome. But what we did not foresee is that it is our physically handicapped friends who are foremost in extending that welcome to all who come. More practised in living, divested of self and therefore more open to others, it is they who most

A moment of joy, Le Toît, Brussels

clearly spell out their welcome. Our house could not survive without them. We all of us need their courage, the lesson in living which they give in their slightest movement, the confidence in life itself which they demonstrate for all to see. Those who come to help them and look after them quickly realize that they are in fact receiving from them, and what they are receiving is the essential; in Denis's phrase: "What is essential is to live relaxed and calm, and to do that, you must look to the Lord, as he goes his way." It is in such meetings and through the joyful smile of those who lead us into them, that we come to discover a whole new world.

Yet life for such people is often hard to bear. Who can claim to measure the extent of their suffering as they bear with a body as burdensome and crushing as the cross? When they can bring themselves to allow us into the heart of their heart, the amount of sheer suffering, of thwarted desire and acute, ingrown loneliness we discover leaves us stunned and overwhelmed. One must have experienced that kind of rejection – and who would dare sound it to its depths? – if one is to realize what yearnings and what disappointments a broken body hides. Acceptance is their only salvation, so easy to proclaim, yet how impossible to achieve, unless they are surrounded by ties of friendship strong enough to give proof of an equal acceptance of every form of aggression. Such friendships create the climate of hope in which a way out and upward can be found.

One such person confided to me: "I am happy because I have accepted my handicap." Others, who are not yet so far advanced, must hold their own with what dignity, strength and courage they can muster sometimes wounding their would-be friends because, in their desire to serve, they forget that first they must listen and be receptive.

If, every day, you have to depend on others, even for your most intimate needs, and if you accept that dependence, whatever the moment of need, and whoever the person beside you, will you not learn to be open to anyone and everyone? True welcome is just that.

But it is impossible to exercise that welcome if one has not first been accepted and welcomed oneself. Yvan puts this very well, in one of those flashes of shrewd wit so typical of him: "When I'm in my wheel-chair," he says, "I'm the one who's pulling the one who's pushing me. And sometimes the pulling is hard, because he's such a weight . . . it must be the chocolate."

At the end of the day, they are the ones who look after us, who take charge of us and bear with us. And they do it with such delicacy. One day Patrick welcomed a young man into the house and asked him to give him his meal. Sad to say, when the time came to eat, and everyone had found his place at the great table set for twenty-five, the young man had disappeared. Patrick's reaction was to blame himself: "I didn't give him time, I shouldn't have asked him such a thing. He got scared and left."

By sharing their lives we come to discover how the physically handicapped person can become spokesman for the mentally handicapped person, in that he can give expression to feelings which the latter cannot formulate. He is like the elder brother who takes the younger under his wing, showing him the path and defending him against every injustice. (The most frequent injustice the mentally handicapped person must endure, and the most irritating, is paternalism.) The physically handicapped brother or sister can speak in his defence, or protect him, by the way he refuses to accept that the mentally handicapped person can be treated without respect. Such an understanding between a physically handicapped person and someone who is mentally handicapped is especially moving when the one who is mentally handicapped, in a surge of generosity, puts himself at the service of the other, regarding him as especially handicapped and surrounding him with all his love and affection. What a beautiful thing it is to see Marie-Thérèse, a thirty-seven-year-old woman with Downs Syndrome, giving Geoffroy his food, interrupting herself to explain: "Geoffroy never stops talking . . . and he wants to be a monk!"

A mentally handicapped person's presence is like a smile lighting up a home. The simple, shrewd comments he lets fly in moments of severe tension set off gales of laughter, which can neutralize mounting aggression. We need him with us. He is the sign of our multifaceted humanity, there to remind us of the respect which we all need.

We cannot live with such a person in accordance with so-called normal expectations. We have to attain a level of discernment at which things invisible to the eye become visible to the heart. Even the highest reaches of the mind must bow before a heart which is yearning for love, ready to give as much as to receive. Mentally handicapped people, though weak in their intelligence, and unresponsive to education, have a personal quality and strength of heart which, if we allow them to be revealed to us by living with them, can flood a home with light: a light which shows up our sense of power and security for the fragile thing it is, teaching us to be ourselves and nothing more.

Unabashed by their own poverty, their presence is a living appeal to all that is deepest in the heart of man. It is in this sense that mentally handicapped people are the forerunners of a new world where love comes first, where open-heartedness is daily renewed and where fidelity reigns over all our human relationships. A home or a community is rich insofar as its life is a sacrament of forgiveness constantly offered and received, a perpetual celebration of the power of love, whose source can be found in every man.

Yet there are many tensions and jealousies within such persons: dreams of being and living like everyone else, so that marriage inevitably attracts them. But the way they regard marriage makes us realize how a bankrupt society can turn even the living reality of love to its own profit.

Mentally handicapped people may become envious of the physically handicapped people who so easily attract attention; but how painful it must sometimes be to know within themselves that fundamental lack which makes them permanently dependent on others. Therein lies the source of so much aggressiveness, so much yearning. We could show you many a broken chair that speaks of a broken heart.

There is a place at Le Toît, and in other houses, for many young men labelled 'social misfits'. Some spend only a short time, some come to stay by choice; others are there in hopes of something better. Their message to us is that we must take nothing and no one for granted. They have a place among us. One young man came to us through a Belgian family who had stayed at the hotel where he worked. He looked them up after their departure and they sent him to us. Another was sent by a judge, a third by a social worker. The telephone keeps ringing and you have to keep listening, understanding, sharing a burden, sometimes saying "Yes", more often "No". We always try to invite the caller to a meal: "Come and meet us." Such brief and superficial forms of welcome can be burdensome and often appear useless. But they reflect our true situation. They help us to remain conscious of our limitations, but also to keep believing in the impossible.

To be open and welcoming to all who come is to embark on a venture in which our solidly structured security must give way to taking many risks, the risk of disappointment, the risk of self-deception, the risk of foolishness, which can all be inevitable on such a path. Nevertheless, this is the path we must take. But we cannot venture on it alone; it needs a community of people to bear and share the burden of one another's limitations, weaknesses and disappointments, so that together we can offer the welcoming face of confidence and hope in man which is our secret faith.

Such is the life we are called to by our handicapped friends; because we share their lives, we witness the quality of soul which shines through the wounds of their bodies, and the wealth of loving kindness which a poverty-stricken spirit cannot hide. The pain of their life's history demands some reparation and, at the least, our affirmation that what comes first in life is love.

I am thinking of that young man of twenty-two we took in one day "so that he wouldn't go to prison", as the social worker said. He had been rejected by his mother at seven months. He stole from us, he cheated us, he deceived us again and again. And he will go on doing so, for it will take more than one person to give him the one thing he never received – a whole heart.

I think also of the boy who came to us when his school life was collapsing, the child of separated parents, rejecting the one, rejected by the other. We knew something of his burden because we shared it with him. At every twist in the path of his growth, and in the events of his life, we tried to reaffirm our faith in him. He wrote to us, on the birth of his son: "Thanking you once more for all you did for me, for everything I learnt from you, even though you were in the end mistaken about me; everything you did for me throughout that time still seems a miracle. Greetings to you, with the hope that I may one day be able to do to someone else all the good you then did to me."

More than once we have been deceived and made to look ridiculous by the subterfuge resorted to by people wishing to enter the community. Do we not all, at some time in our lives, resort to lying and deceit as the only possible defence, thus showing ourselves as other than we are? Lying is a form of poverty, the poverty of a life so lonely that no one and nothing seems to offer any stability. No yardstick of truth is left to set against the possible gains to be had through bluff or unverifiable assertions.

We have had foreigners with us from the start, and they too have a meaning for us. They are a symbol of our exile, reminding us how fleeting is our life here below. People from Vietnam have constantly crossed our path. How ponderous and muddled we feel when faced with the calm wisdom and self-control of the Asian man or woman. These people have so much to give us. Many of them will not be staying with us long, but wherever they go their experience with us will remain engraved in their hearts: we feel bound to them forever.

We have visitors from other European and American countries, and what a gift their friendship is to us. For the last five years, Paula has been coming over from Detroit to spend her three months holiday with us. Likewise Christian from Switzerland with his sister Cornelia, and other friends from Italy, Spain and Poland come to share our life. They have so much to give in affection and hope to those of us who, being unable to travel, find happiness in the visits of these far-away friends.

Several of our visitors have since married. They have set up house close by and continue to help us. In a way we become their own Belgian family, the one which stood by them in their early days. Others have stopped coming. We failed to give them the love and understanding they needed.

It sometimes happens that when young people come to be with us they are often surprised to discover that our life is not impossible for them to live, though sometimes they find it hard and make their visits less frequent, so as to avoid being caught up in such a growing network of friendship.

We are surrounded by many friends, all of whom have a full part to play in the community, even if they do not live in the house: married couples with children, young people who come to share in our activities, and old people who come to help us.

One characteristic of our little homes which quickly came to light is the special place given to the elderly. Each house has come to feel the need to have a grandmother. We call them "our aunties". They are a source of peace, and the consideration which is their due calls out the good that is in each one of us but is too often hidden behind fear, rejection and insecurity. Their presence makes us better, bolder, and maintains our peace and serenity.

Our friends, we discover, are not those who give, so much as those who need us. This attitude is hardly in keeping with that of a country where a family gives fifty francs to the local authority for the right to put up a sign at the door "Begging forbidden". Such families die because they have never dared to invite a stranger to their table. What we share is the measure of what we receive.

Everything we have learnt through our humble experience stems from this little word "sharing". Everything has been given to us, and some houses, such as Le Toît, depend for half their expenses on things given or shared without being requested. But the sharing that is friendship goes deepest of all, friendship with those who have dared share this life with us, with those who have come close to it, with those who went away, disappointed. Each brings a necessary, vital contribution.

We become what we are through those who share our lives, bear with us and constantly remind us of the beauty of a life which is shared and which radiates out from those who are humblest and most rejected.

Christ did what was folly in the eyes of men. He gathered together ordinary workmen, very simple people, and created a marvel, a community of the poor extending a welcome to the rich. Wherever there is a community of the poor living in joy and love, there the rich man, burdened by his wealth and the cares it brings, burns with desire to come, in order to be close to the happiness of simple people. What he then learns from the poor is the secret of being rich without being sad, avoiding the self-reproach of being happy alone and asking himself instead: "Does my position of privilege consist in daily putting myself at the service of the humble?" Abbé Pierre[1] says: "It is a crime to have privileges and render no service."

Obviously, the openness which we try to live entails many contradictions and failures. Time after time experience teaches us modesty, humility, and not to be too quick to claim success. Sometimes it is the growing autonomy of the handicapped person which makes him unsatisfied with what we can offer him and starts him searching beyond us for further means of development. This is where we must show our respect for the person by bowing to his wishes, which are the expression of his freedom. Sometimes our sense of failure comes from the family which placed excessive hopes in us, taking us for miracle workers, we have to live with their disappointment. Often it is we ourselves who have gone too fast in our desire to help someone out of a difficulty, when we ought to have spent time listening, suffering, being with that person. How naive and presumptuous we can still be.

Our long history of failures constitutes a salutary lesson for us. Often it is lack of time which prevents us from bringing peace at the right moment and the right place. As Auntie Minou, one of Le Toît's pioneers, kept telling us from the start: "More calm, less agitation, less hurry. We never have time to talk among ourselves; it's always hurry, hurry . . ." Again, lack of time can rob us of the desire to get together, to put our heads together, to make sure we're all "with it," to open ourselves up to a deeper questioning, so as to become more daring and yet remain at peace.

The life-style of our communities equips us to welcome people. Our limitations and weaknesses make us less self-assured and therefore more open, with our way of life less regulated and more precarious.

The only thing that can help us believe, despite our weakness and failure, is the Gospel. "Keep a strong hold on the Beatitudes,

[1]Founder of the Emmaus communities in France.

on a boundless confidence in Jesus, to whom everything is possible. Live your insecurity with security." That was Auntie Minou's testament.

The whole secret of this attitude of welcome, so passionately cultivated, but often so clumsily adopted, lies in faith in the person who comes, and who shows us his whole being behind the demands he makes. We believe he has come for our salvation, we must respect him and be attentive not just to his request but to his person. We must proclaim our belief in him and our need of him.

All of this, Jesus summed up in the phrase "Love your neighbour". When he told the story of the Good Samaritan, Jesus was not just saying that the man who had been attacked and wounded was the neighbour we must look out for and love; he also sets the Samaritan before us as the figure of man rejected and become saviour, but able to save only when he himself has first been accepted by the one he wished to help. The intuition by which we live is expounded and explained in that parable. Every man has a history, every life has its meaning. Even an entire community can feel it is being helped, and so become a fount of salvation.

At its deepest, our experience never ceases to remind us that God was the first to believe in man, for "What you did to the least of my brothers, you did to me." L'Arche helps us to live that Gospel, despite all weariness and failure, drawing from the poor and the humble the strength we need to carry on, to hold fast, to go on and on believing.

11

A WITNESS
IN THE NORTH AMERICAN CULTURE

Janice Risse

Janice Risse, an American from Michigan, came into contact with l'Arche through a Faith and Sharing retreat in Birmingham, Alabama in 1973. Before that she had studied at Harvard Divinity School and at the time of the retreat was working for the State of Alabama's Mental Health Department, directing several community residences in Mobile. Hope, the Arche community she founded, is made up of two homes and eighteen people.

While still serving as director of the community in Mobile, Jan was elected by the other North American communities to serve as North American co-ordinator, assisting several others who serve l'Arche in North America in a co-ordinating capacity.

I find that a community of l'Arche in a Western culture, and particularly in a North American culture, is a real challenge, an exciting challenge, a challenge that has to be met. The North American culture, like all cultures in some way or other, casts out people who do not fit into it harmoniously. These are the marginal people who then fall into an excruciating loneliness. They need a home, friends, relationships, a feeling that they belong.

But how difficult it is to create community in a culture that is very different from the Asian or African cultures, for instance, cultures where there is still a sense of the family and the extended family. Our North American culture values individualism, the seeking of personal riches, and tends to demand success at any price. There can be a pursuit of external success which is not much more than popularity. In so many ways, our culture kills the interior life and over-emphasizes external things which become status symbols.

L'Arche Wishes to Create a Home

In North America you don't bring your work home. At least you are not supposed to if you want to be mentally healthy, physically fit and emotionally fulfilled. The home is sacred. It is here you can be yourself, be comfortable, be safe and refreshed. Even if that means just a beer before the television after the children are in bed, it is still a haven from the world. Home may also be a setting in which to display possessions and entertain selected guests. A couple may spend much of their energy pursuing the wealth necessary to surround themselves with conveniences, comforts, and objects of beauty, without which they feel they cannot get along. The things bought are often symbols which confer status in relationships. They make certain social transactions possible. A woman may place a great deal of value on maintaining her career, maintaining the house and maintaining herself as both decorative and entertaining. Strangely enough, while the home is held sacred, the unit of relationships it represents may receive less and less attention from family members. A man may work so hard to succeed that he has little time (let alone energy) for a relationship at home with each member of his family. Children may be involved in an extensive round of activities outside the home or spend hours watching television within it.

Whether old-fashioned or contemporary, parents want their grown-up children to get settled and create a home. By this, they obviously mean take a secure job with a pension, marry, buy a house, and begin another nuclear family, which they hope will be safe from social problems.

No matter where a family is on the social and economic scale, these are familiar images. They seem to be glossy, magazine images. Old people, handicapped people, awkward, perhaps marginal, relatives don't fit in. There is too much pressure on various members of the family to make it possible for them to bear the disturbances such people cause. They are too busy. Perhaps, more truly, their emotional resources are too poor to cope. The unsettling fact is that each one of us is awkward and difficult at times, and nearly everyone becomes too impoverished to cope in a brittle world, where there can be a gradual flight from the demands of the most ordinary relationships. It could be that, in our milieu, relationships can no longer be said to be ordinary. For many people, family and home are broken and empty realities.

In the community in Alabama, where I live, we too are trying to make homes, but in a somewhat different way. Our community is five years old; we now have two houses and about eighteen people in the whole group. In many ways we are like other Arche communities, so that what I describe can be taken to be fairly representative.

Americans are generally very hospitable – to those who "fit in". But they tend to put up hard barriers to those who don't, who are too "different". The road we try to take is one of welcome rather than exclusion. We too want each person to find a place to be safe, refreshed, comfortable. But we struggle to make such a place by living with people who may have been rejected and by trying to live through the disturbances which come from their suffering. We want to live this way while still keeping our ties with the wider cultural milieu. We don't want to be a ghetto closed in upon ourselves. Members of our board of directors, and our friends who are professionals, help us in this. Within our community, we have representatives from five Christian denominations and we all go out to our own churches. We attend social events in our town, and going out to work is important to most of us. Many families are close to us and invite people from our communities to be with them for a meal or an outing or a weekend. Neighbouring ladies, whose children are grown up, come in and bake bread, do the mending, or some typing for us. A book-keeper, who is a friend from my parish church, volunteers his services. In this way, we never become severed from our environment.

We don't want to create a sect which is fanatic or which becomes counter-cultural. Integration into the local environment is important for us so that the handicapped people can be known and find their place. Yet it cannot be denied that the way we try to live in l'Arche is in tension with most of North American culture.

One of the obvious tensions comes from the fact that many assistants live and work in the same place, because our aim is to create a community with handicapped people. This is our life and it is our work and it is not always easy to combine the two. Furthermore, in most of our homes there is little or no privacy for the assistant. Even if I have my own room, I hardly ever go there to spend time alone. Most mentally handicapped people seem almost to be constituted as community people. They are generally around in the common rooms of the house looking for someone to share a letter or a cup of coffee, eager to engage in some horseplay, to have you do a little work alongside them, or just sit together with you before the fire, playing with the cat and singing some songs. Some communities favour going out to the pub, depending on the local views toward alcohol. Whatever form the sharing takes in Arche communities, it is the handicapped people who call us together, sometimes by the limitations on their abilities. From time to time, indescribably precious moments come, like the quiet passage of God in the still small voice.

If the handicapped person is at the heart of the community, it is also true that assistants must find a particular rhythm of life. Their hearts and spirits must be nourished in order to be able to live in a situation so contrary to the usual culture. I suppose many of us are helped to live in this way by a sort of prophetic element which we sense in the handicapped person. We must not idealize or exaggerate but there are those precious moments which give meaning to our lives and nourish our motivations.

The Heart of our Homes

We pray together at the close of each evening. One of us will light a candle and put it on the living room floor. Those who want, gather quietly around, sitting on the floor. We may sing a song, but usually it is a time of quiet. Someone may read a text from scripture or share a spontaneous prayer. We conclude with a prayer

Familiar scene at l'Arche, Missoula, Montana

that is commonly used in l'Arche, and the Our Father. Often the time after prayer in our community is one of repose during which we talk quietly, laugh and joke, or just be there a few moments longer before going off to bed.

One evening Elise spoke after the night prayer. She is a girl of twenty-two and has been with us several years now. She was then still quite disturbed and rarely spoke except during hallucinations. Terry had been helping her at meals for many months, yet she had never spoken to him directly. That night she took his hand after the prayer was finished. "Terry. Um hmm. Terry, Terry," she said, nodding her head and looking at him with a luminously beautiful smile.

Of course, moments of quiet presence are not the only ones. Sometimes a chest of drawers or a window is broken, a ceiling is soaked and falls down because a drain overflows. Perhaps the times of peace are possible only because of the crises. People are more precious than ceilings or windows or furniture and the language of distress is preferable to the silence of death. Often such a crisis marks an important moment of growth for the particular person in difficulty and for the whole community. I cannot say I receive such messages with calm, but maybe if I did I wouldn't be getting the message.

Culture and Community

E. F. Schumacher in his book *Small is Beautiful* speaks of the footlooseness[1] that fast transport and instantaneous communications have produced in developed countries over the last fifty years. The bigger the country, the greater the mobility, and the more total the breakdown of structures.

In North America this footlooseness has become a value. The carrot of moving on dangles before us: to a better job, to a better sexual partner, to a bigger city, to the West, to lose the past. The deeper our future orientation grows, the greater our fear of age and weakness, the greater our need to hide the aged and weak. This sense of mobility goes very deep into everyday life, permeates relationships or perhaps, to state it more accurately, destroys them. Strong personal involvement or consistency in long term relationships seems impossible to many people, particularly to many young people. They have reached this conclusion from observation of their own and others' experiences. Talk of decisions and commitments can be so tentative as to seem silly.

Living with handicapped people has helped me to put down roots. It is evident that they cannot grow without being surrounded by consistency, firmness and fidelity. Slowly they call forth these qualities in me. As this happens I discover that I too am growing. I learn with some amazement that I can be consistent,

[1]E. F. Schumacher, *Small is Beautiful*, Abacus (1973), p. 58.

firm and faithful. I learn this with the rest of the community because we are always having to put our heads together in meetings, and our hearts together in prayer, to discern what is happening and what is to be done. Our experience is that together we flourish, but not by fleeing our difficulties. Somehow, with God's help we have to go through the middle of them.

For example, when a severely mentally handicapped person within our community steals, it is just as intolerable and destructive to the level of trust in the group as it would be anywhere else in society. This is true especially if the situation is denied, ignored or dealt with half-heartedly and fearfully. We lived through such a situation and for a long time we thought there was no solution. Obviously we couldn't send the woman to jail. The most obvious resort – giving up and sending the woman back to the institution – was equally odious.

Fear kept us from facing the situation, especially as this woman tends to erupt into violent temper tantrums at any correction. Finally, after many petty thieveries, our nerves reached the breaking point. A key which we really needed was stolen. The locksmith would be expensive. The inconvenience was acute and so was our unwillingness simply to suffer the expense and get on with things. We knew who had been doing the stealing but individual authoritative attempts to deal with her offences had been of no use. Everyone was intimidated by the violence of her tantrums. Sitting down together at table and acting as though everything was all right increased the tension. Hatred and anger were vibrating in the air. We had to put our heads and our hearts together.

What we found was that the whole group had to give up some of its liberty to focus on creating a milieu where it was neither necessary nor easy to steal. Our first response had to be to solidify ourselves as a community, to convey the message clearly and with strength that as a whole community we could not tolerate stealing. We all had to dramatize how much we suffered from stealing. We refused to eat our meals together until the person who stole the key would return it or pay for the locksmith and apologize to us and to God. (The person in question is very religious.) We would cook some food but we would not sit down at the table together.

We learned something about our meals that we had not known before: they are the most important time of community in our day. They give us security, a moment of happiness and celebration, a chance for everyone to be listened to, to rejoice in our work because we all take turns preparing the food. We were all tense and got indigestion embarking on this deprivation. The outcome was unknown and there was no turning back.

We met together frequently during that week. We shared our alienation, our anger, our inability to tolerate continued lack of trust. The guilty person was always right there in the middle, nervously observing what was going to happen. Each person spoke, even the least articulate did their bit to say how troublesome stealing is. We read God's law from the Bible. We enumerated past incidents for which we knew the person to be responsible. We continued to ask for apology and payment. The week dragged on.

When Sunday came, we all went off to our own churches as usual. The woman with the difficulty experienced some grace in her church. She must have prayed in a special way and she went up to the front for a blessing. She came home and humbly announced her desire to apologize.

She had to wait until evening when all the members of the community would be home. We all gathered around a lighted candle as for prayer. The assistant, who is the main reference person for this woman, helped her with her apology because she is very limited in speech and helped her to count out the twenty-eight one-dollar bills to pay the locksmith. In vast relief we all prayed together for forgiveness for her and for ourselves if we had ever stolen anything. The week had sharpened all our consciences. Then we each went to the woman and embraced her so she could feel received back into the group. We were so happy and hungry for each other's presence that we opened a bottle of wine and some bars of chocolate. We ate and drank and sang together. I think we discovered how the celebration for the prodigal son felt.

Handicapped People need Professional Help but above all, Relationship

People can only grow through their deep emotional and psychological difficulties if they are involved in deep and lasting relationships that are comforting and challenging.

Before I came to l'Arche I used to work in a State centre for mentally handicapped people. In conversation with a friend who also worked there, I was asked why I worked with mentally handicapped people. "Because I like them," I said. "That's impossible!" came his quick, almost involuntary reply.

To work with mentally handicapped people is seen as a career choice for many people in North America. Special education, behaviourist training, diagnostic and testing skills, speech therapy and endless other therapies are becoming highly technical. I think, however, that mentally handicapped people are commonly regarded, in the professional world, as a mistake of nature. This view can fail to see the handicapped person as primarily a person rather than "handicapped". It can fail to acknowledge that he or she is a complete human being, unique and mysterious and created providentially, as each one of us is, for an unrepeatable purpose in God's order. It can also fail to notice that, while (or perhaps because) they are less intellectual, they are often more loving than others.

Professionals in mental handicap have, by and large, had a scientific education. The philosophical bases of such an education are the grand ideas of the last century which have now fully worked themselves into popular thinking: evolution, natural selection, relativism, positivism and Marxist or Freudian interpretations of idealism. I refer again to E. F. Schumacher in his description of education. Perhaps it is logical, out of these bases, to view a handicapped person as an unfortunate happening, even a disaster.

The hearts of most people have not quite received the message that the head has been fostering. Future generations may do so, especially as pre-natal diagnostic technology improves. It is not news that abortion is becoming the commonly proposed solution to the "problem" of mental handicap, even as the more common presence of nuclear waste threatens the genetic make-up of those same generations. One now hears frequently, in North America, that publicly raised charitable funds for birth defects are used to finance abortions as well as research. Yet a world of perfect people is hardly in sight. We are close enough to remember that Nazi Germany envisaged such a world.

The action of professionals in the field of mental handicap in North America can seem pretty confused. Radical behaviourists declare that they can produce improvement, but what they mean by improvement is not clear. Appropriate behaviour? Appropriate to what or to whom? Person, meaning, suffering, value, are not admitted as realities. I cannot forget the way behaviour modification principles were used in an institution where I once worked. It was really ridiculous when they gave the same token fine for sexual intercourse in public as for failure to hang up one's coat.

Less radical professionals may still propose a sexual norm for handicapped people that they would never propose for themselves or their children. This may be seen as a substitute for relationships, because the handicapped people have nothing else. Normalization originally meant that handicapped people should receive all the necessary additional supports to lead as normal a life as possible. This can be reduced to techniques which make handicapped people look ordinary and be useful to society so they can "pass". Training for work can mean entering the competitive market. Meaningless industrial work, with money as the sole motivation, can be de-humanizing. Some handicapped people simply cannot be motivated by money. They may be regarded as having less potential for work. Training for independence may mean learning to live alone in an apartment: a sort of individualist ideal but one which is hardly suited to any human being, much less to a handicapped person.

It is heartening though to meet many clear-minded professionals who do regard their clients as people like themselves. Professionals who are generous and compassionate, and who work with uncompromising integrity for a more human situation for handicapped people. They may be quite hidden, working humbly, but their influence can be strong.

Wolf Wolfensberger, a long-time professional in the field of human services, urges that those who work with mentally handicapped people get their philosophy and morality straight. Wolf means that the plumbline is the old-fashioned law of God. He feels that the weak are in danger in North American society, that in many cases they are in danger at the hands of professionals. Wolf's hope is that people will become completely concerned and start to defend those who cannot defend themselves.[2]

Elise came to us quite anguished. She is a beautiful young woman, tall and well built, with the hands of a queen. She gestures slowly and elegantly with her long, slender fingers. They are almost translucent, flaccid from disuse. She had been described as profoundly retarded and catatonic. When she came she had been cut off from contact with other people for ten years. Being cut off was probably a gradual inner choice of her own. It may have begun after some brain damage left her less capable than she might have been, but it was a choice from which it seemed she was eventually unable to return. Locked in a tightly enclosed world of her own, she spoke only in "crazy talk" and screams, engaged herself constantly with pacing in circles and hallucinating. Nearly every technical means of dealing with her illness or its resultant problems to others, had been tried: shock treatments, years of confinement in a mental hospital, drugs and surgery.

Confused by her difficulties, we wondered if there were any physical problems which might be a clue. Our doctor suggested some tests in the university hospital. I was with Elise in her room there when the consulting psychiatrist came in. His covey of students followed him. They clustered at the foot of her bed and he began teaching them about her, in her presence, as though she weren't there. He put his foot up on the lower part of the side rail of her bed. Gesturing over her, he spoke at length. The words were polite, professional. They all added up to one – "Hopeless". Elise twisted in the bed and rubbed her hands across her face crying out as he talked, "Let me die. I can't live!"

In a while she was released from the hospital, the tests having

[2]Wolf Wolfensberger, from a lecture in Springs of New Hope, Daybreak Publications, Toronto, 1978.

shown she had no physical complications. We had been advised to continue with the consulting psychiatrist. He had begun a heavy drug régime in the hospital and would continue seeing Elise on an outpatient basis.

Joe, another Arche assistant, Elise and I sat in the psychiatrist's office on our first visit there. Joe and I asked the doctor questions. He spoke politely, again in professional terminology, and at length. Again, the conclusion was the same. He said that nothing we would do would make any real difference. We should get used to her the way she was – hopeless. Elise sat, rocking back and forth, bent over, her head nearly down to her knees, drooling and wiping her mouth. I hadn't heard her say much that made sense to me in weeks.

The doctor offered his plan of treatment. Even this didn't stand much chance, he said, but it was the only possibility. He wanted to give her, as he said, "the blue-plate special". This would mean putting her on a psychotropic drug and raising the dosage until she became toxic. He would do this over a few months to see what level of the drug was most effective in controlling her illness, improving her behaviour.

When he had concluded his plan and dealt firmly again with our rather feeble questions, he stood up and moved to Elise saying, "I'm going to take her blood pressure." Suddenly she became still, straightened up to her full height and looked at him through steel-blue eyes. Slowly, deliberately, she said, "I hate you!"

This was several years ago and we did not go back. With a little additional outside help we found the courage as a community to live with Elise in our own way. She is still very fragile and awkward but peaceful now, clearly a gentle soul. She no longer paces and her hallucinations disappeared gradually. She now lives in the present, although perhaps a little more ordinary and less queenly in her manner. She does not initiate much but she responds verbally and her clear eyes and lovely smile remain a little enigmatic. She can do simple tasks, shows an interest in things, and is quick to laugh at foolishness among us. When we pray, her prayer is simple: "Thank you". She has found the security of a home and a community that accepts her and affords her safe and permanent relationships.

But to live this sort of relationship isn't easy in a North American culture that accentuates techniques and professionalism. There are not many resources in the culture to encourage and fortify us in these relationships. That doesn't mean to say that the techniques and professionals are not necessary: we need psychiatrists and psychologists, and behaviour modification can be useful if used well. There are many professional people who are deeply conscious of the necessity of true relationships. But it appears that our culture, which tends to over-accentuate technique and under-estimate fidelity and clarity in relationships, ill prepares people to live at l'Arche. Many assistants leave because the demands are simply too intense. Sometimes I myself would like to run away. To stay I need to know my resources. They are not ones which are at all encouraged in North American culture.

My Own Resources

When I said I would come to l'Arche, it was a total decision. I knew that God had led me and called me here and I was sure that I could absolutely count on Him to help me. This conviction has not left me and it is my most central resource. The community itself is his gift, a resource to me as well as to others; it gives me peace and equilibrium. Times of solitude are also necessary for me: a regular time for silent prayer alone each day; my day off each week which gives me a few hours alone to rest and read and pray. I find I do not pray because I ought to, but because I need to as I need to eat and sleep. The Eucharist is an everyday necessity to me. There are one or two good friends who can help me when I'm inwardly low, who listen to my difficulties, who can themselves draw some encouragement from our community. They help me to continue.

The fact, of course, that we are part of the big family of l'Arche is a great support. The regular meetings with other community leaders of l'Arche in North America are a time for sharing and helping each other. So too are various meetings we have on different levels: between communities in the region, within North America as a whole or the international meeting of representatives from all our Arche communities in the world.

I find encouragement, too, in the spiritual gifts of the handicapped people. Many have lived through incredible suffering. There are no words, for instance, which could encompass the experience of being institutionalized for thirty years for no crime other than epileptic seizures and a measure of mental deficiency. Leonard is a man who carries such a past, yet he carries it with surprising simplicity and good nature. Having lived with him for a few years, I realize now that he was not simply insensitive to his surroundings.

He has always loved the Bible and likes to listen to stories from it. Sometimes he will sit for long hours and attempt to copy it, starting at the first page and drawing each letter. Apparently he had never been a member of any church in the past. It seems that over the years many institutionalized people were visited by clergymen, but usually did not go out to church. As I understand it, few were ever baptized. With us, Leonard went to several different churches until he decided the one he wanted. Then he began to declare that he had not been baptized and wanted to be. He knew about Jesus. He and Mike were moving some furniture given us by a convent and came across an old crucifix. Leonard loved it and hung it in his room. When guests come, he likes to pull them up there to see it. "That's Jesus," he growls. "He died on the cross for you."

Leonard has been baptized now, but I don't think following Jesus is new to him. Once at our night prayer he kept asking us to sing "Walk with Jesus". No one seemed to have heard of that as a song. We all said we didn't know it. His insistence mounted: "Sing!" he demanded, refusing to give up. "Why don't you sing it for us, Leonard?" Tim asked quietly. So Leonard sang in his rough voice a nearly tuneless song, one which is perhaps his own: "Walk with Jesus . . . All the way . . . Walk with Jesus to the cross. Walk with Jesus all the way. Walk with Jesus to the grave."

A Community of Sharing

It is not easy to live with hurt people in a culture which teaches each of us to "look out for number one". The everyday world of American advertising fosters multitudes of desires and urges fulfilment of them all. People are pushed to develop a grasping attitude and there is an undercurrent of violence which is deep and pervasive. It frequently expresses itself in the national face we present to the world, and this is particularly true of the United States. These currents are present in our culture, and the trouble with culture is that it is one's own and not just 'someone else's'. In all our North American communities, we are trying to live a lifestyle which is poorer, in a sense, than North American culture dictates, but which is a sign of the value we give to relationships. It is a style which values the creation of "family" ties; just being there in times of suffering, crisis and the simple joy of celebration. But it is not easy to let cultural barriers drop and authentic meeting come about.

Nearly everyone who knows l'Arche knows of Bill and Frank at Daybreak.[3] Both were long-standing, very personable, well-loved members of the community. Each had Downs Syndrome and each developed Alzheimer's disease, which many people with Downs Syndrome suffer as they get older. Daybreak, with great difficulty and stretching of its not-inconsiderable resources, has been able to care for both of them in their long illnesses. Frank died at Easter but Bill continues to hold on to a thread of life. I know Daybreak does not particularly want to be held up as an example; they feel what they are doing may be impossible to people or communities with fewer resources than theirs, they know how great the cost has been. Yet it would be difficult to count the number of people who came in to help, or to measure how deeply their lives were touched, more difficult still to measure the number of those who supported Daybreak at a distance and in prayer. When Frank died, his funeral was a jubilant Easter celebration for his family, for Daybreak and for friends. I mean to describe this humbly. I have been one who supported at a distance.

[3]Arche community in Richmond Hill, near Toronto.

On the other hand, I think it is impossible to gauge how wide is the influence of such an effort of love and how deeply God can work in the hearts of many people through it.

Each Arche community in North America is different. Some have government funds, some have not. One may be more or less materially better off than another. It remains true that no one stays in l'Arche for money. No one stays to gain status. No one stays for professional advancement. Whatever the reason for coming, one stays only because of the relationships one is drawn into, and the community one finds to be "home".

12

COUNTRY PEOPLE

Brian Halferty

Brian Halferty, a Canadian, was a student at St Michael's College,
Toronto, where he met Jean Vanier. He came to l'Arche, Trosly for a
year in 1966 and lived in the original Arche home, working with Steve
Newroth on a maintenance team.

Back in Canada, he married Mary Lou and they both joined Steve's
community, Daybreak. After two and a half years at Daybreak, with a
deep desire to live an Arche way of life in the country, they bought some
land in Ontario. In 1975 l'Arche, Frontenac began. The community now
includes Brian, Mary Lou, their five children, and ten handicapped people.

In the country, away from the cities and towns, you are always
closer to the elements of nature. You feel surrounded, immersed
in nature, and at times compelled and controlled by it. When it
snows, you change your plans. When rain comes, it is felt as the
general condition of the world. When the wind blows, it does
battle with the house and sweeps up all in its path. When the night
is clear, the mass of stars is overwhelming. And when it is quiet,
then you are blessed with a silence and peace that is one of nature's
greatest, though little-known, gifts.

It was these natural elements, in particular the silence of the
forest, which helped in the first place to persuade me and my wife,
Mary Lou, to move to this farm in 1970. Standing together on a
path in the middle of this forest, we marvelled at the rugged beauty
of the rocks and trees, and at the grandeur that nature could
provide through its silent and constant growth. We felt small in
the middle of two hundred acres of land; it made no sense to talk
of "owning" all of this (even though in legal terms we did),

because it was there before us, and in spite of us, and would be there, we knew, long after us.

We determined then that, if we were to remain here, we must find some way to share what was here with others. We were not thinking then of beginning an Arche community. Our dream of sharing the land was vague and non-specific. Only with time, and after some experience together as a family in a Arche community, were we clear that we should put our efforts into planting the seeds of l'Arche here on this rugged terrain.

When we began to think specifically of an Arche community here, Mary Lou and I were faced with two major questions. The first was an interior question. Were we prepared to enter into a long-term commitment of this sort, and would we be able to sustain that commitment? Living in the community of Daybreak for two and a half years helped us to answer that question in the affirmative. Not knowing exactly what the future would bring, we none the less became convinced that we were being called in the direction of l'Arche, and that we would receive the graces and supports we would need to carry through our commitment.

The second major question at this point was an external one. Was our farm, in fact, a good place for an Arche community, given its geographical location?

The Problem of Isolation

Our farm is located in a part of rural eastern Ontario which is at some distance from larger centres of population. The region is sparsely populated, and lacks many of the services taken for granted in the city. We are, as many people observe, *isolated*.

We grappled for a long time with this question of isolation. Would it be wise, we wondered, to gather a number of handicapped people together here when medical services were far away, when there would perhaps be no work in the area, or very little, when many other services were lacking, or very distant from us?

These questions took on even more urgency for us when, during our time at Daybreak, we began to learn about the principle of

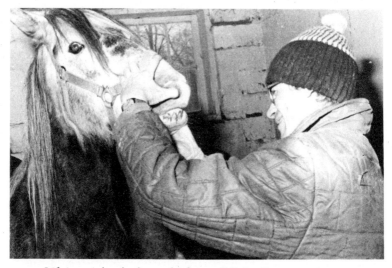

Life is varied and calm on the farm at l'Arche, Frontenac, Ontario

normalization. We came to know Wolf Wolfensberger, and became involved in workshops at the National Institute on Mental Retardation in Toronto. We learned there about providing services for the handicapped based on the principle of normalization, about the history of services for the mentally retarded, and other such matters.

It was a revelation to learn, for example, that institutions for the mentally retarded in Canada and the United States began, by and large, in the country. Housing was established for the mentally retarded on large farm properties. Gradually more and more people were placed there, in the "safe", isolated environment of the country, until the small and medium-sized institutions became large and overcrowded ones. The past decade or two have seen an increasing effort to dismantle these large institutions and to move people back into the normal flow of life, in the town and in the city. And here we were, contemplating beginning a home in the country.

Of course, we were not really afraid that the little house we were contemplating would turn into a big, "death-dealing" institution. But still, we did not want to do anything which would be detrimental to mentally handicapped people, or which would further stigmatize them in the eyes of society.

More pressing were the questions in our minds regarding the opportunities for growth and integration of handicapped people in the rural community. Normalizing community services for the handicapped must take into account and make use of the different services that exist in the community. Handicapped people should have the opportunity, like anyone else, to receive the training they require, and to have the possibility of working in the community at a regular job; to get around on their own as much as possible, and to use public transport; to go shopping or to the cinema and other recreations in the community. In accenting these and other freedoms, the principle of normalization puts the stress on growth and autonomy for the handicapped person and seeks to minimize elements which restrict this.

By contrast, when we looked at our farm, we could see a lot of these options missing. The closest shop is two miles away – within walking distance, but not for everyone, and not at all times of the year. The closest village is five miles away. There is no public transport at all in the region, except for two buses that stop once each day at a village twelve miles from the farm, one bound for the city of Toronto to the west, the other for Ottawa to the east. Thus, virtually all transport has to be by motor vehicle. The nearest doctor was then thirty-four miles away, the nearest hospital forty-four miles away. Needless to say, there were no theatres or other major recreational facilities nearby. Mary Lou and I were willing to move from the city to the country and to accept whatever disadvantages there might be. However, would it be right for us to decide, in effect, for others – for handicapped people – that they should live here too?

These considerations were of such concern to us that at one point we were thinking of trying to find another location, or of offering to do something for l'Arche in some other way. But our love of this area and its natural beauty kept alive in our minds the hope of doing something here. Eventually, a number of things happened which confirmed this hope and helped to bring it to realization.

First, we began to feel the support of other people for our dream. We spoke with friends and acquaintances in the local area of the farm, and they expressed their agreement and support for our project of initiating an Arche community here. Our friends in l'Arche encouraged us too, as did certain professionals to whom we spoke. This growth of support was important because we knew that, if a community did come about, it would not be simply because we had dreamed of it; it would be the result of the efforts of many people.

Another element in confirming our decision was our growing awareness of the range of needs in the region, especially those of the handicapped people who were already living there. Also, we witnessed the efforts of others to answer peoples' needs. For example, the successful establishment of a permanent clinic with a resident doctor in the area, and the formation of a local association for mentally handicapped people, and its initiation of a workshop programme for adults.

Finally, we found ourselves with a growing conviction that, if it is normal to live in the city, it must be just as normal – if different – to live in the country. This was not a rejection of "normalization" on our part. We simply felt that it cannot be necessary, nor realistic, nor in fact respectful of the individual and his needs, to consider moving all handicapped people into cities or towns. There must be ways, we decided, to provide an atmosphere of growth for people in a rural setting – in particular, for those who would choose to live, or to continue to live, in the country. So we moved ahead with plans for the farm.

Thus, in the summer of 1975, Ian came to live with us and our children, Erin and Peter, in our little farmhouse. He is a man who, at the age of thirty, had lived more than half his life in institutions. He had some problems to work through, which presented difficulties for us all at times, but he came wanting to live and work on a farm. His love of hard work was a big help to us all in those early days.

Many helpers came and went in those first months, each one

bringing the farm a little further along its way. These included neighbours, who helped us with the renovations to the house. Ron, a man on parole from prison, joined us for several months, and our little community grew a bit more. We grew again with the arrival of our third child, Mary Beth. We had begun, and were experiencing, all the joys and pains of living together, getting glimpses of things yet to come.

With our decision to proceed, the problems associated with our "isolation" did not disappear. However, we have been able to look upon them in a positive way, as an invitation to become aware of our advantages, and as a challenge to seek creative solutions. For the most part, we do not feel isolated at all. In fact, the flow of visitors to the farm sometimes leads us to the conclusion that we are not isolated enough!

The Growth of Community

When we had made our case to the departments of government that a home for mentally handicapped people was needed in this area, we suddenly found ourselves in a phase of quick growth. There were architects' plans, and many meetings. Soon we were watching from the windows as bulldozers began building a road through the field near our house, in preparation for construction of the new residence. Then there was the construction itself (largely paid for by the government) and our daily visits to the site to watch the new house take shape.

The number of us under one roof grew from seven to eight, then to nine. Finally the day came when Donna Marie and Wayne moved from our house into the new house, ready to welcome our new residents, and then the furniture which came later. Gradual arrivals over many months brought the house up to its capacity of eight handicapped people (four men and four women) and five assistants.

Mary Lou and I originally intended to continue to have handicapped people living with us in the old house with our family, even after the building of the new house. With the support of the rest of the community, however, Mary Lou and I were able to make the decision that we needed more private living space for our young and growing family. It was a good decision, but a difficult one at the time, and it meant asking Ian to move to the new house. He agreed, even though it was a difficult decision for him too.

Not all the handicapped people who came were originally from rural areas, but we tried to help each one, as much as possible, to make the decision about whether this was really the place where he or she wanted to live. Most of the assistants had no previous farm experience so we moved slowly, though fairly steadily, in our plans for the growth of the farm. Not everyone is cut out for farm work, and from the beginning we had to respond to the different capabilities of each person. For the handicapped people in particular, the outdoor work, or work with the animals, had to be supplemented with other types of indoor work, especially in the winter time.

So we began a small workshop programme in the basement of the house, experimenting with making various wood products. During the first year of the new house, everyone was living and working either on the farm or in the house. This was not by choice, but because there were no other work options available. As the house grew towards capacity, this became harder to bear, and was a source of real tension. It is much healthier and more fulfiling for everyone, handicapped people and assistants, to have different types of work to choose from and a division of responsibilities.

Gradually it became possible to arrange for some people to go to the sheltered workshop run by the local association for mentally handicapped people. This going out regularly to work has been a good experience for Rita, Mark, Edna and the others. Gradually, we have also been able to expand the amount and types of work on the farm. It has also become possible to arrange for some therapy and academic programmes for some of the handicapped people. Ken, for example, goes with great excitement each after-noon to the adult day school in the neighbouring village where he is learning to read and write. Finding or developing this variety of options for people is certainly part of our vocation here.

Country People

From the beginning, we have relied heavily on the support of both city and country people. Our board of directors is made up of both. We have often sought the services, the professional support and the financial resources of the city. These are necessary to us, as they would be to almost any organization. But we do not lay too much stress on this aspect, because at least equally important is the support of various kinds that we receive from country people.

In fact, the other people who live in the country are the chief resource for anyone living there. This may appear to be a truism, applicable to any situation, and in a general way it is; but there is an important difference in the dynamics of human relationships between the city and the country.

In the city, one can easily slip into a pattern of life and work in which close relationships never develop. It is possible never to meet, let alone know, your neighbours. Most people encountered in daily life are encountered in terms of the structures that exist and their role in these, rather than as individual people. The pace of life is usually too fast in any case to enter into relationship with so many people.

In the country, one could not function at that sort of level and expect to survive. The forces of nature, the isolation spoken of above and other factors, combine to demand of people a certain level of mutual dependency which is generally accepted as a fact of life and a responsibility. When you need help, you call on your neighbour; when he needs help, he calls on you. Tools are lent back and forth, heavy work is shared, advice is given and received, and in an emergency you know there is someone there.

I suspect that this ethic of mutual support has waned somewhat from former times, but it is still noticeably present in the area where we live. It is an ethic that fits well with our goal as an Arche community – to be a presence within the community at large. It is something we try to be conscious of, and work hard at, because it must not be taken for granted. Our neighbours have been good to us, and have helped us in many ways. Likewise, it was good to see Ian and Ken going out to help a neighbour build a fence, or Dave, Al and Ken rushing to assist him with a difficult birth of a calf.

Many times, when our community has had a special event, the ladies from the various churches have been quick to provide food and baked goods. In return, our house has worked hard to provide food for a supper in the local community centre (and then we have gone there, en masse, to help eat it). These are small things, but so very important in a rural community like this.

Availability of activities and relationships like these are of particular importance to the handicapped members of our community, as occasions of enjoyment and growth in self-confidence and maturity. We see the circle of those who know and are friends of our handicapped members gradually widening. Occasionally we hear a report of someone's negative attitude towards the handicapped people, but this is far outweighed by the openness of so many other people, which is certainly of mutual benefit to the handicapped people and to the community at large.

The Pace of Life in the Country

Relationships between people have an immediate bearing on the pace of life in the country. Here, people generally take time with each other when they meet. Going to a neighbour to borrow something may take an hour or two, because there will be a conversation about the weather, or how the gardens are doing. A trip to the shop for a couple of items might take all morning, while you chat with the shopkeeper, and he chats with other customers. This sort of thing is difficult for city people to get accustomed to.

I remember, though, the time when Mary Lou and I first moved to the farm, after living in the city all our lives. Three months went by before we went back to the city for a visit. After a weekend there, we were frazzled and completely exhausted. We had slowed down, and we could no longer stand the frantic pace of the city.

For the community of l'Arche, Frontenac, there is a benefit in this slower pace of life. There is also, however, a tension in it, since we are often faced with so much to do and so little time in which to do it. The farm makes demands on us, to which we must respond. There is a time to sow, and a time to reap; and in our climate these things must be done on time. In between, there is a time to pull weeds. Trees must be cut if we expect to have wood to burn during the winter. The animals, too, teach us regularity and fidelity. They must be fed and given water regularly; eggs must be collected; the cows must be milked twice a day, seven days a week. Of course, there are also the hundred and one tasks, big and small, which must be done to keep the house in order and people fed.

There are times when two or three people are able to handle all the various farm chores, and it's good to see Ken or Ian being able to take responsibility for these, and feel pride in what they have done. At other times, everyone turns out to help, as on the day when the pigs are loaded into the truck, kicking and squealing, to go to market; or the days in the summer when our massive garden needs weeding, or the vegetables need to be harvested, and then stored or frozen; or in the spring, when everyone takes turns collecting sap, and tending the maple syrup as it boils.

Even those who do not carry a specific responsibility for the farm work are able to enjoy many of these aspects of farm life, and to try their hand at something they have perhaps never done before. Larry was afraid of animals when he came, but is now quite capable of caring for them. Edna's fear of animals has largely passed, too, and she enjoys getting on the horse, with some help, to go for a ride. Ken, who at first had difficulty making the transition of moving away from home to come here, sums it all up for us when he speaks proudly to visitors about "our farm".

Apart from this vocation to the farm, we face a whole other level of responsibility. As a residence for mentally retarded people, funded by government, we have administrative and professional responsibilities. These, I am sure, do not differ greatly from those of other Arche homes, and we recognize their importance. With the help of a visiting psychiatrist, a speech therapist, and anyone else whose help we can get from time to time, we try to devise programmes which will help people grow, and help us to know how best to assist them in this. To learn more about this aspect, the assistants go away occasionally to training sessions.

As our community has grown in size and in depth, we have found various types of meetings to be necessary. Members of other Arche communities will know what I am speaking of when I say how frustrating it sometimes is to be held back from doing what has to be done, by the need to meet about something else. But we must function at that level too; and the growth in our internal organization in turn necessitates growth in the size and complexity of the administrative functions and in the amount of paper work to be processed. We are not an average farm.

Our functions as a community are also part of the pace of life here. These include the quiet moment of prayer that we have as a community once a week, the special dinners or parties, the big "open house" events with many people invited, and the days when visitors seem to arrive in waves.

We are sometimes exhausted by all our activities, and by the diversity of them. At the same time, we know how important each area of the community life is, and how important it is to remain, in the midst of everything else, a place of welcome. In fact, we feel we need to be even more welcoming, being out in the country. When a visitor travels an hour or two or even more to come here, the least we can offer is a meal and time to rest.

In all of this, there is something else that the farm can teach us, when we are able to slow down and listen to it. The land and the forest are simply there; so much of the work that we see in it is work that we ourselves devise. We all tend towards a desire to control things; but nature will not be controlled.

In the end, there is far more there than we can do anyway, and so we must do some of the work, and content ourselves with leaving the rest. This is good therapy for the soul, and is part of the local wisdom: what you cannot do today will just have to wait.

At Daybreak, Toronto, Peggy makes the daily bread

Our Vocation: the Role of a Rural Community

All the communities of l'Arche, wherever they may be, aspire to follow the inspiration of the charter of l'Arche. In doing so, each community tries to discover its own particular vocation, its own expression. Each community is, therefore, different from the others in many respects. Even those in similar circumstances differ. Thus, what I am saying about "L'Arche in the country", based on our experience at l'Arche, Frontenac, may differ from what others are experiencing in other rural communities.

After nearly five years, we are still very much in the process of discovering and defining our vocation. When we began, there was only one other community of l'Arche in North America which was really "in the country", namely, Maryfarm. Daybreak is on a farm, but in close proximity to a large urban area. So we had few models to work from. Now, besides ourselves, there are three other rural communities, two of them in our region: La Caravane, Green Valley, Ontario, and Le Printemps farm at St Prospère, Quebec. We are learning a lot from them about different types of farming and division of labour, about co-operative farming and work projects with people in the area, about trying to make a small farm self-sufficient and other things.

Likewise, we rely strongly on other Arche communities, in our region and elsewhere, for their presence and support. From them we also learn many practical skills and approaches to things, and receive help with our growth towards community life. We also watch carefully for opportunities to learn ways of improving our life and work, from other farm projects or residences outside l'Arche. Still, it is evident that more than anything else, it will be the needs of our own people and of our local area, and our response to those needs, which will determine our vocation.

Much of the growth of the handicapped people is not related specifically to our being in the country. Much of it is simply a function of the family and community life here, such as Rita's peace and stability increasing as she came to see this as her home. Some of the growth is due to professional intervention, such as the fantastic improvement in Doretta's physical and mental health as a result of her heart operation. But there are, of course, the things that have been mentioned which are particular to our surroundings, which are accepted and enjoyed, and contribute to our life together. We often sing a song about "this old farm" which includes the line, "Hey, it's good to be back home again."

This will not always be home for everyone here. Assistants come and go (and sometimes come back again). Some of the handicapped people will undoubtedly make their home elsewhere eventually. But even in looking at these foreseeable changes, we feel that the farm is already, and will in some way remain, an important "home for the heart" for us, even for those who move on.

Within our community, we are constantly learning about the areas of our life in which we need to grow: inward growth, growth in abilities, growth outward towards others. Because we all live on the farm, and there are periods of time without much contact or activity beyond our own community, we must be sensitive to people's need to have time away in other settings, and to be quiet or to be alone. Trips, whether individually or together, are one important change of pace. For some time also, members of the community have been expressing the need for a quiet room or chapel, a place where one could go to be alone. For us, this need seems to have found an answer in the donation to us of a small former church building, just down the road, which will be for us a small chapel and place of retreat.

At the level of interior or spiritual growth, each one of us is at a different point. But there has been an awareness growing of our need, as a community, to deepen in this area. We are trying to find the right expression for this, and also the support and teaching we need from outside. Linked closely to this is our need to learn more about community itself, and to grow more stable and closer together. Again, we sense strongly the need for inspiration from outside our community. This is perhaps no different to other communities, but for us the input from outside is a bit harder to find because of our isolation.

We are gradually becoming more aware, as well, of the needs that exist around us in the community at large. One of the things we aspire to do is to share with others, in a small way, the life of our community, thus answering, we hope, the need for more acceptance and understanding between people.

We have also come face to face with the dire poverty that exists in our region. There exists, in the area, a whole subculture of people whom social and economic progress has passed by, and who live in circumstances which are handicapping them and their children. What we can ever do for such people, or whether we will ever be able to do anything effective, are questions that force themselves upon us.

There is little work available in our area on a regular basis, and so there are many people who are unemployed, all, or part of, the time. Sometimes when jobs are available, people lack the necessary training. In order to fulfil them in this context, the need for work presents itself to us as a much larger question than simply providing training for a few mentally handicapped people, when it is not even clear what the training would be aimed at. Would a work project be possible in which various people could be employed, handicapped and non-handicapped? Could something be devised to build upon the latent skills and resources in the region; work that would be of benefit to many? These are the directions our dreams are taking.

In reality, for the present, we are taking very small steps. One cow, then two; some chickens, some pigs; a little woodwork for sale, then a little more, all produced in our basement. None of the longer range steps are clear yet, and perhaps that should not concern us right now. We feel hopeful about the future, and that we will be able to play some small role in changing things. But we have to be patient too, with ourselves, with others, with the situation. People and events cannot be forced along too much in the country. People have their pride, and events take their own time. Mutual confidence has to have time to grow.

The reality of present economic times must also be considered. Rising costs, shortage of funds, and the energy crisis will no doubt hit harder in an area like this than in others. Already the farm has taken on for us a more important aspect than just something to do. It provides much of our food. It also provides wood for at least some of our heat. We are supported financially by government subsidy; but to what extent will we be supporting ourselves through our work as time goes on? In what ways will we have to change our expectations? In what ways will we be called upon to accept a simpler, poorer style of life? It is good that we are forced to ask ourselves these questions, for it brings us closer to, and renders us more understanding of others around us.

Dying Lifestyle: New Lifestyle

In our society, farming is a dying lifestyle. Statistics have been produced to indicate how many acres of farmland go out of production every hour in Canada. The population in rural areas continues to dwindle, while that of the cities grows by the day. With the drop in rural population, services also decrease, things become more expensive, more people move out, and the cycle repeats itself.

However, there are also some people moving, in small numbers, to rural areas. There are many people who live near us who have chosen to live in the country, to do business here, or to farm here, and to accept whatever hardships may be entailed in moving here. To see this happening is a hopeful sign for us, being ourselves people who moved to a farm with little practical knowledge.

There is a fullness in living in the country, on a farm. There is a fantastic blessing in having open space around you, and all the other beauties of nature. Mary Lou and I see this in the enjoyment of our own children and their relationship with the land and the animals. We see it too in the enjoyment that others also take from what we have around us. It is a richness that a decreasing minority of people have access to, and that many spend large sums of money to experience even for a brief holiday period.

We have to temper our romanticism and enjoyment of the country with a realism about the work entailed in living here, and the commitment to people. Both living in the country and living in community may be new to people, assistants especially, when they come here, and there is therefore much to learn. So we are trying to learn some of the old ways, and apply some new thinking too. We are trying to combine work and enjoyment of life, isolation and being together.

May we be able to work, through our own frailty and lack of constancy, towards a fuller exemplification in our community of some of the qualities of life mutely represented to us by our forest: quiet and peaceful, strongly rooted and ever present, faithfully growing and constantly being renewed.

13

THE FOLLY OF L'ARCHE IN CALCUTTA

Gabrielle Einsle

Gabrielle Einsle is a German woman, who founded the Arche communities in India in 1969. Gabrielle met Jean Vanier at a workshop on "poverty" which she had organized at the centre for foreign students in Montreal, "Carrefour". From their friendship grew the vision of l'Arche in India.

In 1970, the first community, known as Asha Niketan or Home of Hope, opened in Bangalore, welcoming Gurunathan, and Joeboy. A few years later, Gabrielle sensed a new call to start an Asha Niketan in the heart of Calcutta. There, in an old rectory (with the basement of a church for a workshop) given to l'Arche by the Archbishop of Calcutta, Cardinal Picachy, Asha Niketan, Calcutta, began, and has now welcomed ten handicapped men.

Two other Asha Niketans sprang up, and Gabrielle was asked to co-ordinate the Indian region, a task she fulfilled until 1978. At present she is living with the community at Asha Niketan, Calcutta.

Shy and alone, he was sitting on the bank of the river Hooghly, behind the little village of Noorpoor, some forty miles from Calcutta. Out here, near its mouth, this branch of the Ganges is mighty and beautiful. The ferry had just arrived, bringing the villagers from the other shore to the bus for Diamond Harbour, the terminus of a railway line from Sealdah station, Calcutta.

It was March 1973. Chris and I had come on the morning train from Sealdah, where we were about to prepare the opening of a second Asha Niketan in India. We had come to see the Missionary Brothers of Charity on their big coconut farm at Noorpoor where they had welcomed some hundred boys and men, found by the Brothers or by Mother Teresa's Sisters in the streets of Calcutta. After being saved from an almost certain death of rejection, hunger, disease or exploitation, they had been brought to this farm. Their physical or mental handicap gave them little chance in Calcutta of being accepted or helped to become independent and earn a livelihood.

The boy of about fourteen or fifteen, sitting on the bank of the Hooghly was one of them. He was a bit nervous, looking now across the river, and now by stealth towards Chris and me. The Brothers had told us what they knew of him: Father Christadas had retrieved him – naked, starved to a skeleton, shivering and sick to death, without a soul who knew or cared for him. Where he came from and how he had survived was his personal secret, which he would start to reveal only very slowly and carefully, after years at Asha Niketan, to Anand, Swapan and Martha. The Brothers said his name was Kashi. We asked them, if Kashi himself agreed, whether he could come to live with us in a small community of l'Arche, which I intended to start within a month or two. He would be with Peter (whom we had met at the office of Dr Davis, a psychiatrist) and one or two other assistants. And so it was that he moved to Sealdah in May 1973 – one of a hundred at Noorpoor one of a million in Calcutta: Kashi.

The desire to start a second Arche home in Calcutta was born in August 1972 when Judy and I, working at Asha Niketan, Bangalore at that time, visited Calcutta for a week. There, we had met Mother Teresa who had taken us to visit several of her projects. We had contacted Dr Davis, who was later to become a member of our Governing Council. We had spent a day at the Home of the Dying in Kalighat, feeding and washing the sick women on their cots. We had discovered Chowringhee Street and its side lanes and were fascinated by its people, shops and theatres. We had waded, up to our knees, through muddy water in the little lanes of Pilkhana, Howrah with the Missionary Brothers of Charity, visiting their friends.

I had returned to Bangalore, "drunk" with Calcutta. Before the end of the year I was back there with Jean Vanier, and everything started to fall into place. Dr Reddy and Miss Padmasini Asuri, of our governing body in Bangalore and some Bengali recruits for a local governing council met with us at the Raj Bhavan (the house of the Governor whose wife was to become a patron of our new home), to form the legal body which would be responsible for the new home. The Archbishop, who had heard about our search for a home, offered us an almost empty parish house as a foothold, to start Asha Niketan. Tucked away behind little carpenter shops and tea stalls along the main street in front, the two storey house is separated by one wall from Sealdah station, where half a million people arrive and depart daily, and by another wall from St John's Church and its cemetery. The big basement of that church was offered to us for a workshop. And thus, a new venture of l'Arche could begin, with all the painful growth that the life of its communities invariably holds in store.

I must admit, there are times when I feel a bit like Moses (I don't think he will mind my presumption). He must have felt weary in the desert with all those people who, though each one was following God's call, were stuck with him there because he had heeded the voice out of the bush. Each time one of our four present Asha Niketans goes through a crisis of life and death (and they seem to take turns in this) I become scared that someone will turn against me, saying: "Why did you have to start these crazy communities here at all?" I do not think that any arguments would justify or explain the folly of l'Arche in India, and especially in Calcutta. All I feel able to do is to tell a few stories of people who have shared this folly with me. In this, I have to draw on my personal experience, unfortunately neglecting many new developments initiated by the younger generation of assistants who have followed me.

When I look today at Kashi, my co-founder of Asha Niketan, Calcutta, a handsome young man in his self-earned, impeccable clothes, handling all the different steps of our work contract with complete autonomy, I find it difficult to imagine him six years ago, I remember him then as a bit silent, quite tense, reserved, often nervously knocking some object hard on the table as if he wanted to say: "Look, I want to talk about something!" Three years later, it started to come out in bits and pieces: "Look, I am from Bangladesh, my father had a beedi[1] shop there. He was

[1] Indian cigarette

A simple meal at l'Arche, Madras

always quarrelling with my mother, and one day he left us. Then
I was with the refugees, coming down to Calcutta, but I did
something wrong, and they kicked me out, shouting: 'Get out, get
out! . . .' " What happened then, is still too hard to put into words
for Kashi. The next thing we heard about was Father Christadas,
who saved him.

Unlike Madhu, who came with Shankar to us from Noorpoor
Farm a year later, Kashi for a long time never joined us when we
went to the Home of the Dying or to the little clinic Antara where
mentally ill people from other homes of Mother Teresa are
brought, or to her clinic in Tithagar for people suffering from
leprosy. For the time being, he avoided any occasion to meet those
with whom he was once identified: the homeless, the sick, the
dying. Today, this has changed. Kashi knows he is a big brother
with many responsibilities and he is sure of his place, not only in
his own home, but also in the world-wide community of l'Arche.
In 1978 he was one of the delegates of the Indian region at the
meeting of the international federation of l'Arche in France, where
he behaved like a fish in water.

Madhu, on the contrary, was always keen to visit the Home of the Dying, where he had spent four years, suffering from countless sores which wouldn't heal. Was it there that he learned the remarkable and gentle art of reading people's needs? What does it matter that Madhu invariably holds any book or newspaper upside down as long as he can decipher, with a rare insight and attention, people's faces and gestures, responding to their wants with a marvellous spontaneity and generosity. Any visitor, coming in from the terrible heat of Calcutta, need not ask for a glass of water when Madhu is around; they will soon receive a cup of his excellent brew of tea and a saucer to pour it on for cooling.

Asha Niketan has really become Madhu's home. But if there were more people than the fifteen living together there now, it would no longer be a home. And without our daily work that calls us outside, it would be more like a nursing home. Our contract with Philips India Ltd, has allowed us to provide the men at Asha Niketan with work adapted to individual capacities, involving steps with various degrees of difficulties, cutting, twisting, stripping, soldering and counting of radio wires. Our earnings allow us to pay for the daily food.

This contract we owe to a man who is an incredible mixture of a Bengali revolutionary and a respectful upholder of wholesome traditions, an extraordinary connoisseur and lover of Tagore and a highly qualified engineer. He is also the heart of a place called Students' Health Home, a clinic and hospital, giving free medical services to thousands of students in Calcutta. It is run by doctors and other ex-students who spend every free hour of their lives in this voluntary service. How many times – though we are not exactly students – have we found relief there for our stomachs, chests, skins, and ears! Nandan Bhattacharya (the name of our friend) was seduced by *The Place of the Mentally Handicapped in the Modern World* by Jean Vanier, which Chris and I had passed on to him at our first meeting. There are people who criticize the fact that "mentals" are given a decent home and work, when so many "normals" do not even have the essentials, just as there are people who criticize Mother Teresa for responding to too many people and for not concentrating more on an individual follow-up. It is not easy to cope with human needs when they are as pressing as in Calcutta.

"Now there are varieties of working, but it is the same God who inspires them all in every person . . . To each is given the manifestation of the Spirit for the common good" (1 Cor. 12:5–7).

During the winter of 1973 Mother Teresa had started a shelter at Sealdah Station, where she distributed hot milk and bread in the evenings. As we lived so close, she had asked us whether we could prepare and heat up the milk from the tins and cut the bread. We volunteered to bring it over and distribute the food among the hundred or so people (the number increased as the message spread) when the Sisters could not come. But alas, there was total chaos when we actually faced our new task. Like a swarm of excited birds the crowd fell over us and the milk and the bread, and there was much shouting, splashing and throwing. Our report to Mother brought two of her Sisters to the spot the next evening and we watched an unforgettable lesson on how to deal with Calcutta's crowds. Where there was consternation on our part, there were the orders of the Sisters. I can still see the tin of one man, who tried to queue up twice, rattling across the street, kicked by one of the more spirited Sisters. She wasn't too proud of her kick when I expressed my appreciation, but simply said: "What to do?"

Barun's coming to Asha Niketan opened up to us the world of a wonderful Bengali family. His mother, Barun-ma, an ardent follower of Gandhiji and a proud and devoted Bengali woman, became a mother and friend for all of us. She never came without one of her special sweets. Though a simple lady, it was she who insisted on my going to a real Bengali theatre, and her son, with his not abundant salary, periodically takes all the people from Asha Niketan to a high-quality film or to the world-famous Bengali Children's Theatre. What appears like an ocean of suffering to the guilty Westerner, is the home of millions of Bengalis, rightly proud of their beautiful language, of their Rabindranath Tagore, of their profusion of theatres and poets and their famous universities.

I occasionally visited Barun-ma on the top floor of her narrow house where she lives with her husband and two other grown-up sons, in one rather small bed-sitting room. It was there that she invited ten of us for a four-course meal, and I still don't know how we all fitted on the floor, with our banana leaves as plates in front of us. The people in Calcutta have developed an incredible art of making the most ingenious use of every inch of space for storing their belongings, to create room for living. On Deevali Festival, we all climbed on the roof of Barun-ma's house for a magnificent display of fireworks which competed with the crackers of all the neighbours, whose houses were crammed together just as ingeniously as the objects in Barun-ma's living room.

Our welcome in this family strengthened our belief and hope that it is possible to live as brothers and sisters in one home, with people from all types of families as well as with the homeless of Calcutta, even though we had been warned that our intention to open our Asha Niketans to all classes, castes and religions, was bound to fail.

If Barun, of course, had any power or influence on public opinion, Gandhiji would soon see his dream that all men become brothers, come true. But, alas, Barun's tremendous gift of bringing people together is sometimes wasted on those who have no eyes to see or ears to hear. I once visited a hospital with Barun, Noel, one of our dayworkers, and a Canadian friend. Sensing our handicap of not being able to talk with the patients in Bengali, Barun automatically took it upon himself very politely to introduce us individually to each patient, inquiring at the same time very delicately how they were feeling. But the nurse cut him short every time with a factual and quite indiscreet description of the patient's sickness, which in most cases was terminal. Another time, we went for a picnic on the bank of the Hooghly. Barun was delighted when a boat crowded with many people passed by, and he started to cheer and wave down to them, only to cause each face to straighten up in embarrassment. Yet, the people were on a "pleasure trip"!

Not only those crowds, but we too at Asha Niketan, can often be so serious and worked up with our projects, our opinions and our hang-ups that we cannot tolerate or live up to Barun's playful and marvellous vision of life. But when he succeeds in drawing us into one of his brilliant, creative dances, our tensions dissolve and we can see roads again where there were mountains.

One person who enjoyed Barun's dances with every fibre of his being, though he never took part in them with his crippled feet, was Kudhabaksh. I will tell his story in a somewhat detailed way, because it makes one feel the heartbeat of Calcutta.

I met Kudhabaksh first outside our home in front of the little carpenter and tea shops, holding out a battered tumbler to the tea shop man. He looked at me with that candid, trusting and non-defensive expression of a person who cannot argue, pretend or cheat. He explained with his hands that it had been a bad day for getting food. Two days later, I met him with Marlene and later with Fred. All of us felt drawn to him immediately, but we remained discreet, not wanting to involve the inevitable crowds in our encounter. Then again, one evening, when I bought some bananas, someone tapped gently on my shoulder from behind. There he was again, breaking out in happy laughter as I looked back. We now started to look out for him, and one evening, Fred and I invited him casually to follow us. He came as far as the gate, then waved goodbye and went back to the streets with a huge smile. One morning, when he crossed my way again, I turned back to the house, and this time he followed right through the gate. He had tea with us, but then went off again quite decidedly, hopping like a bird on his crippled feet, one going east, one west. He did not speak in words, nor react to sounds, his age could have been twenty-five or thirty-five. His way of greeting, and a little amulet around his neck, seemed to indicate that he belonged to the Moslem community. That day we had to take a decision about a new man joining our community. Should we consider the requests from some rich families or take a homeless man? I started to pray for our new friend of the streets. In the afternoon, Fred came to tell me that he was back with an old bag, stuffed with dirty clothes and a stick. Fred started to heat some buckets of water, for it took hot water to get through the crusts on his arms and legs to the skin. He obviously enjoyed the procedure and showed that in better days he had acquired the habit of washing himself. He gladly accepted the clean clothes we gave him, but his bundle of dirty torn shirts he kept preciously in a corner. Next day we washed them together, and he folded them up with a striking care and know-how. When he took me afterwards for a little stroll along the pavements where his old friends sell tea, sweets and beedis I was struck by the kindness with which they greeted him as he saluted them all. No one laughed at him. He somehow managed to convert other people's attitudes, even if now and then he caught a scornful look.

We had to find a name for our new brother. When I had to speak to a group of students at Loreto College about Asha Niketan, I told them about our new friend and asked the Moslem girls in the group what name they would suggest for him. One girl came up with the Urdu word "Kudhabaksh" – "Gift of God". Soon the name caught on with Kashi, Albert and Peter, who had started to call him "dancing man", because of his bouncing walk.

The following weekend we all went to Ramakrishna Temple. Our new brother was wearing his freshly washed French-style beret – God knows where he found that! The man next to him on the seat in the bus did not look too happy about his company, but other passengers responded to his irresistible salutes and smiles. What a peaceful day we spent at the ashram, where you feel deeply, through the prayerful gestures of the pilgrims, the veneration for a holy man who had truly yearned to see God. As we sat with our new brother on the lawn in front of the Temple, beside the holy river, it occurred to me that he too, in a very hidden way, was a manifestation of God for our times.

Weeks passed, and Kudhabaksh had started to work in the workshop. One day he went out to buy a beedi and did not return for several hours. We started to ask ourselves: what does a regulated life of work, meals and rest mean to a man who has survived all his life through the hazards of the streets of Calcutta? As Fred said: 'His world out there is precious to him and we are taking it away from him all of a sudden.' He did come back though, ringing the door bell with great vigour, banging on the door, laughing and thoroughly enjoying his welcome.

This coming and going went on for several days, till one day he did not come back all day. Nobody talked much about it, but there was a sad atmosphere in the house. When I went out at nine o'clock at night, I saw Kudhabaksh standing in front of a tea shop, with an empty tumbler, cold, tired, hungry, without his precious beret, in a posture of great hopelessness. He was so absorbed in his thoughts that he did not notice me right beside him. Finally, he looked up, then took my hand without a smile and slowly led the way to the house. He devoured the food we had kept, then tried to convey his story with quite excited gestures. Someone had taken his beret from him and kicked him out from somewhere. He looked preoccupied and sad. Albert, Kashi and Peter received him upstairs with much warmth, though at other times they had tended to laugh at him. Sitting on his bed, he asked for a beedi, and as I had none, he searched in his pocket. He found one there, and, holding it up in triumph, he burst out laughing – and the sad day was over!

During the six months that Kudhabaksh had shared our life, he had become slowly aware that work was not a purely voluntary affair in the house, but part of a daily routine. He had also discovered that the people in the community were not saints, and they in their turn no longer idealized him but were aware of inconsistencies in his generally amiable attitude towards life and people. Perhaps he also experienced the hopes, labours and pains of relationships which the closeness of people in a community can cause. He started to reflect a lot. And then, one day, he told us through his gestures that his world was "out there". He did not come back from his daily stroll through Sealdah Station, and Kashi, from the first floor balcony of our house, spotted him, sleeping on the platform. The next day he came to tell us the decision of his final departure. We let him go. He closed the door behind him with an apologetic and consoling look. We were grateful for the time together which had taught us so many things and left us with many more questions. He refused to take anything whatsoever with him, not even a tumbler or a plate for begging. The next part of his story has often made me wonder why.

For a few more days we saw him hopping through the crowds,

assuring us with a good-natured smile that he lacked nothing. Then we lost all trace of him, till one day Barun's brother phoned to tell us he had met Kudhabaksh in a rather emaciated state at Howrah Station, one of the two biggest free hotels for countless homeless people in Calcutta in those days, the other being our own Sealdah.

It was during the monsoons and, when I got up at five o'clock the next morning, the rains poured down, within hours changing all the lower part of the city into huge lakes. Hanging on to the last double-decker bus to Howrah before the traffic went dead, I was wet through by the time I reached St Aloysius Church, near the station. The priest and his two little Mass servers noticed me only when I started to clear my throat, indicating that I too wanted to hear the whispered Gospel. After another downpour during mass, the floods started to stream into the church, and I found it appropriate that the church was dedicated to Our Lady, "Star of the Sea". I really needed a star by now as I waded through the flood, twice almost disappearing into the sewer system of Howrah, with its big open holes in the pavement.

What a sight the station was! (It was before the big renovations there, which improved conditions considerably.) The people living on the streets below Howrah Bridge had moved into the waiting-halls where the water stood less high than outside; they were sitting or lying around, with their few belongings, like little heaps of misery. Wandering along the platforms and through the halls, I was hoping, and dreading, to identify one of those emaciated bodies, looking more like corpses, as that of Kudhabaksh. A stiff little man, lying on his stomach, made me hold my breath for seconds. No, his feet did not belong to Kudhabaksh. The way people avoided coming close to this body, however dense the throng, confirmed my fear that he was dead. Nobody admitted the fact, because nobody knew what to do. I tried to convince myself that the man was sleeping, because I did not have the courage, exposed to the gaze of the crowd, to bow down and touch his body. Oppressed, and feeling guilty and helpless, I stumbled on for a while, returning home finally, deeply disappointed not to have found our brother.

Two days later another phone call from Barun's brother indicated where he had seen Kudhabaksh again. When I reached the spot, I found two other men lying there. They answered my gestures, imitating Kudhabaksh by mimicking an ambulance. This could only mean Home of the Dying, for no hospital ambulance would pick up people in this state from the streets of Calcutta. And sure enough, when I reached Kalighat, Kudhabaksh, thin and with a huge beard, was lying on a cot. His good-natured smile had completely disappeared from his face. Within a short time he was well enough to be brought to Prem Dam, another home of the Missionaries of Charity, for his convalescence. One day, the sisters asked me if I would take him to Noorpoor, to make room for other convalescents. I had no choice, for I knew that work at Asha Niketan was not his "thing", and of his life in the streets he seemed to have had enough. So I took that same train and bus with him which had brought me the first time to Noorpoor, when I had found Kashi.

Kudhabaksh is there to this day. When I last met him, it was with Father David and all of Asha Niketan, on Holy Thursday. As some of us were asked to help wash the feet of the handicapped men at Mass, it fell to me to wash those of Kudhabaksh.

He had come to Asha Niketan at a time when our little community was facing an interior crisis. We were few, Mario from Canada, who had helped us for some months to start the home, had died of pneumonia. There was a continuous turnover of assistants and someone always had scabies, rashes or diarrhoea. The daily work was still slow and tedious; without the clippers which we got later, all the wires from Philips had to be stripped with razor blades and were easily damaged. Hardly anyone understood what we were trying to do in that big parish house with a few handicapped men and some men and women who were not even Brothers or nuns.

Why did Kudhabaksh's arrival give us new life? Without words or theories on social work, he brought an answer to our searching from the streets of Calcutta. In touching our hearts through his gentle concern for people, through his incredible jokes in the face of difficulties and through his utter sadness in the face of abuse, he spoke to us of the love, the courage and the violence of Calcutta's people who, through him, became our people. He told us in so many ways – or rather looks – that we should not feel too bad if we could not bring a massive solution for the "problem" of the poor or the mentally handicapped in Calcutta. (No one could say in which way they were handicapped or not handicapped, and it did not really matter.) We should rather worry about ourselves and people who cannot see or hear what God wants to say through his poorest and weakest children. I think it was necessary that someone should help us at that moment to define Asha Niketan in Calcutta, and Kudhabaksh had the personality and the grace to do it. Dr Bagchi, the chairman of our governing council in Calcutta and also a well-known professor of neurology, had certainly recognized Kudhabaksh. He asks me about him each time I come to Calcutta.

He has a weak spot for Dinesh as well. Dinesh once broke his arm and had to wear a plaster cast. As it was hot, he took it off after a few days, and we were relieved when our good friends at the Student Health Home fixed it back on. However, our relief soon turned into anger, when Dinesh managed to undo the thing a second time. I dragged him to Dr Bagchi's hospital, and decided to appeal to all the doctor's authority to give Dinesh a lesson before proceeding to the outpatient department. But Dinesh, who is an artist with a very fine sensitivity (he paints) and a bit of a crook too, was going to handle the situation himself. Each time the professor opened his mouth to give his lesson, Dinesh very astutely knew how to distract him. When at last we found out that the outpatient department was closed and the next day was a Sunday, Dr Bagchi had his nurse bring the necessary equipment for plastering right to his office and started doing the job himself. We soon had a circle of curious doctors around us. When all was finished, and final instructions about the length of time the plaster had to be worn were about to be given, Dinesh said: "Ah, I forgot to tell you, Doctor, I went to see the Sholay film with Gabrielle. Homa Malini was dancing, but she showed too much stomach!" I imagine his younger colleagues had not heard many patients talk like this to their boss, who obviously thoroughly enjoyed it.

I believe the message hidden in the folly of the presence of l'Arche in Calcutta is found in such simple but authentic little encounters between people. Are we not all craving and yearning for true, trustworthy relationships – in Calcutta as in Paris, in Toronto as in London or Oslo or Moscow?

I am not suggesting that to share one's life with mentally retarded people means constant bliss. The first years of any of our communities are hard and trying years, because too many wounds of rejection and anguish have to be healed before trust is born. And we would be unfaithful to our call if we simply relaxed and enjoyed the company of those who have found hope and freedom at Asha Niketan. Together with them, we become responsible for the healing of others, which always takes a long time.

Only once have I seen a quite spectacular healing of one of our men. We called him Koko (a Chinese word for "little brother"), instead of "mad boy" as he was named by his Chinese mother and her neighbours. He had never left the overcrowded apartment block of poor Chinese people in Calcutta, where he was frequently beaten up by everyone when their teasing made him angry and desperate. He was the most frightened being I had ever seen in any of our homes. Unable to sit for more than half a minute, he stood in corners, knotting and unknotting the strings of the rolling shutters, getting hold of any door-lock to tear off his fingernails till they bled, in a constant attempt at self-destruction. Fred had started to keep him on his lap, from which he escaped every minute, to return again and again like a frightened bird. At night we sat for hours with him. Noticing that he tended to empty out receptacles, we made him fill a basket with weeds in the garden and empty it on the compost. The joy he experienced when he discovered one day that he was doing useful work through this! And soon he started to learn many things with quite unexpected speed. A transformation which I have seen taking years with other people, took place within weeks. Our meals with Koko became a delight for all. Did God want to give us a glimpse of the eternal joy with him which Koko would enter soon? I cannot find any other explanation, for after a mysterious and terrible skin disease, combined with pneumonia, Koko died within a few days at the Isolation

Hospital. When Fred and I came back from the hospital, we simply put up Koko's photo amid all the blossoms we could gather in the little garden around the house. At lunch, there was a sudden outbreak of such joy and laughter, with Barun and Madhu imitating Koko, that a visitor was scandalized by our reaction to death. But we knew that Koko had found life in abundance and wanted to share it with us. It was like a manifestation of that Hindu belief which says: "If, at the beginning of a common venture a member dies, and if he was a good person, this enterprise will always last."

Surely, our communities are not ends in themselves, but are vital for the growth of people and the wholeness of society. But I humbly want to ask God to sustain this fragile little Asha Niketan in Calcutta and to help it become a witness of how much He loves the weakest.

I read this chapter to Maggie in Bangalore. "Yes . . .", she said. And then, after a moment's thought, she put it all in a nutshell: "Yes, in the great needs of Calcutta, our folly is to choose to love a few individuals deeply."

14

L'ARCHE IN HAITI

Robert Larouche

Before coming to l'Arche in 1974 Robert Larouche was a philosophy teacher in Rouyn-Noranda, Quebec. Deeply touched by a Faith and Sharing retreat, he came to live at l'Arche, Trosly where he worked in the pottery workshop for a year. He accompanied Nadine Tokar and Jean Vanier on a trip to Haiti and Brazil and felt called to stay in Haiti. In 1975 the first house in Port-au-Prince began.

With the help of the local board of directors and mainly Haitian assistants, the community has grown. There are three different homes (or "kay" as they say in creole), a small school for the children of the community and of the neighbourhood, a workshop, summer camps and many links with Faith and Light groups.

As regional co-ordinator for l'Arche in Haiti and Honduras, he comes regularly to the meetings of the International Council.

When Jean Vanier, Nadine Tokar[1] and I were invited to Port-au-Prince in 1975, we had no definite plan of what l'Arche ought to be in Haiti, nor did we know if l'Arche should have a place there. We were unfamiliar with the place of the mentally handicapped person in the Haitian family and society, and we realized that the model of community that we had in Europe and North America should not necessarily be imposed here.

I had been welcomed for three months in a Haitian community, the Communauté Sainte-Marie,[2] which is in a poor neighbourhood on the outskirts of Port-au-Prince. While there, I was able

[1]Nadine is responsible for the Arche community in Honduras.
[2]The Communauté Sainte-Marie brings together about 200 families in the manner of a parish. The team which animates it lives in a *Foyer de Charity*, which is a place of prayer where retreats are held. I had been welcomed by those responsible for the *Foyer*.

to learn a little of the language and to discover several aspects of the culture. I also had the opportunity to visit the families of several people who were handicapped, principally from the poorer neighbourhoods, as well as several children and adults who had been left either at the asylum of Signeaur[3] or at the psychiatric centre in Port-au-Prince.

In the slum areas, it is extremely difficult for the handicapped person to find his place. Life is very intense and each day there is the struggle to find one's daily bread. From a very early age, each member of the family feels the pressure to contribute to the well being of his brothers and sisters. The child brings water from the public fountain or goes shopping at the market-place; young people and adults will hold down a small trade or go out looking for jobs in order to keep bread on the table from day to day.

When faced with a situation of such basic need, the apparent uselessness of the handicapped person is constantly called to mind. In general, being handicapped is seen as a trial to which the only possible response is resignation. In Canada, as in France, this perception of the handicapped person as a heavy burden sometimes leads to his being excluded and placed in a special institution. Here, the feeling is the same but it is less camouflaged; it is expressed more openly through the mockery and jeering of neighbours.

If the life of the neighbourhood is built around the buying and selling of basic goods, it is also characterized by neighbours helping each other out. Constantly confronted by the basic necessities of life, this give-and-take guarantees a sort of "life insurance". The person who is handicapped often knows how to take advantage of the situation, becoming not only the fool and buffoon of the neighbourhood, but the beggar as well. In this way, he succeeds in bringing his share to the support of his family. However, he gains absolutely nothing in terms of his own dignity, either in his own eyes or in the eyes of others.

For those families who keep their child from begging and who want to protect him from mockery, the situation is often hard to control. The rejection and hopelessness are often expressed, by

[3]This asylum is a centre which welcomes the chronically mentally ill and those who are handicapped. Most of those there are without families.

saying that the child will never bring anything to the family. There are few services, either public or private, to support families. Those that do welcome children or adults in schools or special workshops are simply flooded by demands. The institutions, usually administered by the government, are reserved for those whose need is extreme or who have been abandoned altogether. It is the family who must take care of their child, and in general there is no other choice but to leave him with his brothers and sisters while father and mother go out to work and to the market. As he grows up, however, there are problems with his increasing need to leave home from time to time and to be like everyone else.

Marie

Meeting Marie at the psychiatric centre made it clear for me that we would open an Arche house in Haiti. Marie, who was about ten years old, was an emotionally disturbed child. She used to run up and cling to passers-by in the streets of Port-au-Prince, singing out at the top of her voice. She had been gathered up from the streets and placed in the psychiatric centre. When I visited the centre, Marie had already been there for a year. I learned that, in that time, no one had succeeded in tracing her family. She was the only child on that ward and, in these conditions, her future was hopeless. The director of the centre asked me if we could eventually accept her in l'Arche.

Up to that time, no community of l'Arche had accepted children, but Marie's distress was great, and her need to be in a warm, personal environment was very clear. The psychiatrists, who were with the unit, offered their collaboration and, together with several others, were able to help us form a board of directors that would support a community of l'Arche in Haiti.

Roland and Matthew

While visiting the asylum of Signeaur, I met Roland who was probably about thirty years old and had cerebral palsy. He didn't

speak, but he could understand. I explained to him what I hoped
to create and asked him if he would like to come and live with
me, and lend a hand in welcoming Marie. Roland hurried away to
change his shirt: he was ready. I later understood how much he
must have been humiliated in being "tossed" into the asylum. His
loneliness was much greater because he could not communicate.
This handicap hid his maturity and his sensitivity from those who
were around him.

As we continued to visit the asylum together, we met Matthew.
Matthew was probably about ten years old and spent all his time
crouched in a corner. He gave signs of being autistic and he had
been brought to the asylum after a year in the general hospital
where, I learned later, he had been abandoned in the emergency
room. He had regressed considerably in that time, and because of
the excessive number of patients at the asylum, he could not be
offered the individual care that would have allowed him to come
out of himself. It was also believed that he was unable to hear.
Matthew had epileptic fits every day and the medication had not
brought them under control. I knew very little about autism and
its treatment, but I believed fundamentally that an attentive presence and stable relationships would be able to help Matthew.

Our Home

In starting our home, I looked for a house that would not be too
far away from others, but rather at the heart of a neighbourhood.
Because of Marie's emotional disorder, I knew that we would need
a certain amount of living space. On the other hand, I also saw
that it would be futile to attempt to create a therapeutic milieu that
was closed off or isolated. If we really wanted integration to be
possible for the children, it was necessary for us from the beginning, to make ourselves part of the life of the neighbourhood. And
the life of the neighbourhood was made up of relationships –
helping each other out as needed, and paying neighbourly visits.
I also believed that our presence could be an occasion for meeting
with other families with a handicapped member, as a stimulant

and support for them. The house also needed a lifestyle as close as possible to the one that Matthew, Roland and Marie had known. This would avoid separating them from their own milieu, and facilitate their return to their own families should this become possible.

I found and rented a house in a poor area named Carrefour, composed basically of working families, at the edge of Port-au-Prince. Carrefour is a heavily populated area. The houses are packed together. The alleyways are more easily negotiated on foot than by car and they are filled with children playing soccer or marbles, as they cannot go to school. All along, they are lined with the stalls of merchants selling their produce from straw mats on the ground or from little tables – rice, fruits in season, soap, oil, – all the basic goods. Mixed with the sound of merchants announcing the price of their merchandise to passers-by is the constant din of radios, the bells of itinerant street-vendors and the sounds of disputes among various people in the streets. All this makes up the music of daily life in the neighbourhood.

In contrast to other houses in the area that have only one or two rooms, ours has five, together with a little courtyard and several fruit trees. A tiny river that runs through the area passes close by. This is the place where the women meet to do their laundry.

After obtaining permission from the Department of Social Services of the Haitian Government, I went to get Roland. Hélène, a Haitian woman whom I had known at the Communauté Sainte-Marie, came and joined us to do the cooking. Two weeks later we went to get Matthew, and then when Louise, a Canadian nurse, joined us, we went to get Marie from the psychiatric centre. Since Roland had a special devotion to St Joseph, we named the home Kay Sin Joseph.[4]

The days had a very simple rhythm; preparing meals, keeping house and taking care of personal needs. Each morning, Louise, Hélène and Marie went to draw water from the well and buy food at the market. It was necessary to go out several times each day since we had no refrigerator. Preparation of the meal also took

[4]Kay Sin Joseph means the House of St Joseph in Creole, the language of the Haitian people.

a very long time, but this allowed the children to really participate: cleaning the rice, shelling the peas, grinding the spices. During this time I worked with Roland and Matthew, doing some wood-work and keeping the courtyard and garden in order. The educa-tional aspect of the home centred around the daily activities that every Haitian child needs to learn at an early age, to be able to serve his family better.

The Early Days

The first days were not the easiest. At that time, we didn't know the gravity of Marie's and Matthew's disturbance. Very soon Marie began to have severe temper tantrums, becoming deeply insecure when we approached her and wanting to reassure herself of our intentions. Matthew was more reserved and refused to open up. He would sink into depression or become self-destructive, refusing to eat.

Marie ran away from us and looked for us at the same time. Her tantrums increased at home, and she would run out into the streets. She had an immense desire to be loved and, at the same time, the conviction that she was unworthy of love. One day, when she was willing to dry a plate for the first time, and she succeeded. Louise said to her, "Marie, you are good!" Marie an-swered, "Me, good?" She couldn't bring herself to believe those words. Another time, Hélène, wanting to congratulate Marie, said, "You are a very pretty little girl!" Marie burst out swearing and ripped her dress. She wouldn't be a pretty little girl! Marie's entire sense of herself was marked and broken. It controlled her entire bearing as well as her behaviour.

Sometimes when she ran away, Marie would go to one of our neighbours' homes, or wander in the marketplace as she had done before, asking repeatedly for money, food, clothing and other items. When refused, she would break into a tantrum, throwing everything from the stalls up into the air. At first, the people in the neighbourhood became indignant at seeing a child brought up so badly and making so much trouble. They told us to beat her, to lock her up or even to tie her up.

It was even harder to accept the reactions of the children in the neighbourhood. Marie and Matthew weren't able to play. Marie was destructive, not able to be one child among many others. She had a very strong need to be the centre of attention, the only one being cared for. The other children made fun of her and enjoyed provoking her. This often led to scenes in the neighbourhood. Often I had to intervene. I always tried to explain to the gathering of parents and children what might have brought Marie to this point, and that neither blows nor insults nor molesting her in other ways would help her to grow. Sometimes I firmly defended Marie when she had been unjustly provoked.

Often we had the feeling that all the vigilant work of encouraging Marie to let go of her image as the *enfant terrible*, was unceasingly compromised by the continual remarks of those around us, and of our visitors. They saw no hope for Marie. She was "disordered", mad, poorly raised. It was only with the first signs of growth and calmness in Marie that people began to be more positive and confident.

At home, it was indispensable to share together each day. Together, we were able to consider everything that had happened to Marie and Matthew and look for its meaning. Roland stayed very close to Matthew, teaching him and treating him with a brotherly affection. Matthew wasn't hyperactive like Marie. He revealed himself more through his reactions: refusing to eat, anxiously repeating the same words for hours on end, or hitting himself when he was upset. Our own therapeutic approach was rather unusual, and sometimes even our Haitian assistants questioned it. Our demands of Matthew were interpreted as being quite hard, whereas we seemed much more permissive with Marie. This required a cultural adjustment by those of us who were foreigners, and a much greater understanding of the disturbed child by all of us.

Our School

Little by little each person began to feel the stability of the sur-roundings and of the relationships: people, activities, meals, the washing of clothes, bedtime. Everything followed a regular pat-tern, the same each day, and what we expected of one another was also the same, even if Marie didn't tolerate this easily. Despite provocation and testing, the daily patterns remained. Relationships became firmer – at first in a somewhat frenzied fashion with jeal-ousies and possessiveness, but little by little they became freer and friendlier. The coming and going of new people was always a source of tension, but also of growth.

For the children, a second environment, separate from that of the home, seemed necessary. Very close to the home we had built an arbour with a thatched roof and a cement floor. This became the school, complete with a teacher, other assistants as references, rules and timetables. This allowed Marie, as well as Adeline, who was ten and had just come to us from the asylum, to open up and breathe more freely within a new set of relationships. The children went to school one at a time, each for a half hour and then shared an hour there together. They really liked school and the little successes that came through learning. It was also a sort of refuge: if there had been problems at home, they were ignored at school. Everything started off on a new foot.

Seeing the progress of each person brought life to us. It also affected the attitudes in the neighbourhood appreciably. Those who kept stalls in the marketplace enjoyed seeing Marie in a clean dress and Matthew out buying the bread with money he carried. It was as though there was a new trust everywhere. While other peoples doubts at the outset had made our work in the home difficult – it had seemed to us then that everything we accom-plished at home was destroyed in the streets – now, Marie and Matthew were growing as a result of the confidence and welcome of those around. Some of the other children in the neighbourhood even began to make friends. The children were able to go out more freely without fear. It was as though, little by little, there was affirmation of them and within them, both at home and in the surrounding area.

The Family

Of all the moments of the day, it was bedtime that remained the privileged one. Once tucked into bed, Marie, Adeline and Matthew were most attentive and open to our words and songs and tenderness. Matthew was afraid of going to sleep, and often he had nightmares. We needed to spend a long time with him, tucking him in, before he would go off to sleep. Marie always spoke much more freely in these times of her fear of the devil hiding in the trees, of the hard moments of the day, or of her own family. This was the time she would name all the people who had been near her as a child. She was confused as to who was her sister, her mother, her uncle, but she wanted to join her family once again. We felt deeply this need of Marie to find herself loved and confirmed by those who had been close to her as a child. It seemed as if this reconciliation with her family was a profound condition for the healing of her disturbance.

We found Marie's family. It was then that a new path opened up for all of us: Marie, her family and ourselves. However, at first, the members of the family didn't want to receive Marie, not wanting the problems and worries that they had known before. On the other hand, from her side, Marie strongly desired to be with them even though she was very afraid. We began by going with Marie each week to spend a few hours with her family. Afterwards we would leave her there for an hour or two, then a day each week. Her aunts and brothers and sisters really saw her progress, but were disturbed by the occasional regression. It took a good three years for the mutual defences to begin to break down so that she could finally be welcomed in a full way. One day her aunt told her that she was looking forward to her next visit the following Sunday. Marie broke into joyful laughter. It might have been the first time she had ever felt that anyone in her own family was waiting for her and wanted to see her.

Marie still dreams of returning someday to her family home. But she will always be fragile psychologically, and her family, even though much more open, isn't ready for her to return permanently. Someday Marie will have to accept this separation. She will also always need the security of the Arche home, with all the relationships she finds there. But though she remains fragile and handicapped, she will be able to live happily and progress more and more in many ways.

For us, Marie's evolution has helped us to understand the immense importance of family ties for the children and adults whom we welcome. We saw how necessary it was, especially in Haiti, that we be attentive to these ties, never allowing the family to believe that their own responsibilities had come to an end. This would not have been right for either the family or the child. This development was often tumultuous for the children. Roland sometimes showed this through fatigue, for he was constantly concerned for Matthew and Marie, and undeniably linked to them. But he needed a quieter milieu for himself. We had thought of renting a small house with two rooms very close to our own where Salusien, a young Haitian man of twenty-two who was interested in l'Arche, and Roland could begin to live together. This was the beginning of what later became our second home. Roland also found fulfilment in being able to go to a workshop each morning that Jerome, a Haitian man of twenty-eight, had begun in another neighbourhood, Brooklyn.

A Haitian Shepherd

The workshop and the second home were founded by Haitians. It would have been very difficult for a "white" foreigner to direct a workshop in Brooklyn. Very quickly, a foreigner is seen as someone who "possesses", and who has come to do a "work of charity", or even as one who stands to gain in some way. Without doubt, this perception is linked to the abuses of colonialism, and understandably so. It isn't readily perceived that one is coming as a "brother" to accompany other brothers and sisters along their way. The fact that Jerome was this brother, and that he was Haitian, certainly affected the development of the workshop in Brooklyn. It gathered together about twenty people who were physically handicapped, and who used to beg in the streets of Port-au-Prince.

With Jerome, there wasn't the same distance as with a foreigner, but trust was still not at all apparent in the first days. On several occasions, especially when there was a real problem, Jerome would invite everyone at the workshop to get together to share and to see what they really wanted to live together: Was it essential to earn the biggest salary possible, and thus to eliminate those who were slow or whose emotional problems made it hard to contribute to the productivity? Or was it to give priority to the person, and the growth of each member in a real working community?

There is sometimes the danger of the Haitian leaving everything entirely in the hands of the foreigner. But with Jerome, they learned to carry, and even wanted to assume, responsibility for their workshop.

It was the same with the home that we began with Salusien in Carrefour where today there are five men who are mentally handicapped and three assistants. There is a sense of solidarity that was born between the neighbourhood and the members of the home, as all its members are Haitian. Those who pass by become more co-operative, and sometimes become friends. These new friendships in a neighbourhood are always a great strength for a community.

Even the traditions of the home – the welcome of visitors, meetings, prayer, leisure activities, conversations – are marked by the fact that they are all very Haitian. In the eyes of the foreigner, there may be less order in the home. Meals aren't always on time, and the work at the workshop may be less productive. But both the people who are handicapped and the assistants are growing quite well and according to their own rhythm because, fundamentally, life flows among the members of the home and there is a unity in the house itself.

It is important for the child who is welcomed, and also for the handicapped adult, to find a "shepherd" among his own people with whom it is possible to identify.

The Assistants

Why do the assistants stay? There are fifteen assistants in the homes, the school and the workshop. They are almost all Haitians who, in most cases, come from a poor background, and who have received only a very basic education. The allowance that each receives is sufficient to enable something to be put aside on a monthly basis, and many use it to support their parents. A young Haitian, when he leaves home, always retains a strong sense of duty and solidarity with his own family. The fact of the allowance together with medical insurance is certainly a security that l'Arche offers, and an attraction. On the other hand, choosing to live in community means letting go of several other options, such as, obtaining more education or a more profitable trade. For many this choice must be made each year.

But, on another level, for several assistants, l'Arche also has meant the discovery of the person who is handicapped and his gifts. In each of our meetings where we share our experiences, we always come back to the same words, "The person who is mentally handicapped is a real person, like me. God lives in him. And even more, he needs a friend." Also there is the discovery of a community where foreigners and Haitians, people from different regions with entirely different backgrounds (from the northwest, the south, the countryside, the capital, men of "letters", and the illiterate) share and make decisions together, seeking unity around the most poor and living with a certain equality. This runs counter to the tradition of a country where the distinctions of classes and social origins deeply affect relationships.

For the majority, the community also provides the opportunity to live their Christian values. The little bit of material security and the values of community life would never be sufficient to justify for many the decision to leave their families to live with the poor in a socially mixed group. All of this does not fit in too well with

Haitian traditions. But I think that for many, the discovery of the person who is handicapped and the discovery of community go together with the discovery of a new dimension of Christian commitment. This commitment is not simply at the level of an apostolate of prayer and of the Word, although prayer remains important and is a source of unity, but of little things given flesh through a regular daily life.

Chantal

Several parents came to us believing that they would find an institution where they could place their child who was either handicapped or disturbed. For those who lived closest, according to our resources, we were able to suggest our school or workshop or one of the services operated by another agency in Port-au-Prince. For those who lived at a distance, the best we could do was to give a few words of counsel, and reassure them that the family itself was the most appropriate environment to promote the growth of the child according to his own possibilities. But I always hoped that we could support them in another way, and that was to invite a member of the family circle to come and share the life of our home for a few weeks or a month.

This happened with a family from the village of Chantal, a village of 3000 people in the south of Haiti, 125 miles from Port-au-Prince, in the area called Cayes. The parents of an eighteen-year-old woman, Anite, had asked if we would take her into our home. Anite seemed to be surrounded by her own family, and I wasn't able to see the point of separating her from her own people and the village where she had lived, by welcoming her into our home at Port-au-Prince. I understood the concern of her family for her future, but I wondered if it might not be much more valuable to go to Chantal, ready to lend a hand to Anite's family in which she was already integrated, rather than to take her from her situation.

One of Anite's aunts, Mme Constant, came to live with us for three months, went back to Chantal, and began to take a few hours each day to show Anite how to care for her personal needs and to look after the house. They went for walks together, which not only pleased Anite, but also the other villagers who had not seen her very often, but who knew her.

Subsequently, during a visit to Chantal, I came to know seven other families with a child or an adult with some kind of mental handicap. The rejection of the person who is handicapped is much less pronounced in the rural areas, where the traditional way of life is still very much alive, than in the city. The solidarity at the heart of the family, faced with the difficulties of life – a beautiful solidarity which is very typical of Haitian society – means that the child who is mentally retarded, even if he is sometimes misunderstood, is accepted and cared for by those who are close to him.

It was in order to help the families of these children that Maryse, who was responsible for the school at Port-au-Prince, was willing to go to Chantal to begin a small school. With Mme Constant, she found and rented a house in the village. Each day, they welcomed the seven people who were handicapped, spending the morning singing, doing pre-school exercises, playing educational games, and practising observation. They then began a more advanced educational programme for those who were ready. In the afternoons, Maryse and Mme Constant would visit the homes of their students and in this way a link of mutual support was established. We called together a group of citizens from Chantal to form a local governing committee for the small school.

It was very difficult to realize that what their child learned might not be what they had dreamed of, but rather what he was capable of doing at that time. We had to help parents discover and appreciate the importance of the effort that their child was making towards the development of attentiveness. This was an essential step towards a greater freedom. The child needed his parents and those in the family circle to see him in a new light.

Subsequently the community council of Chantal, during a meeting that brought together the principal directors of the village, voted to put at the disposal of l'Arche two large buildings that belong to the village. The local committee of l'Arche expects to use them as new accommodation for the school and to open a home for several handicapped people, from neighbouring villages, who are unable to come to the school because of the distance. These children, at the most six, will come to the home during the week and spend the weekends with their families. This gesture on the part of the people of Chantal is not only a sign of appreciation for the work that has been done, but is also the expression of a new openness to the needs of the person who is handicapped. In a village such as this, our work would be impossible without the co-operation of the villagers.

This development also poses a question: "How can a support community for the handicapped child or adult, and their family, be created with a very simple structure that can be carried financially by an area such as Chantal?" The board of directors at Port-au-Prince, and the local committee of Chantal look at this continually. It is necessary that all the projects of l'Arche be financed and directed locally, and that families are always asked to participate according to their means, both financially and in kind. None of us would encourage a project based solely on foreign support.

The Board of Directors

It is not only the question of our financial self-sufficiency that has been a concern of the board of directors.[5] Our board was also called to support, control and consolidate all the varied directions taken by the work: the daily life of our homes, the workshop and the schools. If the board wanted to create new schools or plan a training programme for the formation of young people to help families in the countryside, this was examined in relation to the structures of the community, both at Carrefour and Chantal. A year ago, at Carrefour, we created a community council. Previously, our method of discernment and decision-making varied with the need of the moment. Then one day we decided to elect five people, from those who had been with the community the

[5]The board of directors responsible for the Arche Association of Haiti has twelve members who, in most cases, are professionals engaged in education, medicine or development.

longest, to make all the decisions that concerned the internal affairs
of the community. The more general questions were retained for
the board of directors. A month later, we added to the council two
members who were friends of the community and who lived in
the neighbourhood. We thought their presence at the level of the
community council would help us to grow towards a better integration into the neighbourhood. This was a turning point for all
of us. A new sense of responsibility emerged. When we discerned
together, we found that we made much better decisions and that
each person was much more enthusiastic about their implementa-
tion because they had been part of the group that made them. This
made us discover our capacity to assess situations, and our shared
vision became much more complete. In the beginning assistants
came to help with a work that they admired, but without necessarily an appreciation of it from within. From now on it was
together that we would ask our questions of one another. "Where
are we going?" "Where do we want to go?" The board of directors
also took a role in answering these questions.

The choice to live in a poor neighbourhood also posed questions.
What was our role in the neighbourhood? Was it not our responsibility to contribute to the development of our neighbourhoods
through the example of our way of eating, the care of our home
and our standard of hygiene? But at the same time, how were we
to maintain this principle of solidarity with those around us? We
were concerned to maintain a way of life which was familiar to
those we welcomed.

Our board was also concerned that our work be joined to that
of other associations and Haitian groups dedicated to special education. At the level of life within the community, our board often
reminded us of the necessity to unify the spiritual life and certain
professional demands implicit in our life together. Although the
board members did not live in the intensity of the daily routine of
the community, they remained responsible for its fidelity to the
essentials of our shared life and its integration into the wider
society.

Scene from Kay Jan Batis (St John the Baptist Home), Port-au-Prince, Haiti

Growth

Since 1975, the community has grown around the emerging needs of those we welcomed. The school, the workshop, a second and then a third home were founded as we came to feel Marie, Roland, Matthew and Adeline's need for them. It was their cry that called forth our commitment and the commitment of others. But if at the beginning there was only the cry of Marie, Matthew and Roland, it sometimes still seems to me, after several years, that we are continually called to new projects. Today, there are three homes located in different parts of Carrefour. They welcome fifteen people who are handicapped. There is a small school with two classes; one for the five children who are profoundly handicapped, and the other for eight children who are much less handicapped and who can attain a basic level of education. There is a workshop as well for the adults – there are six adults from the neighbourhood who are handicapped in addition to those from our homes – working on subcontracts from a neighbouring factory. Altogether, fifteen assistants, of whom three are foreigners, direct these projects. A community has taken shape. With the arrival and departure of assistants and the welcome of new people in the home or workshop, one must continually renew the community spirit and work towards unity. But we are only at the beginning of this in terms of our community life. We feel deeply that we are in the process of learning. We simply see a little bit better the form that growth in community may take, and many of the questions we need to explore together. How are we to assure a proper formation for those who come to help in the homes or the workshop? How are we to become a support to the many families around us who have a handicapped member? We are also learning how to be open to those in the neighbourhood, and yet to keep a few privileged times to ourselves such as meetings and fiestas exclusively for the members of the homes and workshops and their families. This is necessary so that each person can come to a better sense of belonging, knowing the limits of the Arche family, and how to situate themselves within it.

Confronted with people in times of crisis and faced by the

tensions that can suddenly appear in the home, we feel that our competence is still rather limited. Our community, as well, still needs to become much more "Haitian". In Haiti, there is such a wealth of welcome, of spirituality, of music and dance. There is a disposition toward communal life that we still have no idea how to integrate. And we continue to have friends in the hospitals and the asylum whom we visit, or who are with their families. They wait. For the time being we are not able to help them. All of these questions show us our limits, while calling us to a greater hope.

15

INTEGRATED INTO A VILLAGE

Nadine Tokar

Nadine Tokar, from Paris, was trained as a speech therapist. While working with a voluntary organization for mentally handicapped people she first met l'Arche. In 1972 she finished her studies and came to live at l'Arche, taking responsibility for a new home in the town of Compiègne. After four years with l'Arche, Trosly, and after a trip to Haiti and Brazil with Jean Vanier and Robert Larouche, she sensed a new call to create a community in Honduras.

She spent her first year in Honduras living with Doña Maria and her family in Nueva Suyapa, a poor area of Tegucigalpa, the capital, learning the language and customs of the people. In 1977, with the help of the local board of directors, and the loan of a former church school, Casa Nazaret was opened. The community now has eleven members and Nadine is the community leader.

L'Arche in Honduras had a providential beginning. During a flight back from Brazil, at a time when I could not have even located the place on the map, I mentioned to Jean Vanier that if ever I would want to live in Latin America, it would be in Honduras. I do not know to this day why I said that. But God knows, and he must have been listening! A few months later Jean was asked to give a retreat in Honduras. And that is how Providence works, I think: tipping us the wink. And so, in November 1975, I came to the district of Suyapa where the Virgin Patroness of Honduras has her Basilica, to which crowds of pilgrims pour each Sunday from every corner of the land.

Suyapa is a poor quarter of the capital, Tegucigalpa. All the efforts made by the tourist office to conceal the fact, by dressing up the façades on the Square, could not change it. Suyapa is more like a village than a city area, with its improvised grocer's shops set up in private houses, its overcrowded school, its fifteen *estancos* or taverns selling *aguardiante*, the national liquor; its tiny market where women sell fruit and holy pictures and *tacos* which they prepare on little stoves set up along the pavement; its children playing football all day long in the square. On the mountain, the other side of the river, is Nueva Suyapa, even poorer and more neglected than Suyapa itself.

The district's history began in the wake of hurricane "Fifi", one of the greatest natural disasters to have struck Honduras. In those days, large numbers of poor people who had seen their homes, their possessions, and in some cases their families swept away by the flood, came in from every part of the country towards the capital, in search of a better life. They occupied the area behind Suyapa and began to make shelters for themselves, some with planks or cardboard, others with branches and newspapers. As time passed, they improved these shelters to make them a bit more like home. Many of the derelict outer districts of Suyapa started off in this way. And now, five years later, though there is hardly any water supply or electricity and no tarred roads or means of transport, nearly five thousand families have settled here.

It was in Nueva Suyapa that quite by chance I first met Doña Maria, Don Umberto and their five children. When I came back to Honduras, with the idea of spending several months sharing the life of a Honduras household to learn their language and customs, their beliefs and intimate daily life, it was Doña Maria and her family who welcomed me into their home, with the simple generosity of the truly poor. I spent nearly a year with them, learning the essentials and discovering the true needs of man. I came to realize how little a man needs in order to live and be happy. As I learnt the true value of water and food, a new feeling was born in me: the fear of waste. Here everything is precious; nothing is wasted. One eats because one is hungry, the same invariable diet. Each day it is rice, beans and tortillas. Yet every plateful is the fruit of such an effort that it tastes better than any meal in a restaurant. I have come to see that to struggle for life is the very opposite of a settled life, living for oneself, living without commitment. Often the poor are without even the essentials, but there is always someone who has less. So you share, because tomorrow that someone might be you. And even though violence is an aspect of their lives which cannot be denied, this sharing which is the gift of self, brings them true life. When I consider all the forms of aid which are directed towards the countries of the Third World, this sharing between one poor person and another seems to me almost the only form of giving which respects the person of the receiver.

Doña Toncha, mother of Ephraim and neighbour to Doña Maria, spent her days quarrelling with her neighbours and had many enemies in the district. But when she fell ill, those same women with whom she fought continually, carried her by night many miles to the hospital. The same women saw to it that her five children were fed during her absence, got hold of a truck to bring her back from the hospital and watched beside her day and night until she died. I saw young people bringing her their mattresses because she was lying on cardboard. After her death, these mattresses were burnt, for reasons of hygiene or superstition, and to this day those young people are still sleeping on planks. Doña Toncha's son, an alcoholic for years, didn't realize until a week later that his mother was dead. Her other children were taken in by one or other of the neighbours and given an equal footing with their own children.

It was during those months at Nueva Suyapa that I came to know Doña Eugenia and her severely handicapped daughter of eighteen, Lita. When we first met Lita, she seemed to be shut off in her own world. She sat naked all day on the mud floor of their hut. I also met Doña Maria who was constantly looking for José, her sixteen-year-old son who was epileptic and a vagabond. Then I met Norma, who is paralysed and spends the whole day shut up alone in a little shed. Her mother leaves by the first morning bus and comes home about eight o'clock at night, just in time for dinner. And then Julia, who is twenty-eight, who lives off almsgiving and sleeps with the dogs, and Miguel who is bedridden and has to be carried down on Sunday mornings to the church square, and back up in the evening, his saucer full of pennies. Nine months went by and I longed to find a house right there in Nueva Suyapa and to start a little Arche.

Living Like Everybody Else

It didn't take long. Finding no house for us, the parish priest of Suyapa let us have an old disused school. Régine had come out from France and our adventure began. The other day when our neighbour, Consuelo, was retailing the latest local gossip, I jokingly said: "Strange that there hasn't yet been any gossip about us." Her reply came at once: "My dear, everyone can see you are not living in luxury, you don't have anything they haven't got. If it weren't so, they would have called you prostitutes long ago and invented lovers for you on every street corner." Turning her remark over in my mind, I began to recall our very first days in Suyapa, when Régine and I were living alone in the house. The neighbours came and went constantly whether to borrow money, or for a little food, or for an aspirin because a child was feverish.

L'Arche, Tegucigalpa, Honduras

Such constant demands were hard to bear, and yet they were scarcely surprising. We were two foreign women and the word *gringa*, which is the popular term for a foreigner, carries with it the meaning of wealth and also knowledge. This made us realize how careful we must be about the smallest details of our way of life if we were ever to meet these people in truth.

I remember little Eligio and his four young sisters. In those early months, they spent nearly all their time with us in the house, at least when they had no work to do for their parents. We loved the way they came and went freely at any time of day, getting in our way, going about touching everything (we had no fear they might take anything because nothing in the house was strange to them anyway), even during our siesta, which would be disturbed by their voices and laughter in the same room with us, some on the bed, some playing on the floor. For they are quite without a sense of privacy in their own homes, and we never thought of sending them away with a "come back later". In fact, nothing was too much for us if only they could thereby come to lose that curiosity and fear about what goes on in a house so much larger than their own.

Later on, when we took in Lita who can neither walk nor speak and at first had little or no contact with people, it was something of a problem to have them around all the time, especially as other children had joined them. Even so, we were aware how important it was to allow them to invade us so as to satisfy their childish curiosity about someone like Lita, who must have seemed so different from themselves. That they should learn to form natural relationships with her and with each person we were to take in was far more important at that time than any "educational work" we might have started with Lita. The important thing is that we should not be seen as living a life of privilege; that we should stick as closely as possible to the reality around us, and that we should need our neighbours as much as possible, as they too may one day come to need us.

For example, one of Suyapa's problems is lack of water. There are two public taps bringing water from the river, water which is often muddy but good enough for household chores. A few houses, ours among them, have direct access to this water, thanks to a tap in the courtyard. This allows us to share with our immediate neighbours. As for drinking water, it comes only once a week and only to about ten of the more favoured households. Now some time after we had settled in, our parish priest turned up with a workman, intending to provide drinking water for us too. This we energetically refused and have never regretted doing so. For a young housewife, Carmen, had watched us from the time of our arrival and had made a point, whenever the drinking water came, of calling on us for our bottles and pails which she filled and brought back the same day. This was always a splendid opportunity for sitting down for a cup of coffee and a chat. When we called on her, the same thing happened. Then one day when she came round for our pails, I offered to fetch them back myself but she simply said: "Leave that to me. It's my way of sharing in what you're doing." And so now, although we very rarely go to Carmen's for water because we can supply our needs from another neighbour who lives nearer, we have become very close to Carmen and her family and no longer need water as an excuse for mutual visits. When our reserves run out and there is no rain, it is good to be able to walk with Teresita as far as the nearest supply point. Any pretext will serve for a little chat with people, and everyone is equal in the face of essential needs.

Our difficulty after two years of this life in Suyapa, is not to relax the vigilance we need to carry on the struggle of our early days. Our life is shot through with contradictions. For example, practically all the members of our board of directors are professional people, rich and influential. And it is just as well. Because, while they have indeed been a great help to us up to now in administrative matters, it is also true that they have the same right as anyone else to be touched by Lita, Rafael, Marica or Claudia, and by the reality of the people around us, whom they do not in the ordinary way have much occasion to meet. Our neighbours are people who live from day to day, for whom Monday's toil must pay for Tuesday's food. We, for our daily needs, get money once or twice a month from the bank. I hope this will change one day but for the present, that's how it must be. If Doña Maria, who for two years has been coming every morning to share our life should fall ill, we will send her to the doctor. We will have the necessary tests done and buy the medication she needs. But if her neighbours fall ill, they may die because they do not have the money for hospitals or medication. I myself come from France, and if occasion arises, the International Federation of l'Arche will help me to pay the fare so that I can visit my family. My neighbour hasn't been back to Toutoule, her native village which is five hours by road from the capital, in twenty-five years. She cannot pay the fare and could not leave her companion and her children to themselves. All these contradictions we have to accept, and live with and there are many others. That is our life.

What is essential, is that we should not possess absolutely all the kitchen utensils we need, so that we can now and then borrow a potato peeler or a cheese grater from Eugenia. Our larder should not be too full so that Marcia can go and buy sugar and coffee from Doña Alba every day and Claudia can be taken to Doña Chilita every day to buy *frijoles*. Now and then we should need something from Teresita – an onion, a tomato or a lemon. Not having a fully supplied medicine chest is equally important, if I have a migraine and don't need to buy aspirin from Melanaia, then she won't know I have a migraine and she won't make me tea from mountain herbs; or if Rafaelito has an upset tummy and I have all the medication we need, Rosaria won't come to tell me what she does with her own children in such a case. People here are not self-sufficient. They need one another. And that has got to be true of us also if we are not to live as if on an island in the middle of the village.

Getting to Know the Neighbours

In those early days, when Régine and I were living alone in the house, we were impatient. We couldn't wait to see the work finished on the house. We couldn't wait to get legal recognition from the government so that we could quickly take in Rafael, Claudia and others we had been visiting regularly in the hospital

Daily Life in l'Arche, Honduras

or asylum and who had been totally abandoned by their families for a long time. We were longing to start work with those families of our area who have handicapped children. But our wishes were one thing, reality was another. We had to wait. I mean we had to learn to wait, learn to live detached from clocks and calendars, learn to let go of time. We can now see what a blessing that was.

Because of the political situation, it took us over eighteen months to get government approval. Although we were depressed each time I came back empty handed from the ministry, this period of waiting led us to spend time getting to know our neighbours. For months on end we hadn't much else to do besides taking coffee with Doña Gabriella, gossiping with Ilda or playing with Priscilla's baby. No wonder Doña Maria often got cross with us when she sent us to buy salt and we didn't get back for two hours! People around here don't live in a hurry. They are not driven by watches or the pursuit of efficiency. One of the most common expressions is: "Time caught up on me; I didn't realize how late it was." What better way to lose our sense of time than with our neighbours, talking to them about our daily happenings and listening to theirs?

The truth of this came home to me the day we welcomed Claudia among us; a blind, autistic little girl whom life had wounded deeply and who at first spent the days and nights howling for everything and nothing. If our neighbours had not known us as well as they do, if they had not known Marcia in her wheelchair, and Lita with her smile and her silence, and had not been completely familiar with every detail of our daily lives, we would then have had serious problems. In fact, it was a piece of good fortune that we had to wait so long for Claudia and likewise for Rafael, for several of our neighbours shared that waiting with us. When at last the time came, it was Pedro with his old car who came with us to fetch them. Never a day passes without someone enquiring why the little girl was crying this morning or why Rafael was shouting at a passer by.

Next door to us lives Consuelo, who spends her days sitting in front of her house. Whenever she is asked the way to l'Arche, I imagine she begins interrogating the caller on the purpose of the visit, for she often tells me that there was a woman wanting to leave her child with us and she persuaded her not to. But sometimes she judges otherwise and then she herself brings the woman and introduces her to us, calling again later to see how matters stand. She will even pay another call some weeks later to inquire how things have turned out. We could almost say that because of Consuelo we do not need a social worker!

Then there is Doña Lola, who listens to Marcia's complaints when the house gets too much for her, reasons with her, and then tells us the story with a sly look. There is Sonia who won the lottery on Régine's birthday and brought her a cake. When Doña Maria is ill, Consuelo cooks for her own family and ours too. When several houses, including part of ours, were destroyed by fire, we were evacuated by our neighbours in a twinkling, each taking in some part of our furniture, bedding and linen, and housing all of us into the bargain. This is one more example of an event, unwelcome enough in itself, which drew us all closer together.

It eases my conscience to know that when I spend a long time at Letici's, while on my way to buy tortillas, aware all the time that Rafael is alone among his toys, it will be to his advantage in the end. For I can tell others about his pranks or his progress or his health problems. Surely he has everything to gain from being known as he grows up just like any other kid in Suyapa, since he can't get out whenever he likes to play with others, because he cannot walk and is still completely dependent on us.

It has been important too to waste time with Lita's mother. She had never really accepted her daughter because of the gravity of her handicap. We welcomed Lita but on the precise condition that her mother would have her back every weekend. It has been quite something to watch her mother gradually discover the person and the beauty of her daughter. She was able to do this by discovering the admiration of the neighbours as they witnessed Lita's progress in so many domains, as she began to make tortillas, to wash clothes, to sew, etc. It has been important both for us and for Lita to grow closer to Doña Eugenia.

I feel this is not the place to write about our integration in Suyapa; it is still too early and I don't have the right to use the word. I just wanted to mention our relationships with our neighbours. Even so, although those relationships make up our life and are often a source of joy and of strength to us, we are nevertheless aware that much remains to be done and that we have to cultivate those relationships with every day that comes.

16

IN SEARCH OF NEW STRUCTURES

Alain Saint-Macary

A former banker, Alain Saint-Macary, from the south of France, relates how he first came to l'Arche, Trosly in 1972. He has been living in the same home ever since, serving all the time the larger community of Trosly as well as l'Arche International by assuming various responsibilities.

In Trosly, he first took responsibility for the workshops, then for five years co-ordinated the finances. Last year he became assistant director of the community.

On the international level, in 1975 he was voted vice-co-ordinator of l'Arche International and, in July 1979, was asked to serve a second term until 1982.

In 1972, I came to live at l'Arche in Trosly-Breuil because in some way George had touched my heart and revealed something in me. George is a handicapped man who was particularly distressed at that time. Until then I was rather an intellectual person. I had been working in the cushioned world of finance, with quite a good job in a bank. However, the events of May 1968 in France opened my eyes to the dangers of the consumer society. Over those weeks of "revolution," I caught a glimpse of what a new society could be like, where communication would be re-established between all human beings; where "to live" would be more important than "to have"; where each and every one would share with others. I was convinced that if the world was going wrong, it was the fault of the structures. Thus, the most urgent task was to try to change them.

My chance meeting with l'Arche brought me, at the age of twenty-eight, to a complete reversal of my priorities. Before trying to change structures, I must change myself, drop my barriers, and learn to love those who feel they are useless; I must come and share my life with them in order to help them rediscover their dignity. I had no idea how difficult this would be. Yet my intuitions told me that the people called "handicapped" could teach me how to live, on a small scale, the dream I had for all humanity.

The debate between person and structure is as old as time, yet it is very much a problem of today. How often excellent initiatives in the realm of social services have been stifled by heavy structures; how many sound and liberal ideas have been smothered by institutionalization. On the other hand, it is also true that many communities have not survived the test of time because they neglected to pay sufficient attention to adapting and renewing their structures.

In the Arche community where I live, we now number nearly four hundred people, with more than twenty homes and several work units scattered over a district of twenty-five miles. When I arrived seven years ago, we were about half this size. Over this period we have been trying to adapt our structures to growth so that we may have the ones that best enable us to reach the goals of the community.

People in community tend to be frightened of structures, as if they were threatening and dangerous. Is it not easy for people animated by the same ideal to live together, deciding everything together? Why do we need structures? In my first days at l'Arche, I was astonished by certain reactions to structure. On the Sunday of my arrival, I settled into my new home. Danièle, I was told, was "head" of the house but she destested this title and did not want to be regarded nor treated as such. The following morning I was shown to the workshop – my place of work from then on. My role was to subcontract work from local businesses, to organize and distribute it among the various workshops. I remember approaching the workshops with great apprehension, knowing no one and having no experience in this domain. Much to my surprise, I was eagerly welcomed by most of the fifty handicapped men and women with affectionate shouts of "Hi, Boss!" This rather distressed me as I wanted them to know that I had not come to be "boss" but, rather, to be like a brother, and I wanted to be accepted as such. This initial contact with the home and the workshop showed me that, although assistants might have problems with authority and structures, the handicapped people needed to know their references.

From the beginning of my time at l'Arche, I was struck by the importance given to each person; by how important it was to be attentive to each one, listening to his needs and inner self.

Danièle was very impressive in the home that first year. She knew, far more than any of us, how to encourage and to assist each one in discovering his unique gift. She was not afraid to confront difficult situations, thus enabling tensions to surface. She knew how to relax the atmosphere and animate meals so that each one felt his presence was important, that he was there for more than just food. She had a natural authority recognized by all the members of the home. Yet her refusal to be "head" of the house stood firm. Despite the fact that we had several house meetings about this with the leader of the whole community, no one said to her: "Stop wasting our time with your soul-searching; it is obvious that you must accept the position of "head" of the house."

The fruit of all these meetings was that our house would not have a leader but that each member of the team would take responsibility as co-ordinator for a three-month period. We elected the first co-ordinator and, of course, we elected Danièle, who accepted the position.

From the viewpoint of efficient structures, this process could appear to be a waste of time and energy. I remember my own feelings of anger boiling up inside. But for Danièle it was essential that we take the time to listen to her in order to help her realize that, even if she had personal difficulties with the idea of authority, probably as a result of earlier bad experiences, she had the confidence of us all. Therefore she was the natural reference for the home and she exercised her authority with great honesty, not wanting power but rather wanting to serve.

Responsibility for One Another

Over the years I have discovered how difficult it is to exercise authority without either dominating too much or, by being fearful and refusing to act, evading responsibility. Once, when I was responsible for the finances of the community, I came to the conclusion that our transport problems would be resolved if we purchased a sixty-seater bus. So I met the representatives of a bus firm, bought the bus and announced it to the Community Council. But the Council put me firmly in my place! Without a doubt I had taken too much power upon myself. It was evident that such an important decision, involving such expenditures, belonged to the Council and not just to me! Other times, when faced with difficult situations, especially when there was a lack of full agreement, I evaded my responsibilities, either because I wanted to please everyone or because I was afraid of making a mistake.

In the parable of the Good Shepherd, and again when He himself washed His disciples feet, Jesus teaches us how to exercise authority. True authority implies a vulnerability which is not easy to accept. When you live in community, you cannot hide behind authority or function. You exercise your authority with the same people you live and share your meals with, those whom you need also as brothers and sisters. In the big Paris bank where I worked, our directors were very distant people who hid themselves at the end of long, forbidding corridors. They gave the impression that greater authority was always linked to distance and mystery. At l'Arche, on the contrary, I have learned that I can exercise authority to the extent that I am not afraid to show my weaknesses to those around me. Authority is grounded in trust.

I am also beginning to understand that by listening closely to the needs of the weakest members in the community we learn how to exercise authority. People who are wounded in their intellect or their psyche need not only those who can help them accomplish the ordinary tasks of life and work; they also cry out for an authority that is a mother or father figure, one who understands, reassures, comforts and loves them. They need someone who calls them out of themselves to grow, to progress, to better the broken image they have of themselves and to see their value. This second type of reference is much more vital. It cannot be learned through a recipe nor in schools that give out diplomas which are supposed to grant a certain power. It is called forth from the very source of our being.

The people we welcome at l'Arche are often in a state of confusion. They lack personal and inner structure. To help them restore order inside themselves they need clear and precise references. They need to know *whom* they can ask for *what*, in the home as well as at work. This is particularly so when handicapped people go through a difficult time, when they are in a state of regression and confusion. They then become dissociated and tend to spread their inner confusion outside themselves. In order to help them come out of this, their references must be very clear, and each reference must remain within the boundaries of their authority. The head of the workshop must not intervene in the decisions of the home; the head of the home must not try to take up the role of the psychiatrist. And these different references for the distressed person must learn to work together in harmony. Frequently I noticed that when someone in the home was in special difficulty, he could become a factor of unity for the home. On the other hand, I have also seen that, when there was a lack of unity in the team of assistants, it was the most fragile person in the home who suffered. It is precisely because we are all fragile and capable of egoism, of falling into individualistic ways, that we need structures.

Meetings

In the day-to-day life at l'Arche, just as everywhere else, we soon realize that often when we are feeling lonely and need to talk or share, others are not necessarily available. Little by little we discover all the barriers and stumbling blocks which hinder us from going further in a relationship. If we really want to form community, a good lifestyle where all are relaxed, happy and attentive to others, is not enough. We have to create the time and space for people to "meet". We cannot wait until the occasion spontaneously creates itself.

I remember during that first year in our home we did not have regular weekly meetings with all the members. Thus, when some-one had a bone of contention or a question, he or she would voice it at any time and in front of anyone. Depending on the person and the moment, he or she could get any number of answers. A weekly meeting was established five years ago. It has grown in importance, becoming the place of decision-making in our life together. It is not always easy to live these meetings, for tensions can surface. And it is not always easy to express our gripes and expose our problems in front of everyone at a structured meeting. It is so much easier to do it in another way. Then too, when decisions are made, we are never sure whether our point of view will be sustained or not; we have to take into consideration the opinion of the majority. This weekly meeting has become a basis for our growth together as a community.

In Trosly, a similar meeting takes place every week in each home and place of work. Thus, each member of the community has the opportunity to express himself in his immediate group or groups. However, beyond each home and workshop we belong to a wider entity; the larger community. It is the same for every person on earth: each one has several spheres of belonging; his home, his village or neighbourhood, his region, his country, the world. If we are all called to open our hearts more and more to a universal love, it just is not physically possible to have the same type of relationship with everyone. We must begin by relating to those closest to us. It is very clear here at Trosly that when each small unit – home or workshop – is more loving, the larger com-munity is more alive and united. On the international level of l'Arche it is the same; the communities most open to others are those who, from within, live a rich and profound quality of rela-tionship. Our aspirations towards universal love should not be a flight from immediate relationships. This is why the structures of our larger community aim, first of all, at creating support and unity, starting from small cells which are fully alive and enjoying a large degree of autonomy. Each sphere of belonging corresponds to a type of encounter. There are not only meetings in each home but also between the houses of the same village and meetings of the whole community. We have meetings in the workshops, as well as between the various work sectors (garden, workshop, maintenance, etc.) and a general meeting of all those involved in the work of the community.

In order to develop a sense of belonging it is good, from time to time, to be gathered all together in the same place. For this reason, once a month, at Trosly, the whole community crowds into an old renovated barn. But as we become more numerous these gatherings can only be times for celebration or passing on information. Thus we have had to develop a system of representatives who meet together to participate in decision-making or to share the responsibilities of the larger community. Each home elects its own representatives who meet, as do also the representatives of each sector of work. One of the things that has impressed me most, since I have been made head of the work section, is this monthly meeting of representatives. The handicapped men and women have made me re-discover the concept of representation and delegation, so worn out in our Western democracy. Very limited on the verbal level, often neither able to read nor write, they cannot depend on their own resources; all their attention and energy is centred on being true spokesmen for the sector they represent. Rarely have I seen among more gifted people such transparency, such conscientiousness as I have seen here.

These structures of delegation have been recently introduced into our community. They will have to evolve towards a greater sharing of responsibilities as the members of the community grow in maturity. More and more I am aware of the rather subtle relationship in our community between personal growth and the evolution of structures. As people become more rooted and committed, they learn more how to respect and to listen to others, and it becomes more possible to share responsibilities. The reverse is also true: the more structures are collegial, the more they become a place of growth towards greater responsibility and deeper commitment.

Alain Saint-Macary and Jean Vanier

Structures

That is why, from the very beginning of the community, the structures have been evolving, adapting to the ever-changing reality. At Trosly, when l'Arche was founded in 1964 by Jean Vanier, there was only one house and decisions were made around the dinner table. Progressively, we have come to our complex structures of today.

There were several steps in this evolution, some of which were quite painful. Personally I was deeply marked by the period 1974–5. Up until then the structures had evolved with the growth of the community. Jean Vanier, our leader, had formed a council of six people to share his responsibilities; this council nominated heads of workshops and houses; a core of assistants committed to l'Arche had been created, and a deputy leader nominated. But these structures remained fairly vertical and hierarchical.

Jean Vanier has a gift of awakening a sense of responsibility and drawing out creativity in others, giving them confidence in themselves; but still each one referred directly to him and found their support and, I would say, their justification and authority in him. He himself drew up the agendas and ran nearly all the meetings. So, whenever he was absent, we had to await his return to settle most of the problems. This created many very difficult situations, due to the growing size of the community and the bottleneck which was forming around its leadership. There were long queues outside the community leader's or his deputy's office. Often we would have to wait well into the night for our turn to come.

Something had to be done! It all began in July 1974, when a special meeting of the council was called to study what was going wrong with our structures. I remember how anxious the six members of the council were as we waited for this meeting. For if it is easy enough to say what is going wrong, it is much more difficult to find solutions. Besides we were going to touch on something which seemed sacred: the role of Jean Vanier. If we sometimes suffered from too much dependency on him, we also found security in him. However, a few hours before the meeting started we learned that Père Thomas – who had been with Jean Vanier at the origin of l'Arche and who played an important role in the community – had just had a cerebral haemorrhage and his life was in danger. Thus quite dramatically the whole atmosphere of the meeting was changed. Père Thomas had been, of course, a member of the council from the very beginning; it was difficult to imagine our community without his presence. So the meeting took place in a rather awe-filled and serious atmosphere: we were experiencing the fact that our founders were not immortal and that our structures could not rest on passing pillars. This new acute awareness allowed us to imagine, with audacity, a complete revision of our system of leadership.

A week later, while Père Thomas was recovering, Jean Vanier called a meeting of the permanent assistants to report on this council meeting and to announce his intention of taking a sabbatical the following year: another reason for modifying our structures. I remember how insecure we felt. Until then the unity of the community had rested essentially on the deep trust that each one had in the two founders. Now we had to move on to trust one another. This was a really important passage or "transfer" which was made but not without suffering. It took us six months, with many painful episodes, to reach a final vote for the new constitution in January of 1975. Yet, this painful delivery only gave birth to a provisional constitution, valid for one year.

From then on the council would consist of fifteen members (instead of six), elected by the core of permanent assistants whereas, before, half of the council were nominated by the community leader. This new council would nominate an "executive" comprising five people who would coordinate the overall running of the community. After a year with these structures some alterations were made, and in January 1976, we passed on to a new stage with the decentralization of the houses into geographic areas. The executive, from then on, consisted of nine people who met with Jean Vanier and his deputy. In 1977, new amendments were made to the constitution and, in January 1979, the end of the three year term, it was completely reviewed. Nevertheless, the main principles introduced in January 1975 held good.

We went through a very similar process some months later on the international level of l'Arche. Each community of l'Arche is independent and managed by a national or local board of directors which carries legal responsibility. In 1972, for the first time, there was a meeting of representatives from the five existing communities of l'Arche or those about to begin (Trosly and La Merci from France, Daybreak from Canada, Asha Niketan from India, and Little Ewell from England). From this was born the "international federation of l'Arche". These twelve people wrote the international charter of l'Arche. Eighteen months later, in the autumn of 1973, a second meeting of the federation brought together thirty-five representatives from a dozen communities. It seemed necessary, then, to create a structure which would sustain the links between all these communities. A small council was formed around Jean Vanier, the international co-ordinator, with a representative for North America, for Europe and for India. In reality, this council was never able to meet; the unity of the federation was maintained mainly through Jean Vanier's regular visits to the three continents and his personal links with each community.

In 1975 when we met in Toronto for the third international meeting of the federation – only three years after the first – there were almost one hundred delegates representing thirty existing communities. The communities of l'Arche had become more dispersed, with new foundations beginning in Haiti and Africa. We had to invent something new so that we could remain united in one big family, in spite of this rapid growth. Jean Vanier announced his decision to step down as international co-ordinator. A project for an international constitution was adopted, creating eight regions in the federation, each one coordinated by a regional co-ordinator elected for a three-year term. These eight regional co-ordinators along with the international co-ordinator, a vice-co-ordinator, and Jean Vanier, as founder, formed the international council of the federation. This council was to meet once or twice a year.

I remember we voted on this new constitution in Toronto in a climate of confusion and great uncertainty, if not scepticism. When we proceeded to the vote for regional coordinators and had to imagine an international coordinator other than Jean Vanier, the atmosphere was tense.

As I myself was named international vice-co-ordinator at this Toronto meeting, I can bear witness to how, in the council and in the regions, we have gradually discovered how to give support and help to each other and to each community to remain faithful to our calling. We were feeling our way, not really sure of where we were heading. Yet, in 1978, we saw the fruits of this growth when we had the fourth meeting of the international federation. There were two hundred and twenty-five delegates there, representing nearly fifty communities. For the first time sixty handicapped people had been sent as delegates. A new international constitution was voted in an atmosphere of peace, confirming and defining more clearly the more important ideas which had been adopted "in extremis" at Toronto.

Structure at the Service of People

These two important steps that had been taken, both in my own community and on the international level, are only a prelude to many other steps. In both cases the new structures corresponded to a given situation at a particular moment. But there are certain principles which governed and inspired in both cases and which are important to underline.

The first principle is that structures should evolve. Certainly we must find the subtle balance between security and change. Personally I find a greater danger in inflexibility. All change is a bit of a jump into the unknown, questioning the habits that have been taken by those in authority or in a position of dependence. I have often noticed that those who are wary of structures, as well as those who take refuge behind them, have a tendency to forget that structures are only an instrument at the service of people, and not an end in themselves. We must frequently be reminded of *why* and *how* they have been created in order that we remain conscious of their relativity.

But it is never with great joy or enthusiasm that we review our structures every three years! We must allow a lot of time so everyone can have a say. Most of us would prefer to spend time deepening the spirit that animates us, for when we share on our ideal we nourish one another; we are in the realms of inspiration and the infinite. When we discuss structures we are often disappointed; we are in a very finite limited realm where there is no absolute truth. We have to agree on a terminology which in fact is never completely suitable. We have to choose the least bad hypothesis because no structure or constitution is perfect or ideal. There is a danger of never arriving at any conclusion, because we refuse partial solutions or compromises, or because we lock ourselves up in details, forgetting the finality the structures are called to serve.

Another important principle in the structures of l'Arche, is that the mutual aid, the support, the vision and the decisions do not depend on one person but on the group. Of course, nothing replaces the support one person can give to another. But in my community, the style of the constitution we had in 1974, which

was essentially vertical, had been progressively transformed into
a constitution which was essentially horizontal. At each level of
the community, decisions are taken collectively from within the
group concerned. It is the same at the international level. We could
now define diagrammatically the structures of l'Arche, as a whole,
by a series of concentric circles between which there is constant
flow back and forth. If I took my house as the point of departure,
I could say the flow starts from the house meeting; from there the
head of the house goes to the meeting for all the heads of the
houses in our area. The co-ordinator of the area goes to the community council meeting. The community leader, (who animates
the council meeting, shares with the other leaders of our communities in France at the French regional council meeting. The
links between the circles are not necessarily hierarchical. Progressively we develop the common consciousness of a community,
then of a region, then of the extended international Arche family
– going from the particular to the general. In the same way the
vision of the whole can be reflected in the regions and the individual
communities.

What matters is what is happening in the circles. It is not enough
to have meetings for the sake of having well-structured communities. Everything depends on the quality of the meetings. Since
being at l'Arche, I have taken part in many meetings. I think that,
even if we still tend to look on them as rather irksome tasks that
have to be done, we are beginning to discover how to run them
so they become valued and valuable. The meeting is not primarily
a time for discussion, it is a place where we can share, where each
one feels responsible for nourishing the others. We do not limit
ourselves only to the obvious questions of things to be decided and
done, nor to evaluating balance of power, nor to finding a compromise on the points of contention. Each one should feel at ease, free
to express himself without any fear of showing his weakness or of
being wrong. It is a time of listening, of support, of evaluation
and of reviewing each other's authority.

When it is time to make a decision we discover more and more
that light comes forth from the group, if it is trying honestly to
discern the will of God for the community. The will of God is not

made known in sudden spectacular flashes of light, it is found through a laborious, arid process where each one listens to the other, ready to alter his opinions. I remember a certain decision that took us several days; at one moment the group was completely divided and only very gradually did it come to a consensus of opinion. When we finally reached a decision, we were not only totally convinced that it was the right one, but because of the way we had discerned together each one seemed to be filled with a new strength and enthusiasm to implement it.

The discernment process, where we try to reach a consensus of opinion, does not exclude voting. On the contrary, we even go through several tendency votes before coming to the final one. Gradually we are learning that in the voting process it is important that each one be clear on what exactly the vote is about, the definite procedures to be followed, and all this in a spirit of peace and listening. Most of the time the vote will be made by secret ballot, leaving each one more free. Before voting we specify the majority required and whether there will be one or two ballots. How we conduct the voting greatly influences our growth towards mutual trust.

The third principle is the necessity to define the mandates clearly and precisely, with exact time limits. In general, in my own community, as well as on the international level, responsibilities are entrusted for a three-year period. This is to remind us that authority is a service; that individuals should not be identified with their function and that responsibilities should not remain the prerogative of a club; "veterans" working together. We try to specify what each responsibility involves, regularly giving account to those whom we serve. Thus, the constitution becomes a precise document to which each one can refer.

Gradually, as responsibilities are effectively carried out by groups, we find the role of the community leaders evolving. Their power is diminishing and they are becoming more the coordinators in charge of animating the groups which actually make the decisions. Nevertheless, their role and maybe their authority is even more important now; growing especially in two domains: first of all, they must be very attentive to each individual person, becoming in some ways the discreet shepherd who sustains, nourishes and confirms; secondly, they must be a leaven of unity, and carriers of the vision. The more the group begins to assume responsibility the more the leader has to be vigilant in supporting and defending individual persons, particularly the weakest, or those in some way rejected. At times he must be able to bend the rules of the group so that it is more at the service of each person. In the same way the leader is the one who must carry within himself all the different components of the group. And thus by the fact that he is not engulfed in everyday tasks, and can keep his head above the flow of life, he is the one who must formulate and maintain the vision. I realize that this evolution in the exercise of authority is not so easy when one is a leader. It can be a very painful process for founders of communities. In the beginning they assume all the responsibilities, then gradually they see them diminish until they completely let go so that the community can truly carry responsibility themselves. Some founders of Arche communities have already had to live this "death to themselves."

In my community, I feel a great step has been taken in the past few years in the sharing of responsibilities. But there still is too wide a gap between the council and the grass roots, between the sixty who carry responsibility and all the others. The handicapped people are being progressively involved in the responsibilities of the larger community, thanks to the delegates' meetings, yet they do not have a sufficient place in the structures as a whole.

We still have a long way to go to find structures that are truly for community living. In my seven years at l'Arche I have learned that it is better to have imperfect structures that are adapted to reality than to try to apply the perfect plans which are only in our heads. We must strive to remain free, always eager to perfect and adapt structures for they are indispensable instruments of growth in the community. Our search has only begun.

17

GOOD IDEAS AND BAD INSTITUTIONS

Ann Shearer

Ann Shearer is a journalist in London, writing for the Guardian and other newspapers and journals about health and social services. She also works with voluntary organizations, including CMH (Campaign for Mentally Handicapped People) of which she is a founding member.

In the year 1973–4, Ann lived in one of the homes of l'Arche, in Trosly, working in the mosaic workshop. She was secretary to the International Council of l'Arche for four years and is now a member of the Arche UK central committee.

In 1847, a school for mentally handicapped children opened in England, one of the first of its kind. "We have laboured," said its prospectus, "under the appalling conviction that idiocy is without remedy and therefore we have left it without help. It may now be pronounced, not as an opinion, but as a fact, a delightful fact, that *the idiot may be educated.*"

The school thrived; it attracted royal patronage and public support. It grew; it moved to the country. And there its successor sits today, a mental handicap institution with problems that would be recognized not just in Britain but all over the Western world.

What happens to "good" ideas? How is it that, sooner or later, they seem to lead to what we recognize as "bad" institutions, limiting and dehumanizing rather than being creative for those who live and work in them, their early aspirations for the cure of souls, of minds or of bodies turned to custodial weariness? The question is one for religious communities, struggling to get back to the inspiration of their beginnings. It is a question for the caring establishments which have often become places of deprivation rather than opportunity. It is a question for every venture which has set out with its own good idea but may end up plodding through its daily routine, bringing anything but life to those trapped in it, whether they are carers or cared-for.

The first easy answer would be to say that there was something wrong with the good idea of others; that the institution with which we are concerned has somehow captured a truth which has evaded those with longer traditions. But even a glance at places which have set out in the past shows not how different their aspirations have been, but how similar. The penitentiaries, asylums for people with mental illnesses, almshouses for the poor and orphanages which sprang up in the United States in the early nineteenth century (as David Rothman's fascinating study, *The Discovery of the Asylum*, shows) were designed as anything but the dumping grounds, the punitive controllers of the untidy, that they so often became. The good idea behind them was to rescue unhappy and defenceless people from what seemed a chaotic and cruel society. Their own microcosmic society would, by eliminating the bad features of the one outside, "cure" the delinquent, the insane, the poor. It would also serve as a model for that larger society, which had created their problems in the first place, and so act as a general force for social reform.[1] These aspirations may seem naive now; the components of the new model society may be unacceptable. But the good idea, after all, was not so far from l'Arche's own aspiration to create communities which not only encourage the growth of individuals but act as a "yeast in the dough" of that wider, less than caring society, which it wants to see transformed.

The second easy answer would be to blame the people who run these places. "Bad staff means bad institutions" is a glib and misleading equation, but it still underlies a great deal of the criticism that these places come in for today. Certainly there is evidence enough of the problems faced by any institution which has relied for too long and too heavily on the charisma of its founder, once that leader disappears. Certainly too, there is too much evidence of bad management, and dispirited, time-serving and even sometimes sadistic staff in many institutions. But these are symptoms

[1]Rothman, D. *The Discovery of the Asylum*, Little, Brown, Boston, 1971.

of a decline which has already set in, and not its cause. We can be sure that very few of these places started with the deliberate intent of staffing themselves with people who had no commitment to the good idea behind them; the reverse is true. No institution is exempt, either, from the fact that most human beings have their share of weakness, nastiness, inertia, and despair, just as they do of strength, understanding, empathy and hope. An institution which counted on defending its good idea through recruiting paragons of all the virtues, which waited for charismatic leaders to emerge to replace the one it had lost, would be on shaky foundations.

So how is it that good ideas end up as bad institutions? External constraints may play some part in the process. Whatever the ideal of the founders, the society which in the end has to accept and support its expression, if that expression is to survive, may have different notions. What looks like "welcoming" people from the receiving end may look like simply tidying them away to a society whose underlying, if not crudely stated, concern is that it should no longer have to bother with its untidy members. The institution depends on social approval, funds and recognition if it is to continue. The price of that approval and support may be that the members of the institution lead their lives quietly and without too many reminders that they are there. At the same time, the society will want the assurance that the tidying up operation which it is supporting is effectively done. So a variety of legal and administrative constraints may be imposed; these have grown as support has increasingly become a matter for the state rather than charitable individuals. So conditions and hours of service may be agreed in negotiations with unions; so standards of staff training may be demanded; so fire precautions and safety standards may have to be met. Restrictions may be more subtle than this. People who live and work in residential homes for people with physical disabilities, which rely heavily on charitable donations, often say that they feel obliged to lead a more old-fashioned, "moral" life than is usual in the society around them; the people who give them money want to know that it is being spent in upholding "proper" values – even if they themselves may have discarded these.

These external demands cannot be ignored. None of us likes to be told we are doing a bad job; all of us need approval, especially if our institution depends on it, whether directly through government support or indirectly through the good will of neighbours. Their demands may serve a good purpose. Any institution which is entrusted with the care of vulnerable people, however good its good idea, needs an external check on the way it goes about its business. Hermits can lead the life they choose; caring establishments, which operate as part of a wider network of such places, cannot. At the same time, of course, the demands may seem to run across the good idea by subtly – or not so subtly – changing the way it is expressed in daily life. They can even influence relationships within the institution: an insistence on rigid shift systems, for instance, will affect the degree of mutual support that individual carers and cared-for can offer each other.

But it would be too easy, again, to blame the decline of the good idea on external constraints. Just as it is possible – as thousands of people prove daily – to work a shift with care, concern, empathy, humour and a sense of relationship, so it is possible to work many hours of unpaid overtime with hatred in your heart. The essence of both the good idea and the bad institution is in the quality of relationship between those who care and those who are cared for. And whether that relationship is healthy or destructive is determined by the expectations that are brought to it.

Any good idea must inevitably carry its own expectations; the better the idea seems, the higher they are likely to be. "The idiot can be educated," proclaimed the prospectus for the school for mentally handicapped children. The delinquent can be reformed, the insane brought back to sanity, the poor to industry, declared those nineteenth century American reformers. The handicapped person is a complete human being, capable of great love, says the charter of l'Arche. And in the very faith and optimism of those claims is the seed of disappointment which can grow to strangle the good idea.

When "the idiots" learned, perhaps, to dress and wash themselves, to eat unaided, even to say a few words, but not to lead independent lives; when the incidence of crime didn't significantly

A moment of prayer during an international meeting of l'Arche

decrease; when stress and misery continued to take their toll of individuals; when poverty continued, what happened was this: the institutions, sometimes dramatically, more often gradually, gave up on the good idea. The carefully worked-out regimes, the programmes of education, seemed pointless. Society outside shared the disappointment; it felt cheated of the promised return on its investment of financial and moral support. But one thing had to be admitted: those institutions certainly had kept some untidy people out of the way, and that was useful. Without extravagant claims for "cure," they could do it for more people and do it more cheaply. And so the stage was set for the proliferation of the physically and emotionally deprived warehouses for human beings that now typify everything we understand by the bad institution.

If the disappointment had its effect on the development of institutions, it also had its effect on the relationship between the carers and those who had let them down, fallen short of their expectations, made them feel failures – the people on the receiving end of their care. There are many possible reactions to this sort of betrayal. One of them is for the carers to put as much distance as possible between themselves and the betrayers. The other is to identify with them against a world which seems unsympathetic and underlines the failure by withdrawing its enthusiasm and perhaps even its support. Both these reactions have made their contribution to the decline of the good idea and the creation of the bad institution.

The most dramatic example of the first reaction in the history of those who are mentally handicapped is a denial that the people cared-for are human at all. It is still not uncommon to hear staff in institutions speak of their most handicapped charges as "animals" or "vegetables." It is even more common to hear assertions that "they like to be with their own kind" – as if they were, somehow, not part of humankind at all. Other, less dramatic, perceptions of "differentness" serve the purpose of distancing the people on the receiving end of care from the carers. They are seen as "sick," so are excused from the ordinary demands of life; thus they are clearly distinguished from the "healthy" who look after them. They are seen as a menace, a threat both to physical safety and to the future health of the nation if they are allowed to breed; those who look after them, far from being a menace, are contributing to national security. In these perceptions, the flaw is predominantly that of the people who betrayed the carers by failing to live up to expectations.

When the carers identify with their "betrayers," the fault is seen as that of the society which has rejected both groups. The betrayers may be seen as "eternal children," not responsible for the hurt and anger they have caused and in need of the special understanding and protection that the institution and its staff can give them. They may become "burdens of charity," who may deserve little by way of luxury or even comfort, but who enable those who devote their lives to them to score celestial points. They may be seen as "holy innocents," especially chosen of God, again unable to carry responsibility for the hurt they have caused, understood only by the initiates.

Wolfensberger has shown how these perceptions of mentally handicapped people have both led to and perpetuated many of the characteristics of the bad institution which we recognize today – the disregard for privacy, the often appalling physical conditions, the clinical wards and obsession with physical health, the high walls and lack of freedom on the one hand, the preoccupation with safety, the over-protection, the lack of normal opportunity on the other.[2] But it is their effect on relationships between carers and cared-for, and on the relationship of both with the wider society that is even more fundamental to the transition of good idea to bad institution.

Whatever the predominant perception – and all of them can be held, in varying degrees, in any institution – there will be a tendency for that institution to close its doors to the society which accused it of failure. When the fault is seen to be society's, that tendency will be all the stronger. The sense of mission, the confidence in the originality of the good idea which the institution needed to get started, will be used against that society; no one else will understand in quite the way these carers do. The jargon, which perhaps served its purpose to weld them together when the idea was new, will be used as a weapon to ensure that no one else even gets a chance of understanding what they are up to now; the carers will disdain to explain themselves in society's usual language, or even sometimes to accept it. They will feel no obligation to explain, let alone justify themselves, even though the original good idea may have included a sense of mission to the wider world; they will make no compromise, saying flatly that outsiders cannot understand them unless they "share their life". They will develop their own culture, in which bizarre behaviour among the cared-for is tolerated, even applauded, as evidence that they, the carers, have "special" reserves of understanding and faith.

This tendency to shut out society is dangerous. A closed institution which operates by its own rules, to its own standards, unchallenged by normal social patterns, is likely to become a bad institution. The skewed perceptions of the cared-for, adopted by the carers as their first defence against the failure of their good·

[2]Wolfensberger, W. *The Origins and Nature of Institutions*, Syracuse University, New York, 1974.

idea, will be able to flourish. And flourish they will, because the
carers will find they need them. So the institution will get worse.

The main purpose of these perceptions – clearly in the case of
the first three, more subtly in the case of the others – is to make
it plain that there is an unbridgeable gulf between the carers and
the cared-for, and to give the carers a sense that, even if their good
idea has failed, they still have a purpose. To identify the people
they care for as inhuman somehow makes them more than human
– "what wonderful people they must be to do such a job". To
identify the cared for as dangerous gives the carers points for
contributing to the security of society. To identify them as sick is
both to confirm the health of the carers and to give them an
identifiable role in keeping society free from possible contamina-
tion. If they are eternal children, objects of pity, then the carers
are the adults with compassion. If they are objects of charity, then
the carers must be charitable. If they are Holy Innocents, then the
carers have access to a mystery.

The carers may think they have built themselves a role which
gets them over their sense of disappointment and failure. But what
happens to the people they care for? They are confirmed as powerless, as those who receive from the carers when and how the
carers choose; they will not again get the chance to betray expectations and disappoint. They will be locked into the prevailing
perception of their nature, however far from their individual reality
this may be.

The expectations the carers hold of them will be as unrealistically
low as the ones which led to the initial disappointment were unrealistically high. And as we know, they will be caught in a self-
fulfilling prophecy: they will act disturbed or sick; they will develop bizarre behaviours; they will remain childish and unable to
choose the pattern of their own lives.

And the carers will need to make sure that they do, because their
sense of usefulness depends on it, just as surely as it used to depend
on the good idea. It is not uncommon in homes for people with
physical disabilities, for instance, for the different aids to independence to be gathering dust in cupboards; for electric wheel-
chairs, which may make the difference between total dependence

and an independence of sorts, to be ruled out as "unsuitable" for these patients. The staff, it seems, cannot bear the thought that their patients might become independent of them to any degree: what would that mean for their own role?[3] It is not uncommon, either, for carers in other settings to reject out of hand the techniques of behaviour modification; where would it leave them if these actually achieved what was claimed for them?

The effect on the cared-for is obvious, and we have a whole history of bad institutions which bring stagnation rather than growth to those who must live in them. The effect on the carers may be less obvious; after all, they have got themselves the assurance that they are doing a necessary job. But they are no more categorically exceptional, brave, healthy, compassionate, good or spiritual than those they care for are categorically dangerous, sick, childlike or innocent. In locking their clients into a role, they have done no less for themselves. When the institution has come to rely on relationships which are as unrealistic as this, there must be some escape. And the escape is characteristically one which bad institutions the world over would recognize: into routine and chores. The deputy director of St Christopher's Hospice for the dying in England knows it. He says that when staff are sitting on patients' beds when he does his round, he knows morale is high; when they are busying themselves in the office with routine administration, he knows that it is low. At the limit, the carers end up like the young nurse in a ward for severely handicapped children, who said: "If the children weren't here, it would be OK, but we can't do our work when they're around." They end up like her colleague who said: "All students start off with ideals and want to help the children walk and play, but they have to roll up their sleeves in the end and realize that they cannot waste time playing with the kids."[4] It is when the relationship between carers and those they care for has become a waste of time, and the need to keep the place going has become paramount, that the bad institution is in charge.

If there were easy answers, good ideas would flourish and bad institutions would never exist. But if unrealistic expectations are

[3]Miller E. and Gwynne, G. *A Life Apart*, Tavistock, Publications, 1972.
[4]Oswin, M. *Children Living in Long-Stay Hospitals*, Heineman 1978.

at the heart of the transformation of one to the other, maybe the task of people who want to remain true to their good idea is to find realistic ones. They need to set some realistic expectations, first of all, for themselves: to recognize that their work is hard, that it necessarily brings a great deal of stress, and they are no more "special" in their ability to cope with this than the countless others who have fought to preserve their own good idea in the past. They need to look to outside help rather than relying solely on their own resources, in the recognition that the self-sufficient institution, however good its idea, will bring a kind of death to all who belong to it. They need to be realistic too, about those on the receiving end of their concern, seeing them for what they are – people with their share of strengths and problems, stereotypes neither of beauty nor ugliness. They need to help these people find their own realistic expectations – of themselves and of the carers – so that the relationships between them can be true and not distorted by disappointments.

They may even, between them, need to draw up a few goals, which leave out the big words of the good idea, which pin it down to the everyday; to talk not of unity, but of how the house meetings are to be established; to talk not of sharing but of who needs to learn what to ensure that every member of the institution takes his or her part in preparing the food; to talk not of growth but of what skills individuals lack and want to learn. Mundane matters, perhaps, but they could be the translation of that good idea into practice.

> Go, go, go, said the bird: human kind
> Cannot bear very much reality.
> Time past and time future
> What might have been and what has been
> Point to one end, which is always present.[5]

There is the challenge – to l'Arche and to any institution which ever started with a good idea and is working to find its expression.

---

[5]Eliot, T. S., 'Burnt Norton' from *Four Quartets*, Faber and Faber 1943.

CONCLUSION

Jean Vanier

I am becoming more and more aware of the vast divisions in our world and of the prejudices and hatred which cultivate them. Groups tend to look down upon one another, feeling that they are the best, the wisest and the strongest. In every continent and country there are oppressed and minority groups: the Aborigines in Australia, the tinkers in Ireland, the untouchables in India, immigrants in England, Puerto Ricans in the States, and so on. It seems that every group, in order to feel it exists, must relate to another group that it considers inferior.

The same is true of each person. Very quickly each one wants to prove that he or she is right and the other wrong. A whole system of competition and success, so deeply ingrained in western civilization, is based on the need to prove that "I am better than you."

But alas, if one person or group has the elation of victory, the other has the depression of defeat. For every one that wins a prize there are many losers. And this brings much depression, for the losers are left with the feeling of inferiority.

So it is that our world becomes quickly divided into those who have power and success and those who feel broken. Some have too much, others very little. Those who have, quickly condemn those who have little; these in turn are left with a broken self-image; they tend to condemn themselves.

One of the serious needs in our world today is to learn to walk with our aggression. So often instead of dealing with our negative feelings directly we direct them towards others who are innocent.

There is the story of misplaced aggression. The director of a factory yells unjustly at a worker. The latter cannot respond di-

rectly so, when he gets home, his pent-up frustrations are un-
leashed against his wife who in turn yells at her daughter. The
daughter then kicks the dog who chases the cat. And the story
ends with the death of the mouse!

This seemingly funny story is alas the story of much that happens in groups and among people. How quickly we need to find
someone weaker than ourselves upon whom we can put our negative feelings without endangering ourselves.

Differences among people very quickly become threatening. The
white reject the black, the healthy reject the handicapped, the rich
reject the poor, and vice versa. What is the source of all this hatred
and division, prejudice and fear?

Our modern world has fantastic power and knowledge. Man
has conquered the moon, delved into the secret of matter and
discovered immense energies. Yes, we have amazing knowledge.
But the only real knowledge necessary for the survival of the
human race is lacking: the knowledge of how to transform violence
and hatred into tenderness and forgiveness; how to stop the chain
of aggression against the weak; how to see differences as a value
rather than as a threat; how to stop people from envying those
who have more, and incite them to share with those who have
less. The real question of today is disarmament, not only on the
international scale but in terms of our own personal aggression. Is
it possible for men and women to break down the barriers of
prejudice and fear that separates groups and races and to create one
people? Are we condemned to war or is peace possible?

Obviously l'Arche is concerned by this question for in many
ways mentally handicapped people are the mice of the above story.
They cannot defend themselves; they have no voice; they are not
allowed to express themselves. They are rejected and put aside,
laughed at and considered "mad". They disturb the so-called "normal people", for they do not abide by norms. Can it be that the
broken and neglected of our societies can become a source of peace
and unity if people turn towards them as brothers and sisters, to
welcome and serve them and to discover the gift that is theirs?

The Suffering of Handicapped People

All over the world I find appalling institutions where handicapped people are confined. Parents sometimes are intolerant of their handicapped children or else are overly protective. They have been hurt in their family pride; their child appears a disappointment to them. In some cases they feel dishonoured and shamed. People in the neighbourhood have pointed their fingers at them; their children have been mocked; doctors have told them that there is nothing that can be done, that their child should be "put away" in an institution. The suffering of parents can be appalling.

But the suffering of handicapped children is also appalling. The other day a handicapped man I know phoned his mother to ask if he could go home for the weekend. "No," she said, "never; you are crazy and I wish I had never given birth to you." This mother is obviously deeply disturbed and she can appear to be an extreme case. But so many men and women I know suffer from a feeling that they are not wanted or admired by their parents. This creates a deep wound inside them. They feel worthless, no good, useless. Having no sense of their own identity, they feel confused and have a broken, diminished self-image. They have no positive dynamism. They are often angry, frustrated, and depressed. Some may be violent; some display odd and anti-social behavior; some are closed up, yearning for and yet frightened of relationship. Many live in situations where they are considered idiots. They have no right to express themselves, their ideas and desires. They are pushed aside and made to obey and to conform to the desires of others. It is not surprising that their self-image is broken and that darkness and confusion come to the surface of their consciousness.

Men and women with delinquent behaviour bear the same suffering; they carry the same confusion and lack of identity. But, because of their vitality, they tend to confront society in a more open way. They attack and destroy symbols of a culture that has hurt them. The mentally handicapped person is frequently closer to depression: silent, closed in upon himself, frightened of expressing himself. He can go around in circles, touching, knocking, crying, and laughing.

Relationship of Love

What will transform this despair and spiritual death into life and creativity; this feeling of uselessness into meaning, motivation and hope; this confusion and loneliness into light?

Each one of our Arche communities has experienced men and women, who are chaotic, broken and spiritually dead, evolving – after years in a big institution – into men and women of peace and light. These are not mere words. We have all seen the dead rise. It has happened before our eyes and in our homes. This has told us something about the depth, vulnerability and capacities of the human heart.

Man consists of head, hands and heart. He is capable of knowledge, of skills and of the relationship of love. Activity and work – particularly interesting work – bring a certain fulfilment. But this is not sufficient. He needs a friend, someone in whom he can trust; someone with whom he can have a deep relationship and share his weakness and secrets. Each human person needs to be loved, needs affection and tenderness. Without it, he hardens. But some are afraid of love and relationship. They are afraid of becoming vulnerable and of being hurt in their hearts or of being rejected. They close themselves up and protect themselves. People with handicaps, and especially severe handicaps, are particularly vulnerable, for they cannot hide their yearning for relationship behind hyper-activity. In a way, they are only heart: a wounded, open heart.

The newborn child is totally weak. Without the protective love and tenderness of the mother and father he will die. But if he is certain he is loved, he will be happy and at peace; he will rest in the security of their love. He will not fear his weakness. He will not have to prove that he is good, intelligent or powerful. He just knows that he is loved; he believes and trusts. If his trust, however, is deceived, then he will fall into the pits of sadness. If he feels abandoned, he will die spiritually. Fortunately, many children have that beautiful experience of knowing that they are unique and loved in a special way.

For the handicapped person who has felt abandoned, there is

only one reality that will bring him back to life: an authentic, tender and faithful relationship. He must discover that he is loved and important to someone. Only then will he discover that he is worthwhile; only then will his confusion turn into peace. And to love is not *to do* something *for* someone; it is *to be with* him. It is to rejoice in his presence; it is to give him confidence in the value of his being. It is to listen to him and to his needs and desires. It is to help him find confidence in himself and in his capacities to please, to do, to serve and to be useful.

This healing process can take a very long time when someone like Marie[1] has been deeply hurt, when the wounds of rejection have been violent. She will not open her heart quickly and give trust; she must test and see if it is possible. It will take many years and gestures of love before she can believe she is truly loveable.

Who Will Give Love?

Healing can come if there are healers. And who will be the healers? This is the challenge of l'Arche. It can be professionally interesting and profitable for someone to work with handicapped people as a teacher or a therapist. But who will live with them if they have no family or if they cannot get on with the family? And particularly, who will create a relationship with those who are severely handicapped and what happens if the relationship is not immediately rewarding and gratifying? Who will be prepared to accept anger, violence or depression, hoping that under all the confusion and darkness lies the light of the person? Who will believe and trust in them more than they believe and trust in themselves?

A few years ago I went to see the Mayor of Bouaké in the Ivory Coast, to ask him for land for an Arche community. He had difficulty understanding what I meant by mentally handicapped people. He only knew about "mad" people. Finally I asked him: "Do you know why we do that? It's because we are a bit mad ourselves." "Oh," he said, opening wide his eyes, "now I under-

[1] Cf. p. 204. L'Arche in Haiti.

stand!" You have to be a bit different to live with handicapped
people.

Handicapped people have difficulty living by the norms and
conventions of culture. That is why they are rejected and frequently not wanted. They disturb culture. So too, those who feel
called to live with them are sometimes rejected by culture. They
are pushed into an alternative culture and then they tend to be
considered marginal, utopian, or idealistic – and more so if that
culture, like our western one, is based on competition, success,
efficiency, power and independence.

The motivation of assistants at l'Arche is varied. Claire de Miribel has elaborated on this.[2] But there is something that unites
them all: a desire to live an alternative culture where the weak are
not rejected but are given dignity and where they can live as
people. They all want this culture to be integrated into society,
capable of influencing it, instead of being a ghetto, separated from
it.

I believe that there is necessarily a difference between the culture
of l'Arche and the culture of society. Of course, "normalization"
is important; of course we must try to help handicapped people
live "normally" in a village or a town. But because they have real
deficiencies and because for many marriage will not be possible,
they need communities which offer a real home for their hearts.
If this home is not really a place of celebration, all that is left for
them is work, leisure activities such as TV and occasionally sexuality without real, permanent relationship. A community of
l'Arche that is not a home for the heart, will be but a boarding
house where hearts become shrivelled. The more profoundly handicapped people will be seen as disturbing the routine and peace
of the community; people will have to fit into structures rather
than structures adapting to people; organization and productivity
will take priority over human growth; finances will govern instead
of being at the service of people; and authority will become hierarchical, defensive, rigid and protective, no longer a service but a
place of prestige that has been merited. Assistants will then talk

[2]Cf. p. 69. Growth Towards Covenant.

more about their rights and needs for salary, their days off and holidays, rather than of their vision and concern for the people entrusted to them.

One of the challenges of l'Arche is to provide the necessary nourishment for assistants to find meaning and growth in living with handicapped people, so that they can put their roots down in the community and create permanent and secure relationships with handicapped men and women. If a community does not provide that nourishment, then gradually assistants' hearts will become motivated by the yearnings of society's values. Doubts will creep into their spirit: "It is not possible." But how can we relinquish certain values if other values are not nourished and stimulated?

This is particularly so if assistants are called to remain unmarried. It is important for handicapped people, many of whom are not able to marry, to live and celebrate with assistants who have assumed their celibacy peacefully. It is important that they have models near them who reveal an alternative to marriage. Certainly, to have married couples in a community is excellent. They provide secure relationships. It is an immense challenge for a family to live in a home with handicapped people as do Pat and Jo Lenon.[3] But many handicapped people might not want to live with a married couple. They might tend to identify with the children and then suffer. They might choose to live with single assistants, who have expressed their choice to put their roots down in the community, and to remain single. But such a choice needs to be continually nourished, for in so many ways it is folly. And I believe that this choice can be nourished.

I do not believe assistants can accept and live with people who have real deficiencies, who manifest anger, violence and depression at times, unless they have accepted and touched their own weakness, anger, violence and depression. If assistants see themselves as strong, generous people, then they will not be able to live and rejoice with handicapped people. They will always be putting themselves on a pedestal of superiority and generosity. Only if they have touched their own vulnerability will they be able to

[3]See p. 84. A Place for a Family.

welcome the vulnerability of another. Fred Blum, a Jungian ana-
lyst, says that only the healer in contact with his own wounds can
be an agent of healing for another person. The assistant who wants
to prove something about himself will not be compassionate; he
will tend to be hard. The assistant unaware of his yearning for love
and his own vulnerability will tend to be over-protective and will
fall into the trap of dependent relationships.

In the same way, only the person who has touched and assumed
his own insecurity and weakness will be able to break the chain of
misplaced aggression of which I spoke earlier. The person who is
consciously or unconsciously fearful of his weakness and of the
power of death in him will be hard on the weakness of others. He
will cover up his insecurity in efficiency. Is it possible to accept
one's own weakness if one has not experienced the compassion of
God which many of us touch in the forgiveness of Jesus? Is it
possible to accept the fundamental insecurity of life if one has not
discovered that God is a father who loves, guides and holds each
person and in whom one can totally trust.

The most profoundly handicapped people, who cannot speak
nor walk, need essentially a presence of love – not sentimental,
protective love, but a love that is liberating, challenging and respectful; a love that understands and is compassionate and competent; a love that gives security and is commitment. Through
touch, for words may mean nothing to them, they realize they are
loved and are precious to someone. The assistant who has experienced the gratuitous gift of God for himself, in all his misery and
darkness, will be better equipped to be that instrument which
reveals to the handicapped person that he too is loved with a
gratuitous love. The assistant is thus called to be a sign, a physical
sign, of the tenderness and fidelity of the Father for the handicapped person. He is called to reveal to him that he is loved by
God.

Called to be a Shepherd

Assistants are thus called to exercise in some way a role of paternity
or of shepherdhood. Today psychology recognizes the role of the

mother in education, particularly during the first years of a child's life. But since Freud, and particularly since the abuses of repressive education, the role of the father is not recognized; it is even rejected. One of the great needs of our times is to help people refind and exercise this role. Real authority cannot be lived if it is separated from tenderness and compassion. Otherwise it becomes simply domination and suppression of the liberty of the other person; it becomes imposition. The essential role of a father-figure is to confirm the gifts of the other, to encourage him and help him recognize his real worth. It is neither to impose one's own desires upon another nor to simply let him do what he wants according to his instincts. To exercise a role of paternity is to accept the other as he is, to recognize his life and beauty, and to help him grow to be what he should be. This means that one cares deeply for him and is prepared to make sacrifices for him. But can one exercise this role of a father figure if one does not know how to be a "son"; can one command if one does not know how to obey?

In a way this is the crux of the matter. So frequently in society, authority means domination. One person commands another in a military style. In front of this power, other forces rise up. It is necessary then to find a balance of power. But at the heart of community there is no "balance of power" but instead "shepherds" called to give their lives, to serve and to confirm. If there is no humility in the exercise of authority, it will become repression. How easily in l'Arche we can fool ourselves and live in the illusion that we are doing good work and fulfilling our vocation when in reality we are living a double message: saying one thing and doing another. In the name of God and of "good works" or generosity, we can repress and oppress. This is hypocrisy. I am well aware of the seeds of hypocrisy in myself. That is why I speak of it with ease. Stephen Verney in his book *Into the New Age*[4] says that what is most beautiful in man – his capacity to be generous – can quickly become what is worst: a desire to impose and to dominate through apparent goodness; a desire to be recognized and esteemed for one's spiritual worth. That is pride. I believe that to exercise

[4]Stephen Verney *Into the New Age* Fontana/Collins 1976.

authority in a real human and Christian way is impossible without a special gift from God and the revelation of his Paternity. It means that constantly the assistant must be challenged and questioned, that he must look into himself and call to God to help him live this paternity in truth. For all true paternity comes from God and is a participation in his life.

Of course, all assistants at l'Arche have not attained this maturity. Have any of us? But if we are not seeking and walking towards this goal, then we will close up and fall into the danger of relinquishing responsibility out of fear, or of exercising it for our own power, prestige and feelings of superiority. To grow towards this maturity of shepherdhood, assistants too need shepherds; carers need to be cared for. If we expect too much from assistants they will be disappointed in themselves, as Ann Shearer says; this may lead to guilt and depression. One does not acquire the capacity to exercise authority in one day; it is something one grows into. It is a long process of human maturation and growth in Christian living and love. Who is shepherding the shepherds? L'Arche and similar communities must look into this question and perhaps review the role they give to priests and ministers. They must review also the role of leaders who sometimes fall into the pitfalls of becoming organizers and administrators rather than shepherds, who love their flock and have time to listen.

Relationship is Lived in Community

This deep and healing relationship between an assistant and a handicapped person can only take place in family or community life. In a way it is not just one assistant who lives this relationship but many who are linked together in bonds of friendship and co-operation. I don't believe any *one* person heals another; there is never a unique shepherd. A child needs *two* parents who love each other; in some way, he enters into the creative relationship and love between his father and mother. A dual relationship that does not bear fruit and open out will tend to become closed and then destructive, one wanting to master the other or fearing to lose him. An only child with a single parent[5] will seek to get his own way and through temper tantrums or other forms of blackmail will try to become master of the relationship, jealously guarding the single parent for himself. To love is not only to care for, to protect and to comfort; it is also to challenge the other to growth. This calls for separation as well as presence. An assistant must not fall into the pitfalls of dependency – absolutely needing the handicapped person to fulfil his own personal needs for affection and friendship. Community helps handicapped people to live out not just one relationship but a network of relationships. It helps assistants not to become dependent but to be objective and humble, co-operating together for the one goal of healing the wounds of those entrusted to their care. It is a place where assistants too can be challenged to growth. To grow humanly one needs to relate with people in authority but also with one's peers and with those who are weaker and smaller. This is true for assistants as well as for handicapped people. There can be no peace of heart and human equilibrium unless one has found truth and meaning in these three forms of relationships. That is why l'Arche can only exist and be therapeutic if it is true community, where people are learning to accept and love each other, discovering the covenant which binds them all together, and walking towards the same goals in a spirit of cooperation and respect for each other's gifts.

It is in community and in the relationships it permits that the handicapped person will begin to live and to find hope and peace of heart. As he discovers he is loved in spite of his former rejections and of all the darkness, fragility and handicaps of his being, he will begin to discover his capacity to love. He will not be angry with his wounds; he will learn that he is loved on a deeper level and that he does not have to reject himself, and so he will not have to reject others and their weaknesses.

Community is based on forgiveness, that is, the acceptance of others in their weakness and darkness. Community deepens as hope in growth becomes clearer and more intense. Community is

---

[5]The single parent must continually open the child up to other relationships. Otherwise the child will be stifled. Thus, "community" is born between the single parent and the other relationships.

crowned in celebration, which is a thanksgiving that deepens a sense of belonging.[6]

L'Arche: a Special Type of Community

But where will this community and its individual members find their source of life and inspiration? As it constitutes an alternative and/or a counter-culture, it must find an energy to be able to maintain its identity in front of the prevailing culture and values. Otherwise the prophetic beginnings will erode little by little through compromise. We all know how "good ideas can become bad institutions"; how dynamic communities can close up; and how the seeds of death can prevail. Communities which began in enthusiasm, poverty, dependence on God and a real desire to help handicapped people can so quickly become satisfied with themselves, rich, preoccupied by organization, reputation, influence and the needs of "assistants".

The spirit of l'Arche is based on the Gospels, the good news of Jesus Christ. The Beatitudes are at the heart of our communities. If we forget this initial inspiration, then the real meaning of the handicapped people will be lost; they will no longer be seen in their capacity to live and grow in their openness to God and in the beauty hidden in their weakness; assistants will refuse to enter into a covenant with them. They will tend to use the handicapped people for their own experience or spiritual benefits or in order to build a new way of life for themselves. They will not let themselves be disturbed by them because they do not let themselves be disturbed by Jesus and the truth which he is.

Here we touch upon the fundamental ambiguity of l'Arche which is also our call. L'Arche can only live and progress if there is a strong spiritual inspiration at its heart. The assistants will only be able to stay and deepen the covenant, that they have been called to live with the poor, if they are in contact with the source of their own being. For many this means being rooted in Jesus and the gospels and trusting in the power of the Spirit. Psychological

[6]Jean Vanier *Community and Growth* Darton, Longman and Todd 1979.

techniques can help assistants clarify their motivations, and professional techniques can help them in their attitudes towards the handicapped people. But only the spirit of Jesus can transform their hearts and teach them to love and to live an authentic relationship with handicapped people and thus to live the Beatitudes which are such a contrast to the values of the world.

But how can one live this Christian community if the option of l'Arche is to welcome handicapped people because they are in need and in distress, and not because they are Christian? Our aim is not just to have Christian assistants bound together in Christian love to "look after" the weak and the poor. Our goal is to live community *with* handicapped men and women, to create bonds with them and thus to discover their prophetic call. It is to create a community where handicapped people are fully members. It is to enter into deep relationships that are healing for them and hence for the assistants as well. Handicapped people are so frequently closer to living the Beatitudes than the assistants; to live with them can only constitute a real gain from a spiritual point of view. This unity in community between assistants and handicapped people is the heart and essence of l'Arche. If one day it disappears so that assistants can live a "deeper" spiritual life together, or so that they can have a more reasonable private life, less harrassed, less stressful, then l'Arche will no longer be. Our therapy and our call are based on this "family living" together, where we share, work, pray, suffer, and celebrate together; where we grow together in love, in hope and in freedom of heart.

If many of our assistants are convinced Christians, many are also searching for spiritual values and an alternative way of living but are not yet determined in their beliefs. Perhaps this weakens the "Christian unity" but it can also increase a dynamism of searching and of openness which are important for all our communities. It can also be important for handicapped people to be with people who are searching, not having "found" yet. Of course, it is better to have assistants who are really concerned by handicapped people and their growth, wanting to live with them, than to have people who profess a Christian belief but who are more concerned by their own spiritual growth than by the covenant with handicapped people; unable really to share their lives with them.

So it is that the communities of l'Arche are different from other Christian communities. People have difficulty situating us as sometimes we have difficulty situating ourselves. In our community in Kerala, India, assistants are Christian, Hindu and Moslem. The handicapped people are mainly Hindus. This is not always easy to live and, of course, there can be tensions. But the handicapped people are growing and they are much more open and happier than a year ago; their wounds are healing and their roots are deepening in the community. They are more secure and more hopeful. The assistants are bound together in a common vision and they pray together and live this common life of sharing with their handicapped brothers. People sometimes want to clarify who we are: "Are you missionaries?" "Are you professionals?" "No," we say, for we are not – at least not in the generally accepted sense of the terms. "What organization do you belong to?" "Our own", we answer, knowing that almost nobody has ever heard of us. It would be so much better if we could say that we belonged to the World Health Organization or something like that. Just recently in one country we were told that we were not eligible for funding from Caritas because we were not "Catholic" enough. I understand this because it is true that we do not come under the jurisdiction of the bishop. But yet that hurts a bit.

In Scotland, members of our community come from different Christian churches. It is not easy to live together, to love each other, and not to be able to drink from the same chalice. As Thérèse says in Chapter 9, we can only drink from the same cup of suffering.

Of course, we have no intention of creating a new religion or a new group based upon meditation and quiet prayer. I personally have never felt more the need to eat the body of Christ and to drink his blood at the Catholic Eucharist. And, I am more attached than ever to the shepherd of shepherds, John Paul II. But I realize what a gift it is for l'Arche to have Hindu brothers and sisters; to walk together, deeply bound to each other, calling each other to fidelity. Of course this means that each one must grow in maturity,

in his own faith, in prayer; that Christians be deeply rooted in
Jesus and in their church; that Hindus be rooted in their prayer and
traditions.

Christian Community and Professional Centre

This difficulty for our communities is linked to another. We are
living in an age where governments are more and more concerned
by handicapped people. We cannot be of service to them and
welcome them into our homes unless we receive permission from
local or state authorities. And, of course, these authorities need to
be assured of the competence of any organization before giving
this permission. So it is that l'Arche is governed by a local board
of directors or by committees, which create a "charitable" society,
according to the laws of the country. But it isn't always easy to
work with these boards even if at the outset we chose the members.
It takes a while for them to discover what l'Arche is and what their
exact responsibility is. There are many occasions for conflict until
the frontiers of responsibility are established – and these frontiers
can never be clearly defined once and for all!

As our communities are legally constituted organizations approved by the government, we are subject to the laws of the
country which govern employment. It is not easy to be both a
community and a professional centre; to be both leader of a community and director or employee of an institution. In this domain
there is much room for ambiguity and conflict. In France, there is
a minimum wage and nobody is legally allowed to be paid less.
Yet at l'Arche we do pay people less, precisely because we are a
community. We are trying to work out a solution to this question
with government officials.

In a community, when someone does not want to abide by the
spirit and rules, he can be asked to leave. But in l'Arche, as we are
also a professional centre, thus governed by laws of employment,
someone who does not want to abide by the spirit of community
but who still wants to work (and be paid) in the centre, cannot be

asked to leave unless he makes a serious professional mistake; he is protected by the law.

So it is that our communities are a real challenge. They call for a core of convinced assistants who agree to enter into a covenant with the poor, who carry the vision and are prepared to struggle in order that the community maintains its course and grows according to this initial vision.

When l'Arche began in 1964, we were small, poor and quite insecure. We had no reputation. I personally knew nothing about handicapped people. In our ignorance and insecurity, we needed God's power and guidance. So many times and in so many ways, his saving presence was felt.

Today, l'Arche is big. Most of our communities, if not rich, at least are quite well off; they are approved and helped and financed by governments. There are many committed assistants, and many handicapped men and women are deeply attached to their community and are growing and peaceful. We are better known. This rather exterior security hides a deeper insecurity. If we needed God's guidance and presence in the beginning, we need him even more today. The complexities of our communities are such that without his saving grace we would never be able to continue along the same path. Each time I visit one of our communities, I come away amazed at the peace and growth of the community, but also terribly concerned by its fragility. The problems seem so immense, the tensions sometimes so deep, the fragility of assistants so real, that I wonder how long the community will be able to last. If from the outside the community seems fine and strong, I know that inside it is weak. And yet, it keeps on; the handicapped people and some assistants continue to grow and put down their roots; friends of the community become more numerous and the integration in the local area is better. All these are signs that, in our fragility, God is looking after us.

At times, leaders of communities are frightened by this insecurity. They want to be certain of the future and plan and organize things so carefully that insecurity disappears. That is a time of real danger when the community risks closing up upon itself and becoming static and protective. Our communities can only live,

Eileen Glass of l'Arche in Australia and Jean Vanier

deepen, and grow if they accept their weakness and have confidence in God our father who is looking after them, guiding them; confidence also in the members and in their capacity to respond to the challenge of growth.

This is the last chapter of this book, or is it but an introduction to the next one? I feel that each day and year is like a new beginning for l'Arche. Each day, each year we are, as a community, breaking new ground. We have little security in any domain. In many ways all of us together carry and live the insecurities of our handicapped brothers and sisters. I suppose it is normal for communities, where the weak are held in honour, to be weak and insecure. But maybe this is also our strength, if we trust in the saving, healing power of God and in our own capacity to evolve and to grow.

The divisions of the world are great. Peace will only come if there is freedom for each person to grow and if the rich and the powerful learn to share; if people venture out from behind their frontiers and meet others, discover their beauty and learn from them. Is this a dream or utopia? Isn't it really a possibility if each one of us, trusting in the light burning within our hearts, trusting in others as brothers and sisters and trusting in God, ventures forth out of our frontiers and walks with our vulnerability and insecurity?

The struggle of l'Arche is a struggle for liberation, the liberation on the one hand of handicapped people who are oppressed by the rejection of society and, on the other, of those who live with them. This process of liberation is a long one and it is never fully completed. It implies, as well, the liberation of those living around our communities.

Many others take part in this struggle for liberation from the powers of darkness, hatred, division and from collective and individual egoism. L'Arche wants to take its small place, working with many others in this larger struggle for peace and justice; seeking for new ways of living universal brotherhood where all people, and especially the poor and weak, are held in honour, respected and received. L'Arche obviously cannot do big things. Our lives are with people. We are called to live little things with little people and to create communities of hope and reconciliation. Thus, we hope to help the structures of society evolve. If we cannot do big things, may our communities at least be signs of hope; signs that love is possible and that people from different backgrounds can live together in unity; that we are not all condemned to live behind our frontiers; and that Jesus came to announce the good news of liberation and growth for all:

"The Spirit of Yahweh has anointed me and sent me to announce the good news" (Luke 4:18).

ARCHE COMMUNITIES

AUSTRALIA Emmaus Cottage,
100 Princes Hwy.;
Milton NSW 2538

Genesaret,
29 Guilfoyle St.,
Yarralumla, 2600 ACT.

BELGIUM Ark Antwerpen,
Madona,
8 Janssenlei,
B-2530 Boechout

Aquero,
14 rue de la Cure,
1301 Bierges

L'Arche Brabant,
Le Toît,
83 Avenue de Tervueren,
B-1040 Bruxelles

L'Arche Liège,
La Brise,
53 rue des Muguets,
B-4310 St. Nicolas,
Liège

L'Arche Namur,
La Cascatelle,
Chaussée de Waterloo 118,
B-5002 St. Servais

CANADA Agape,
39 rue Marston,
Hull, P.Q. J8X 1B9

Alleluia House,
831 Broadview Ave.,
Ottawa, Ontario,
K2A 2M6

L'Arche Antigonish,
69 St Ninian St.,
Antigonish,
Nova Scotia,
B2G 1Y7

La Caravane,
RR 2,
Green Valley,
Ontario, KOC 1LO

Daybreak,
11339 Yonge St.,
Richmond Hill,
Ontario, L4C 4X7

L'Ecureuil,
1811 Chemin St Thomas,
Sainte-Thècle,
Laviolette, P.Q.
GOX 3GO

L'Étable,
1446 Gladstone,
Victoria, B.C.
V8R 1S3

L'Arche, Frontenac,
Old Farm Road,
Harlowe, RR1,
Arden, Ontario,
KOH 1BO

L'Arche, Hamilton,
1622 King St. E.,
Hamilton, Ontario,
L8K 1T7

Kara Foyer,
683 Ferguson St.,
North Bay, Ontario,
P1B 1X7

Maranatha,
82 Huron Street,
Stratford, Ontario,
N5A 5S6

Marymount,
808 69 Ave. S.W.,
Calgary, Alberta,
T2V 0P3

Le Printemps,
1385 rue Principale,
St. Malachie,
P.Q. G0R 3N0

Rosseau Court,
420 Rosseau Ave. E.,
Winnipeg, Man.,
R2C 0K8

Shalom,
6107-97A Ave.,
Edmonton, Alberta,
T6B 1E2

Shiloah,
7401 Sussex Ave.,
Burnaby, B.C.
V5J 3V6

The Skiff,
1302 Crawford Bridge S
Verdun, P.Q.
H4H 2N5

DENMARK   Niels Steensens Hus.,
           Nygade 6,
           3000 Helsingør

ENGLAND   The Anchorage,
           25 Fairfield Cres.,
           Liverpool 6

Lambeth l'Arche,
60 Rosendale Rd.,
West Dulwich,
London SE21

Little Ewell,
Barfrestone,
Near Dover,
Kent

Zacchaeus House,
36 Servite Close,
Bognor Regis,
West Sussex

FRANCE   Aigrefoin,
          78470 St-Rémy
          les Chevreuse

L'Arc-en-Ciel,
334 rue de Vaugirard,
75015 Paris

L'Arche,
BP 35,
60350 Trosly-Breuil

Le Levain,
1 Place St. Clément,
60200 Compiègne

La Merci,
Courbillac,
16200 Jarnac

Moita,
St-Germain,
26390 Hauterives

Le Moulin de l'Auro,
84220 Gordes

La Rebellerie,
49560 Nueil sur Layon

La Rose des Vents,
Verpillieres,
80700 Roye

Les Trois Fontaines,
62164 Ambleteuse

HAITI	Chantal, Zone des Cayes, CP 63, Cayes	SCOTLAND	Braerannoch, 13 Drummond Cres., Inverness
	Kay Sin Josef, BP 11075, Carrefour, Port-au-Prince	SPAIN	El Rusc, Lista de Correos, Tordera, Barcelona
HONDURAS	El Arca de Honduras, Apartado 1273, Tegucigalpa, DC	UPPER VOLTA	L'Arche des Voltas, B.P. 1492, Ouagadougou
INDIA	Asha Niketan 308 Acharya P.C. Rd., Calcutta 700009	USA	The Arch, 402 S. 4th Street, Clinton, Iowa, 52732
	Asha Niketan, 53/7 Bannerghatta Rd., Bangalore 560029		L'Arche Syracuse, 1701 James Street, Syracuse, N.Y. 13206
	Asha Niketan, Kottivakkam, Tiruvanmiyur P.O., Madras 600041		The Hearth, 502 W. 8th Street, Erie, Pennsylvania, 16507
	Asha Niketan, Nandi Bazar, Katalur P.O., Meladi Kozhikode, Dt. Kerala 673522		Hope, 161 Michigan Ave., Mobile, Alabama, 36604
			Lamb of God, 1730 E. 70th St., Cleveland, Ohio, 44103
IRELAND	Moorfield House, Kilmoganny, Co. Kilkenny		Mount l'Arche, 637 Alder Street, Missoula, Montana, 59801
IVORY COAST	L'Arche, B.P. 1156, Bouaké		Noah Sealth, 816 18th Ave. E., Seattle, Wa. 98112